The Psychology of Learning

THE
PSYCHOLOGY
OF LEARNING

by E. R. Guthrie

Professor of Psychology
University of Washington

Revised Edition

17462

Gloucester, Mass.

PETER SMITH

1960

Contents

Preface to First Edition

In so far as a writer can account for his own opinions and prejudices this essay on learning is a natural development of the views expressed in a book, *General Psychology in Terms of Behavior,* which was written in collaboration with Stevenson Smith and published some thirteen years ago. Although Smith has had no direct part in the writing of the present book a history of some twenty years of argument with him over the lunch table makes the determination of responsibility for much of what is here offered quite impossible.

Like the earlier book, this essay is written in terms of behavior. My prejudice in favor of a behavioristic attack on the problems of psychology dates from the Christmas vacation of 1910 in which I heard Professor E. A. Singer deliver an address at Princeton on "Mind as an Observable Object." That address remains the most stirring event of my academic life. Singer's contention that a relatively objective method could be applied to the scientific treatment of mind revived an interest in psychology that was waning as the result of an excursion into the field of psychophysics.

The notions described in the following pages are not new. Most of them have been familiar for a generation and some of them for centuries. Associative learning has been recognized in some form or other by every writer on psychology since Aristotle. What has been here attempted is an exploration of the field of learning to discover the nature of the phenomenon of association and the limits of its use in the explanation of learning.

Without a reading by Professor E. A. Esper and editorial comment full of "insight" by Professor Gardner Murphy many more faults would have been included than will now be made public.

Publishers who have very courteously given permission to quote from their publications include the Bureau of Publications of Teachers College, Columbia University, The Macmillan Company, Thomas Y. Crowell Company, Harcourt, Brace and Company, Liveright Publishing Corporation, Farrar and Rinehart, and the *Psychological Review* in which the chapter on Reward and Punishment appeared under the same title.

E. R. GUTHRIE

Seattle, July 27, 1934

Preface to Revised Edition

CHANGES in the revised edition consist chiefly in the addition of four chapters, one dealing with what I have chosen to call the pluralistic theories represented by Tolman and by Maier, another dealing with Skinner's two-process theory, one dealing with Hull's reinforcement theory and its modifications in the hands of Spence, Miller and Dollard. The fourth additional chapter recounts some experimental work done by Horton and myself and includes certain extensions and modifications of the theory presented in the first edition. No attempt is made to cover the thousand and more titles of the literature during the intervening years. The additional material cited is chosen as representing the main developments of learning theory in the period since 1934, when the original book was written. The theory presented remains substantially the same. I hope that my own preference for association by contiguity as the basic principle is founded on certain merits of that principle and not on the tendency for our conceptual habits to be less amenable to change with the passage of years. It is my own conviction that learning theory, which is obviously far from complete, will profitably explore the lines of advance defended in this book.

The views of Tolman, Maier, Skinner, Hull, Spence, Miller, and the many others mentioned are discussed in terms of their relation to association theory. There has been in the last sixteen years a very gratifying amount of writing of high quality by psychologists in the field of learning. The general discussions of theory tend to obscure the fact that there are substantial gains in agreement and common understanding among psychologists writing in this area. When we are comparing men we tend to emphasize their differences and to take the points of agreement for granted.

Some effort has been made in this book to understand the nature of psychological theory. Theories are not true or false. They are useful or less useful. Good theory guides us to important facts and increases our ability to predict and control behavior and, particularly, makes it possible to teach.

One regret on finishing this book is the discovery that its plan has restricted the discussion to particular theories and has not allowed recognition of some of the outstanding general discussions of learning theories published in the last ten years. Spence's chapter in Moss' *Comparative Psychology* is about to be more than matched by his forthcoming chapter on learning theories in Stevens' projected *Handbook of Experimental Psychology*. Postman's *Psychological Bulletin* article on the law of effect, Hovland's chapter on learning in the Boring, Langfeld, and Weld *Foundations of Psychology*, and Hilgard's *Theories of Learning* prove that psychology is making remarkable progress as a science.

My colleagues Roger Loucks and Moncrieff Smith have read the new chapters and their comments have been responsible for clarifications in the text and in my own thinking. Virginia Voeks has also suggested a number of changes in the interest of clarity.

E. R. GUTHRIE

Seattle, February 4, 1951

CHAPTER I

Introduction

—————————

PSYCHOLOGISTS nowhere depart further from common sense than in their notion of the nature of minds. The man on the street acknowledges that minds are rather mysterious, but he is definitely sure that a mind is something that you either have or you haven't. Bricks haven't. He has, and knows that he has. Dogs also have minds. Angleworms? Here he becomes a little doubtful. Angleworms seem very definitely to resent indignities in a way that a brick does not. And their daily round of activity seems to have something of a plan and purpose behind it. A brick reacts to a kick by moving over, but there is a distinctly passive and helpless air about the brick's behavior. And the brick is so dependable; it regularly does the expected thing when it is disturbed. If it behaves differently on a second occasion we can find the occasion for the difference. It is a different brick. If it did not fall apart at one blow of the hammer, but now does fall apart when struck the second time with the same force, we take for granted that the first blow cracked it. If a bridge timber gives way after years of use under a load that it has held up to the present moment, we assume that it is a different timber; dry rot has invaded it or past stresses have cracked it.

But do angleworms have minds? Are growth and reproduction and defensive reaction enough to qualify the worm for that distinction? Plants also grow and multiply and defend themselves not only by their structures but in many cases by movement. Common sense is inclined to deny that plants have minds,

for this is an opinion shared only by a very few detached senti-
mentalists.

What is it then that plants lack that is to be found in creatures
which common sense endows with minds? Strangely enough,
common sense will be found to offer a very good answer to this
question. Growth and reproduction and defense reactions are
life, but they are not mind. Mind is these and something more;
it is growth and reproduction and reactions serving these ends
plus something that common sense might call profiting by experience. The answer to the question of the angleworm's status
will be determined by the answer to the question: Does the
worm always respond the same way to the same combination of
circumstances, or does the worm alter its response as a result of
its past experience?

Of course, a full worm and an empty worm respond differently to the world. This is not what is meant by profiting by
experience. The altered behavior here is like the altered behavior of the bridge timber; it can be referred to differences in the
present circumstances. The difference can be examined and the
response understood on the basis of what is now the condition of
the worm.

Now it happens that a psychologist has established that worms
can profit by experience. Yerkes many years ago placed earthworms in a T-shaped maze and found that if a slight electric
shock was always administered when the worm turned, say, to
the left, ultimately the worm was in some fashion changed so
that it more or less regularly turned to the right and avoided
the shock.

The difference between a worm that has received this Harvard laboratory training and a worm that has not is a difference
that can not be discovered by examining the worm. The training
leaves no observable changes. All psychologists believe that differences accounting for the altered behavior exist in the worm's
"brain," but it is doubtful whether we shall ever be able to ex-

amine these brain differences either during the lifetime of the organism or at a post-mortem. Such traits as an acquired liking for mince pie, or skill at chess, or an ambition to travel, which are all modifications of behavior like the right-turning habit of the earthworm, are not by any -present technique possible of demonstration at an autopsy. We may speculate concerning the nature of the brain changes that lie behind these habits, but that speculation will throw no light on the nature of the habits.

These changes in behavior which follow behavior we shall call learning. The ability to learn, that is, to respond differently to a situation because of past response to the situation, is what distinguishes those living creatures which common sense endows with minds. This is the practical descriptive use of the term "mind." Another use, the theological or mythological notion of mind as a substance, as a mysterious hidden cause of action, we may dismiss at once. Our interest is scientific, and we are dealing only with observable features of the world about us. Mind must be for us a mode of behavior, namely, that behavior which changes with use or practice—behavior, in other words, that exhibits learning.

Learning, as so defined, does not include all changes in behavior tendencies. Fatigue, for instance, is a change in behavior, but it is referred not to action primarily as its occasion but to altered chemical states in muscle and in the blood stream. There are other changes in behavior tendencies which might be included in the term "learning" if we were so inclined. When continuous pressure is exerted on a touch receptor, Adrian has recorded instances in which the receptor responds only for a brief period. Impulses from the sense organ are demonstrable in the sensory nerve only for a few seconds, though the pressure on the sense organ is continued. This is a change in behavior tendency, since the organism will no longer respond, though the stimulus continues; but this is a very temporary change and from it there is a quick recovery.

The definition of learning used by a psychologist selects the facts which he observes and records. Using the common-sense definition of learning as improvement leads to the observation of such items as the number of errors made in achieving a goal, or the time required, or the effort used, or an increased percentage of success. Nearly all the thousands of studies of maze learning by rats have recorded only the facts of improvement, not the facts of changed behavior. These records are of little or no interest to the psychologist who thinks of learning in terms of changed response to a stimulus, because no record is made of specific alterations of behavior at choice points. Only total errors or total time from start to goal are noted. The fact that at the fifth choice point a given animal took the "correct" turn for the first time on the eleventh trial and persevered in this from that trial on is not in the record.

Common sense and many psychologists have used "learning" to refer only to those changes which contribute to the accomplishment of some end or purpose. In this sense learning always means learning to do something, learning to write, learning to skate—learning, in short, which results in an ability or a skill or a capacity for some achievement. This identification of learning with the attainment of a good result is all very well for common sense, but for a scientific understanding of human behavior it will not serve. And the reason that it will not serve is that in the same manner and in the same ways that human beings acquire skills and capacities they also acquire faults and awkwardnesses and even lose capacities which they once possessed. Since virtues and skills are acquired in the same way that faults and awkwardnesses are acquired, it seems unreasonable to limit the meaning of the word learning to achievement. It is true that the changes referred to as "learning" do generally turn out to be beneficial, that they are in the long run adaptive, and this must be looked into; but we have deserted the methods of empirical science if we assume that all learning is good, that every action has its goal. There are psychologists who believe this, not only of their own actions but of all the actions of all animals. The hen lays her egg, not because it has reached an embarrassing size, but because the species must be preserved. She is aiming at motherhood and carrying a torch for her species, not just laying an egg.

In this present account it will not be assumed that all learning is a progress toward betterment. Learning will be understood as change rather than as improvement. Our task is to understand the circumstances under which learning takes place and the nature of the changes that it involves. Our method should be to survey the experimental work on learning, to review what is common knowledge of learning, and to try to discover any generalizations that can be made from our survey. Can we find any rule or uniformity in the phenomena? Can we describe any circumstances which regularly have a certain kind of outcome? Does the animal which has had one kind of history tend afterward to do certain things? *Under what circumstances do the specific changes in behavior we call learning take place?*

If we find such rules, they will not only be an adequate theory of learning; they will also direct the practical advice we give to persons who are guiding learning. Our rules, to be good theory, must be based on observation and verified by observation. This is one requirement. Another is that they shall be as concise and clear as we can make them. Our antecedent circumstances must be so clearly described that from our description other persons can recognize instances of what we describe; and this must also be true of our alleged consequences. If our descriptions are vague or ambiguous our rules can not be verified; nor can they be used for the anticipation and control of behavior. These are the important requirements for psychological theory, and we may note that these would be the most important requirements for practical advice.

If we can find, on examining our common knowledge and

the experimental work on learning, that certain describable, observable, and recognizable antecedent conditions enable us to predict certain describable, observable, and recognizable changes in behavior, we shall have discovered laws of learning. These laws will constitute our explanations of learning, for all scientific explanations are nothing more than generalized laws or rules which cover the event needing explanation.

The search for these laws has certain inherent difficulties. The first of these difficulties has to do with language. Putting events into words is never entirely satisfactory. Here are pupils in a classroom. The teacher gives them a spoken direction. How are we to describe this as a stimulus to the pupils? No two pupils see the teacher from the same angle or hear her voice from the same distance. No two pupils move their eyes alike, consequently no two have the same retinal activity. The optical properties of different eyes differ. What the pupils hear and what they see depends on the form of their present attention and on their previous experiences, which are various. We are forced to speak of the voice of the teacher as a stimulus, but we are forced to speak vaguely. We can never be sure that the stimulus of the voice does not affect different pupils in essentially different ways.

Reactions are just as hard to describe and name. Popular names for most acts are names for end results which may be accomplished in an indefinite variety of ways. Accepting an invitation, going to market, attending a dinner, playing a tune, catching a fish—all name acts, but the acts they name are left indefinite. It is only because the acts we name have a rough practical equivalence that we are able to undertake their prediction. Under these handicaps our forecasts of action are bound to be inaccurate and we must be resigned to finding exceptions to all our rules. We shall be dealing with tendencies and not with certainties.

A second difficulty in codifying the laws of learning has been introduced by psychologists themselves. Experimenters in the field of learning have failed to make clear to the public or to themselves that two fundamentally different kinds of research have been in progress. Some psychologists and physiologists have been interested in the prediction of movement or glandular secretion without any reference to the utility of the movement or to its consequences. Pavlov, for instance, was interested in discovering the circumstances under which a dog will secrete saliva in response to stimuli that were previously ineffective. The ability to secrete saliva at the sound of a bell or at a touch on the flank is of no use to the dog after the experiment, though similar conditioning in natural conditions may be useful. Pavlov was interested in the phenomenon of conditioning, not in its utility. Tolman, on the other hand, records the fact that the rat in the maze reaches food, its goal, and is not concerned about the movements by which the goal is reached. The psychologist whose interest is in the goal-reaching capacities of animals will make goal attainment the entry in the record, and not the means used, which may be varied. One experimenter like Pavlov is interested in the process; other experimenters are interested in the results. It is to be expected that the two types of workers will discover very different laws of learning. The conditions under which goals are reached are not at all the conditions under which habits are stereotyped. A day-old chick will peck at grains and capture a certain percentage of them. Its percentage of success increases rapidly with practice, but if the chick formed a stereotyped habit of pecking in one direction and with a fixed reach it would retrieve very few grains.

The differences in the results announced by different psychologists arise from differences in the modes of behavior that they are intent on predicting. Their findings are not contradictory. Empirical studies, if they are honest, can not be contradictory. Pavlov's question, under what circumstances can a stimulus not previously the occasion of a response become a substitute cue for that response, will have one answer; and the question, under what circumstances will a man or a dog acquire a certain skill or ability, will have another. It is, of course, this second question that has the more practical interest. To it the later chapters of this book will be devoted.

Two sources of difficulty in the formulation of laws of learning have been mentioned—the difficulty of fitting language to the description of the confused and intricate flow of behavior, and the failure of experimenters to record the same features of behavior. There is a third difficulty. We can not record or control all the conditions under which our experiments are made, or record all the details of any sample of behavior. The physicist is less embarrassed by this obstacle. He does not concern himself about the recent night life or the childhood experiences of the bit of metal whose density he is determining, whereas such items of history may lead to very bizarre results in the psychological laboratory. Even with this advantage we find that the physicist tends to flee from reality into a dream world of "ideal" gases and liquids, because these are the only ones that will obey the laws of physics. Boyle's law that in a gas with temperature held constant the product of pressure and volume is a constant is not true of any real gas. And when the physicist turns engineer and undertakes to predict the behavior of actual things in a real world, he protects himself with safety factors of 600 to 1000 percent to allow for any shortcomings in his predictions.

The psychologist must resign himself to the fact that no psychological event is ever really repeated. The second repetition of a stimulus is only roughly and for practical purposes equivalent to the first; his laboratory subject is only substantially or approximately the same person who sat in the chair the day before. Since that time he has slept, eaten a little, learned a little, and this will alter his response no matter what precautions have been taken to have conditions the same. No two responses are alike. Two trips through a maze, two conditioned salivary reflexes may be substantially the same, but they are always the same with a difference.

CHAPTER II

Psychological Explanations

PROFESSIONAL explainers regularly forget that there are two parties involved in an explanation, the one who offers the explanation and the one at whom it is directed. An explanation that does not make the event clear to the person seeking information is no explanation at all. It is not the explainer who must be satisfied, but the listener.

There are now current several kinds of psychological explanations of human and animal behavior which all satisfy their inventers, but the rest of us are left in some confusion. There are no true explanations and false explanations, but only successful and unsuccessful explanations, acceptable explanations (acceptable to us, the hearers) and unacceptable explanations. If we believe in fairies, events can be explained to us as the actions of fairies. The explanation will be unscientific only because the scientific tradition is not acquainted with fairies and scientific men have discovered that they can get on well enough without recourse to spirit agents of just this sort.

An explanation of any event consists in stating the rule or generalization of which the event is an instance. Scientific explanations have a severe restriction placed upon them at the start. They are directed at the prediction and control of natural events, not at arousing awe, or giving comfort, or forestalling questions. Scientific explanations can not invoke the will of God because to explain a happening as an instance of the will of God may lead the questioner to be resigned but it does not lead him to foresee what will happen in such cases. Common sense uses many such too facile explanations in terms of the action of agents, and this is quite legitimate under many circumstances; but knowing that an event is the act of an agent does not give the rule of the act unless we know the ways of the particular agent, and science is a public and impersonal affair, not interested in particular agents. "Your chair," the housewife explains to her inquiring husband, "I put there because I had grown tired of seeing it where it was." This is an adequate explanation for some purposes. The husband knows something of what to expect when his wife is taken with this form of aesthetic fatigue. But this is not a scientific explanation because science can not be burdened with a catalogue of the ways of particular human agents.

Scientific explanations all have much the same form. They state the rule of which the event in question is an instance. A state of affairs which we may call A (for "antecedent") is followed in a certain proportion (say x percent) of the cases observed by another state of affairs C (for "consequent"). If the law has to do with the degree or quantity of some state instead of merely with its presence or absence it will read: State C is a certain mathematical function of state A, or $C = \Phi (A)$, with an observed error of estimate, z.

In such a law both the antecedent and the consequent may be anything whatever, provided that they are observable, describable, and recognizable. The consequent, C, will be something which we are interested in anticipating or predicting; the antecedent, A, will be anything that can conveniently serve as a warning of C. The rule itself, if it is to qualify as scientific, must be the result of observation of cases of A and of C and it should be verified by further observation after it has been formulated.

It has just been said that when a rule of behavior expresses a relation between the degree or extent of A, the antecedent state of affairs, and C, the consequent state, the rule has an expression different from the rule predicting merely the presence or absence of some state or condition.

This difference is important because it marks two radically different methods of prediction. The two may be illustrated by two very different ways of predicting how many times in one hundred a thrown die will come to rest with the six side uppermost. We can make this prediction after throwing the die one hundred times and counting the number of sixes thrown. Or we can argue that a die has six sides and a shape such that there is no inherent reason why one side should turn up oftener than another. Furthermore, no die will come to rest on its edge if the underlying surface is flat. If, therefore, the die is certain to land with some side uppermost and we represent this certainty by 1, the probability that a given side will turn up is one-sixth of 1. This is a deduction from our conception of the die as a physical object with mass and weight.

There are interesting differences between these two methods of prediction. If the particular die we are using has any peculiarities, only the first method can be used. Gamblers sometimes tamper with the shape of a die or weight it in such a way as to favor one side. The study of its actual performance would bring out the idiosyncrasy.

But the second method has its own advantages. It results in a general prediction of the behavior of dice, not likely to be distorted by peculiarities of the particular situation.

The first method results in quantitative laws based on actual observation. The great majority of studies in the psychology of learning have been made in accordance with this method. Pavlov's researches were confined to observing the probability that a given stimulus (for instance, the sound of a bell) would be followed by a given response (usually the secretion of saliva) after different numbers of pairings of the bell and an original stimulus (food) for secretion. The Yale group have produced a wealth of studies of this kind in which an animal was placed over and over again in a situation (A) and the effect on the latency of a particular response or on its certainty or on its energy or on its resistance to extinction was noted.

The first method makes empirical studies of repeated situations and arrives at rules which are essentially empirical curves giving the relationship between two measurable items such as hours of practice and frequency of error, or number of unreinforced trials (trials in which the signal is not accompanied by an eliciting stimulus for the response) and frequency of response; or the relationship between elapsed time and the diminishing frequency with which a response followed its stimulus (forgetting).

The raw data from such empirical studies are always irregular. To draw conclusions from such data or to make any generalizations or arrive at any predictive rules it is necessary to fit an equation to the curve which will express one variable as a function of the other. This equation never fits the data perfectly, but the extent of the fit can be measured. We can calculate the probability that the discrepancies may arise through chance errors of measurement or chance variations in unmeasured factors.

The second method was illustrated by the argument from the characteristics of a cube. Prediction was based on the physical properties of a cube rather than on observation of an actual cube.

In psychology this method consists in devising a conceptual model like the cube. Behavior is predicted in terms of what such a model would do. Psychology is a new science and psychologists have drawn upon a great variety of such models. Freud explained the behavior of an individual as if it were a struggle between a number of persons, the id, the ego, the censor, the pleasure principle, the death wish, all of which had the traits of complete persons—ambitions, likes and dislikes, even certain forms of low cunning. Popular mythology used to explain the weather in terms of similar person-models. Boreas, the north wind, had his own angers and pleasures and grudges and fears as if he were indeed a man. We should not feel too superior to men who speak in such terms because useful information can be thus conveyed. If we know what Boreas likes and a bit about his habits we may be the possessors of real weather lore.

The usual model of psychologists is the receptor-effector system of the body and the afferent, connector, and efferent neural structures, conceived originally by Descartes as fine tubes conveying "animal spirits" which flowed rapidly through the nerve channels. At the pineal gland these spirits could affect the mind, and at this point Descartes' model broke down rather badly.

For many years the nervous system was conceived as basically like a telephone exchange, essentially a system of conductors over which nerve impulses passed from receptors to effectors. The conductors were thought of not as metal pathways over which electrical energy was conveyed at the speed of light but as electrolytic structures in which the electrical changes were mediated by chemical changes.

The first radical objection to this conception came from Köhler, who, responding to an advancing knowledge of physics, conceived the brain and nervous system more in terms of an elaborate electrical grid in which the general pattern of potential could as an integral whole be responsive to local changes. This scientific model did not throw much light on behavior except to underscore Köhler's warning that there could be no prediction of response from specific stimuli, since response was a function of the whole pattern.

Nor can Tolman's proposed model, which asserts that the rat in a maze acts "as if he had a map in his head," really throw light on behavior to come. Tolman uses as an explanatory model the figure of a navigator poring over his charts. The model is entirely too formidable—and too indefinite in its prediction.

Our stock of available models has been considerably enlarged in recent years by advances in physics. In 1914 Stevenson Smith published a short article, "Regulation in Nature," in which he took as a model for the explanation of animal behavior the regulatory mechanism like the governor of a steam engine in which the effects of behavior (in this case, revolutions per minute) serve as the occasions for the regulation of the behavior. When revolutions per minute exceed the rate for which the governor is set, the steam supply is shut down by the instrument, and when the speed falls below the critical rate for which the governor is set, more steam is admitted to the engine.

Since that time Haldane and W. B. Cannon, both physiologists, have explored many instances of regulatory mechanisms in the body which maintain temperature, the concentration of blood, salts, the moisture in the body tissues, and many other "constant states." Norbert Wiener in his *Cybernetics* has elaborated and extended the concept of regulatory mechanism to include recent inventions in the field of electronics that have made possible the calculators which perform elaborate computations at high speed. His suggestion is that the brain and nervous system are best understood in terms of such machines. These machines store information as well as compute. They can select types of information. The automatic pilot keeps the plane or ship on the set course, and the corrected deviations have a strong resemblance to the corrected deviations of a man walking down the street or across a field, or a hand reaching for a glass on the table, or the wabbling of anyone standing erect and maintaining that posture by a continuous series of muscular adjustments to counteract the beginnings of falling.

When we think in terms of such scientific models we are very likely to be more interested in predicting, on the analogy of our model, whether or not certain behavior will occur in a given set of circumstances, than in predicting the measure of the behavior in terms of measured items in the antecedent situation. What response will this cat make on the next trial in the puzzle box? What will the child do on his next visit to the classroom? How will the pilot respond to the threatened disaster to his plane? How will the soldier behave under fire? Will the merchant pay the obligation he proposes to incur? How can we manipulate the situation so that the dog will no longer attack the postman? How can we insure that the school child will say or write "63" in response to "7×9"? Our answer to these questions will have the form C will follow A, and not the form $C = f(A)$.

In his *Cybernetics*, Wiener suggests psychological application of his theory of regulatory mechanisms but selects among the theories of learning that of Clark Hull and the Yale school which is formulated strictly in quantitative terms. Habit strength is regarded as a continuous function of a number of variables. Wiener's calculating machines do not readily fall into this pattern. A calculator into which data must be fed over and over again and which merely becomes more and more sure of the answer would not be of great use. The scientific model needed for the understanding of learning must be able to make complex changes in its behavior as the result of a single experience, not a long series of repeated exposures to a situation.

A generation ago psychologists sought the basic explanation of learning in what was called the curve of learning. It was hoped that by plotting the rates of improvement in typing, archery, maze learning, and a multitude of other activities the curves would turn out to be variants of a basic curve of learning. This hope was illusory, for the curves of learning differed for each activity with no evidence that they were variants of a single master curve.

All of this will undoubtedly prove rather discouraging to a reader who is interested in learning and not in a general discussion of the nature of science, but it has much to do with an understanding of the apparent differences between psychologists who are engaged in the study of learning. The differences between psychological schools lie in what they choose to employ for the A and C of our formula. Many psychologists are now engaged in finding what behavior may be expected from knowing that an individual is a member of a certain species. A great deal of such information has been collected. If our antecedent knowledge is that this individual is a rat we know something of the kinds of things we may expect of it. What can be expected of rats in a maze has been the topic of an enormous amount of investigation.

Information concerning what to expect of an individual if he is a member of our own species is important. But there is a source of information still more important. *This source is the past history of the individual man.* Knowing a man's past history, we can make specific statements concerning how he will behave in specific situations which would be quite impossible if all the information we had concerning him was that he was human. The best information we can gain concerning how a man will behave in a given set of circumstances comes from the record of what he last did in these circumstances. Individual likes and dislikes, idiosyncrasies, response tendencies, the greater part of all that we can predict of the individual man is predicted in terms of the association of specific features of response with specific features of a situation. And the only form in which such information has been offered or can be offered is some form of association theory. Other theories may list the goals which men are often known to reach, but the anticipation of specific action must always depend for the most part on the use of stimuli as the weather signs of conduct and the past behavior in the presence of these stimuli as the indication of what is to come.

It will be noticed that such information will never violate the modes of behavior known to hold for all organisms, or known to hold for the human species. Membership in the species is a very persistent attribute of man.

The Gestalt psychologists have placed a great deal of emphasis on the assertion that behavior is always a response to a total situation. So far as I know, this has never been disputed, and it is of great importance to bear it in mind. But any attempt to predict from the total situation is hopeless. A, the antecedent term in our general formula for scientific laws, can not be a total situation because total situations are never repeated, and science can not deal with events that are unique. We can deal only with recurring aspects of events. The determining occasion for the World Wars could be found only by observing a series of comparable wars and finding which of the antecedents were necessary and sufficient antecedents. This, of course, could not conceivably be done because of the uniqueness of the events. A great deal of human behavior is in this same category. For human actions that are unique, for the work of the creative artist and the original thinker there will never be any adequate scientific treatment because the creation and the thought occur once for all, and there will never be an opportunity to find what details of the artist's training, of his difficulties, of his love affairs, of his chance human contacts were the determining conditions for his work of art.

CHAPTER III

The Conditioned Response

IN A Pacific coast city a number of dogs succumbed to strychnine poisoning. Poisoned chunks of beef were found in the neighborhood. Several owners of good dogs undertook to train their animals not to indulge in stray tidbits by scattering about many pieces of beef to which were fastened small mousetraps of the familiar spring variety. For a time, at least, they had quick success. The dogs developed a very supercilious attitude toward stray meat.

The mother of a ten-year-old girl complained to a psychologist that for two years her daughter had annoyed her by a habit of tossing coat and hat on the floor as she entered the house. On a hundred occasions the mother had insisted that the girl pick up the clothing and hang it in its place. These wild ways were changed only after the mother, on advice, began to insist not that the girl pick up the fallen garments from the floor but that she put them on, return to the street, and reënter the house, this time removing the coat and hanging it properly.

A mature student, a woman, has become so indignant over the noise of the radio in the next apartment that she is unable to study in her own quarters. On the advice of an acquaintance she finds that mystery stories compete successfully with the disturbing noise of the neighbors' radio for a week, and that at the end of the week study is again possible in spite of the noise.

A talkative three-year-old is at the dinner table. Her father has come from his business tired and angry. In answer to her request for something he turns suddenly to her and shouts:

"Say please." The rest of the family joins his demand, but the child becomes excited and for a period of some eleven months has not spoken in the presence of her family.

All of these are instances of the modification of behavior following some experience. The first three are cases in which some person showed a rough knowledge of what to expect as the result of interference with behavior. They are examples of control. The hysterical mutism of the little girl illustrates the lack of such knowledge, and the effect of that lack. Explanations of learning put such knowledge into words, and the real test of any explanation is this: Does it enable us to anticipate behavior and adjust ourselves to it in advance, and does it enable us to interfere with behavior and be prepared for the results of our interference?

The law of least action, that the difference between the kinetic and potential energies for any actual motion in a given time interval from one configuration of a system to another shall be a minimum offers cold comfort to dog-trainers or to parents. And yet any college freshman to whom the cases above are described can give an approximation of the result to be expected. Obviously some form of association is involved. This also the college freshman can state, though his statement may not be as clear as we might ask.

Associative learning has been recognized since there has been any writing on the subject of human nature. Popular sayings have made knowledge of it available for generations. "Once bitten, twice shy." "The burnt child dreads the fire." Aristotle described its nature and used it to explain recall. The oldest and most persistent observation concerning associative learning is the law of association by contiguity in time, a rule that has been noticed by practically all psychologists since Aristotle.

The psychologists of modern times have usually treated associative learning as though it were concerned with the association of ideas, though their illustrations show that they considered action included in its scope. In recent years emphasis on movement as the observable denotation of "thinking" has led to the use of the phrase "conditioned response" in place of "association of ideas," but the phenomenon is basically the same.

The principle has been stated in many different ways. Bishop Berkeley speaks of "an habitual and customary connection" by which one idea is the occasion for another. For Hume there was a "gentle force" by which "one idea naturally introduces another" after they have occurred together. James Mill says: "Our ideas spring up, or exist, in the order in which the sensations existed, of which they are the copies. This is the general law of the 'Association of Ideas,' by which term, let it be remembered, nothing is here meant to be expressed but the order of occurrence." For him this association could be successive or synchronous. The strength of an association could be measured by its permanence, its certainty, or its "facility." The conditions determining the strength of an association were frequency and vividness.

By the time of James Mill the doctrine of association was so much involved with the analysis of consciousness, which was the proper and peculiar domain of psychology, that action and performance were lost sight of. According to Bain: "Actions, Sensations, and States of Feeling, occurring together or in close succession, tend to grow together, or cohere, in such a way that, when any one of them is afterwards presented to the mind, the others are apt to be brought up in idea." Hartley's statement of the law was: "Any sensations A, B, C, etc., by being associated with one another a sufficient number of times, get such a power over the corresponding Ideas a, b, c, etc., that any one of the sensations A, when impressed alone, shall be able to excite in the Mind b, c, etc., the ideas of the rest."

William James states it thus: "Objects once experienced together tend to become associated in the imagination, so that when any one of them is thought of, the others are likely to be thought of also, in the same order of sequence or coexistence as before." He also is referring to ideas rather than to action, but he has prepared for his law of association by this remark: "The laws of motor habit in the lower centers of the nervous system are disputed by no one. A series of movements repeated in a certain order tend to unroll themselves with peculiar ease in that order for ever afterward. Number one awakens number two, and that awakens number three, and so on, till the last is produced. A habit of this kind once become inveterate may go on automatically. And so it is with the objects with which our thinking is concerned."

In spite of this introduction of the association of ideas by the "laws of motor habit" which are "disputed by no one" and in spite of his incidental remark (*Principles*, vol. 1, page 124) in his famous chapter on habit: "It is not in the moment of their forming, but in the moment of their producing motor effects, that resolves and aspirations communicate the new 'act' to the brain," James failed to see the application of the notion of the association of ideas to movement and to action. In his short chapter dealing with habit he is content to say that "our nervous system grows to the modes in which it has been exercised" and to point out the results that "habit simplifies the movements required to achieve a given result, makes them more accurate and diminishes fatigue," and that "habit diminishes the conscious attention with which our acts are performed" (vol. 1, page 112). He does point out that "in action grown habitual, what instigates each new muscular contraction to take place in its appointed order is not a thought or a perception, but the *sensation occasioned by the muscular contraction just finished.*" This implies the rule of the conditioned response but does not expressly recognize it.

The years following the publication of William James' *Principles of Psychology* in 1890 saw a focusing of interest on the problem of associative learning that resulted in a much more definite conception of the nature of association. In 1900 C. Lloyd Morgan published his *Animal Behavior*, containing accounts of some experiments. He placed before newly hatched chicks either bits of egg yolk or bits of orange peel. All chicks will, without previous experience, peck at such objects—even at ink dots on white paper.

The chicks which pecked at the egg yolk continued that activity. The chicks which pecked at the orange peel quickly left off pecking and would peck at neither peel nor egg yolk.

Here was behavior clearly modified by an association. Lloyd Morgan thought in terms of the centuries-old principle of the association of ideas and believed that what the chick had associated was, in the one case, the pleasant taste of the yolk with its yellow color. In the other case the chick had associated the unpleasant taste with the same color and as a result did not peck at small yellow objects. Lloyd Morgan believed that the first chick pecked more vigorously and certainly because pecking the egg yolk had "confirmatory results." His notion of associative learning is that it is dependent on the effects of action, a conception which has become familiar as the *law of effect*.

The law of effect has been most widely publicized in the writings of the late Edward L. Thorndike, who published his *Animal Intelligence* in 1898. Thorndike believed that learned associations are established between a sense impression or cue and an act "with the impulse leading thereunto." The law of effect will be considered in more detail in the chapter on reward and punishment. Here it is sufficient to note that Thorndike, like Lloyd Morgan, believed that the simple association of ideas or of cue and "impulse" is in itself not enough to insure a future connection. He believed that a confirmatory favorable effect was required. This may be described as the prevailing view of association. The Hull-Spence theory uses the term "reinforcement" for such confirmatory effects and holds that mere association in time is not effective in establishing a stimulus signal as the effective elicitor of a response.

It should be remarked here that Pavlov used the term "reinforcement" to mean something very different. By the reinforcement of a signal Pavlov meant only another pairing of a signal with the stimulus that elicited a response. Food causes a dog's saliva to flow. A bell sounded just before food is presented will become a signal for the secretion of saliva. By reinforcements Pavlov meant only added pairings of the stimulus eliciting the response and the new stimulus which is to be made the associated signal.

The position taken in this book in this one feature resembles Pavlov's, but not Hull's. The form of the principle which is in my opinion the most useful is this: *A combination of stimuli which has accompanied a movement will on its recurrence tend to be followed by that movement.* Note that nothing is here said about "confirmatory waves" or reinforcement or pleasant effects.

Although the principle as it has just been stated is short and simple, it will not be clear without a considerable amount of elaboration. The word "tend" is used because behavior is at any time subject to a great variety of conditions. Conflicting "tendencies" or incompatible "tendencies" are always present. The outcome of any one stimulus or stimulus pattern can not be predicted with certainty because there are other stimulus patterns present. We may express this by saying that the final behavior is caused by the total situation, but we may not, in making this statement, flatter ourselves that we have done more than offer an excuse for a failure to predict. No one has recorded and no one ever will record any stimulus situation in its totality, or observed any total situation, so that to speak of it as a "cause" or even as the occasion of a bit of behavior is misleading.

The principle of conditioning thus stated with the word

"tend" merely asserts that on the recurrence of a stimulus pattern we can expect the former response, but with what certainty it does not state. The value of the probability can only be assigned as the result of observations of a number of like cases. If in one hundred instances of the recurrence of the stimulus pattern we find forty-one cases where the movement in which we are interested recurs, we may write this down as a law and add it to our psychological information. *The principle of conditioning is not an explanation of any instance of learning.* It is merely a blank form which explanations of instances of learning may take. It expresses only the conviction that we may profitably look for the signs of a movement among those stimuli which are now present and which were once before present with the movement.

So much for the word "tend." The phrase "combination of stimuli" also requires elaboration. "Stimulus" is a Latin word. The English for it is "goad." A goad is not the entire cause of the movement of the goaded animal, but only its occasion. A goad is ineffective on a stone or on an exhausted beast. Stimuli, likewise, are not the entire causes of movement, but only certain convenient signs of the movement to come. Movements do not always follow stimuli, but so far as the psychologist or physiologist knows, it is true that movements of the striped muscles which are employed in moving the body or in thinking are always preceded by stimuli. Stimuli are the necessary but not the sufficient conditions of movement. The muscles of the viscera, the smooth muscles, may contract and relax in response to chemical changes in their medium, or to internal rhythms. But movements of the striped muscles are generally believed to follow only when motor nerves are excited, and again, so far as we know, this excitement of motor nerves is in all normal behavior preceded by sensory nerve impulses, which are in their turn normally preceded by those changes at the sense organ which we call stimuli.

Having used the word many times we may now offer a be-lated definition: Stimuli are changes in the world order to which sense organs or receptors respond by exciting impulses in sensory nerves. At the risk of going somewhat astray from the topic of conditioning, something further must be said concerning the nature of stimuli. *The views of learning presented in this book are not dependent on any special theories of the physiology of the nervous system.* For the purpose of understanding learning, stimuli could be defined as changes in the physical world that occasion observable reaction on the part of an animal. But I am nevertheless strongly inclined to view the role of the nervous system as a system of pathways connecting sense organs with muscles and glands, pathways over which nerve impulses travel. I am also strongly inclined to believe that the occasion of every thought as well as of every act is to be found in stimuli acting on receptors. Thought is born in action, paradoxical as that may seem to those who notice how often action depends on thought; but it is possible to doubt, as I do, that we can report any thoughts which are not embodied in movement. Activity in the nervous system is, fortunately for the owners of nervous systems, normally dependent on a beginning in the sense organs by which we are in touch with the world and its changes. A train of thought, to be sustained, must somewhere effectively stimulate sense organs. The sense organs stimulated are those which are sensitive to our own movements, the proprioceptors, scattered throughout the skeletal muscles and at tendons and joints.

Stimuli can in a great many cases be observed and recorded. This is the reason that they serve so well as the warning of on-coming action. It is very rarely that we can observe the direct impact of change on the sense organ. What we can observe is the source of light, not the beam that enters our subject's pupil; or we hear or record the sound wave that must affect his ear, the same wave but on a different section of the wave front;

we can see and record movements and changes in posture, but the sense organs that these movements affect are hidden from direct observation. Movement, light, sound, pressure, skin contact, the contact of various substances with the olfactory membrane and with the taste papillae—these are what we mean by stimuli. The world may alter us by other means, by wounds, disease, by the nature of the food we eat, but it is only to changes that affect sense organs that we respond in the manner that is called behavior.

About one class of stimuli there has been considerable disagreement among psychologists and the position taken in this book differs radically from other views. The proprioceptors are the receptors in muscles, joints, tendons, and in the inner ear, which are sensitive to movements of our own bodies. When we raise an arm, this stimulates sense organs in the muscles, tendons, and joints of the arm.

Because these sense organs are buried in the body tissues, and because their stimuli are in a sense private to the individual stimulated, their importance in behavior has been neglected. Actually the continuity of behavior is largely dependent on proprioceptors. Through them behavior is coördinated and what is happening in one part of the body is adjusted to what is going on elsewhere.

The stimuli to proprioceptors are far more open to the observation of other persons than are stimuli to eyes, ears, or nose. It is easier to determine whether or not another person or an animal is running or sitting than it is to determine what the light pattern is on his retina or whether or not he hears what you are hearing. The theory of learning presented in this book makes use of observable movements as important determiners of response.

Through proprioceptive stimuli we are continuously in touch with our own movements and one movement can be related to another. Through exteroceptive stimuli we are in continuous touch with the world about us. The resultant behavior is a response to this total stimulation, a continuous compromise, a continuous integration. It would be hopeless for either psychologist or the man who has no interest in psychology to try to keep an eye on this totality of stimulation. The best that either can do is to select certain outstanding and conspicuous parts of the total stimulus situation and keep some record of their consequences. Among these particular stimuli that are selected for use as warnings of the act to come, we find that combinations of stimuli may have an importance that the component elements would lack. It is possible for stimulus combinations to act as signals of a response when parts of the combination would have no effect.

Skinner (1938) has suggested that the units of behavior observed must be so chosen that they permit repeated observation and the derivation of quantitative laws. His choice of such a unit was eminently successful by this criterion. It was the pressing down by an animal (a rat) of a bar which projected into the box in which the animal was confined. Skinner's very original contributions to learning theory will be given space later, but at this point some consideration of the nature of bar pressing as a unit of behavior is in order.

It should be noted first that the pressing of a bar by a rat does not denote any one movement or combination of movements. Skinner is indifferent to the means by which the bar is pressed, even going so far in his earlier experiments as to have the rat in a box which prevented observation of the animal's movements. The bar can be pressed by using the right paw, the left paw, both paws, or the snout, or by making an indefinite number of other movements and movement series. Bar pressing is an act, in the sense that it names the outcome of movements which are not specified.

Playing a tune on the piano is an act. The act is always accomplished by movements but it can be accomplished by a wide variety of movements. The naming of the act does not specify the movements. An armless man can learn to play skillfully with his feet. On different occasions a tune can be given radically different fingering by a player using his hands. "Going upstairs" may be accomplished on hands and knees, or by bounding up three steps at a time, or by proceeding slowly, with the aid of a hand on the banister. Naming an act like "writing a letter" does not describe or indicate the actual pattern of muscular action. We claim to have written a letter whether this was accomplished by pen or pencil, or by voice with the aid of a machine or a stenographer.

The difference between act and movement is of vital importance in learning theory because our accepted notion of the mechanism of response is that nerve impulses actuate muscular contraction, and if association or conditioning is to be related to changes in the nervous system it is specific movement patterns which must be dealt with.

To return to our principle, something must be said of the nature of the response. The principle was stated thus: A combination of stimuli which has accompanied a movement will, on its recurrence, tend to be followed by that movement. Movements, like stimuli, are complicated. We can not possibly follow or record the total response. All that we can do is to notice some feature of it, and attempt to forecast this. But the movement in response to stimuli is not a detached movement and it is affected by many stimuli which are not on the record. It will be affected by other movements and by our posture, as well as by those stimuli which remain outside our calculations. In other words, we will never get exactly the movement we were looking for. I may pick up a hot object and then hastily drop it. I have been looking at it as I picked it up and as I let it go. If we took the principle of conditioning literally, I might be expected at the next glimpse of the object to go through the motions of dropping it although it is not in my hand. As a matter of fact something like this often occurs. It is, however, more probable that the next sight of it will cause some movement of the muscles used in letting go but that this movement will be much disguised because it is in another context; the hand is not in the same position grasping the object. It may now be in my pocket, or engaged in holding a pipe. The visual pattern of the hot object is not the only stimulus acting; the pipe is in contact with the skin and the muscles used in grasping are maintaining contraction through circular nervous pathways from their own sense organs. These other sources may insure that grasping will be maintained, and the conditioned response may be present only in the form of a minute relaxation of the muscles.

I am taking a walk and at a certain point in the walk I meet a friend and stop to chat with him. When I repeat the walk the context of stimuli in which I met the friend may recur, but in the absence of the friend and in the strong tendency for an activity like walking to maintain itself through learned, associated sequences of movement I do not on this occasion stop and converse with the empty air. All that is evident of the conditioned response may be some remnant that constitutes thinking of the friend. This may include some traces of the greeting. We say that we are reminded of the friend at that point.

The conditioned response will thus never be the exact duplicate of the original behavior; but it will on many occasions be enough like the original behavior to make its prediction important.

Razran (1933) and Rexroad (1932) have each suggested an extension to the principle of conditioning which would recognize the fact that the dominating response has an advantage over a dominated response. Rexroad would formulate this as follows: "A stimulus gains effectiveness for a given response when the stimulus is followed by that response as a dominant response."

To illustrate: If a dog is offered food and at the same time struck a blow, his response is a compromise between eating the food and avoiding the blow. Neither whole-hearted eating nor complete avoidance will occur. If this situation is repeated, there is no rule by which we can tell in advance whether the final result will be that he will slink away on seeing that particular food, or that he will eventually secrete saliva on receiving the blow, making the blow a mere appetizer. This is not an absurd result, because Pavlov's laboratory found that blows, pinpricks, or burns could be made signals for eating and saliva flow, and the traces of the original protective movements practically disappeared. Rexroad's principle would hold that the dominant response, the response that was most in evidence, would eventually win.

I believe this extension of the principle of conditioning as it has been stated in this chapter is of very doubtful use. The principle of conditioning states that the movement that occurs will be the movement conditioned. The only test of dominance is the occurrence already provided for in the principle of conditioning. In the illustration just offered, the result of the first experience will undoubtedly be that both food and blow tend to call out the compromise. This may last indefinitely, and the dog for a long period may take that particular food under those particular circumstances with little enthusiasm, even though the blow is not repeated. For one response or the other to occur there must be further training in which the "dominant" response is facilitated, or in which the dominated response is lessened or inhibited. Dominance is a function of the relative intensity of stimuli and of facilitation and inhibition from the remainder of the situation. There can consequently be no general rules for dominance in advance of the event except experience which indicates that one response rather than the other *will occur*, and if it occurs the principle of conditioning indicates that it will be the response conditioned.

One more feature of the principle of conditioning as here offered may be noticed. It is confined to simultaneous association. The stimuli present *as the response occurs* are the future cues for the response. How this may be reconciled with the experimental findings that responses are associated with stimuli which precede or follow them, sometimes with an appreciable interval between, will be described in the chapter on time factors in conditioning.

The most extensive laboratory investigations of the conditioned response have been made in Russia, following the pioneer work of Pavlov, whose interest in the conditioned salivary reflex dates from the 'nineties. Laboratory experiments have brought out a large number of characteristics of the conditioned salivary reflex and of conditioned motor reflexes. Razran (1933) has made excellent summaries of the results of the early work on the conditioned reflex, including much material not before available in English. We may list separately a few of the best-established generalizations, most of them suggested by Razran:

1. The simple conditioned reflex is most readily established when the substitute stimulus is given shortly before the original stimulus (the stimulus used in the laboratory to elicit the reflex to begin with).

2. Simultaneous and backward conditioning are possible, but less effective than forward conditioning.

3. A substitute stimulus which, to use Pavlov's language, has been conditioned to a response loses this effect when it is repeatedly given without reinforcement from the original stimulus. This Pavlov calls *temporary extinction*.

4. This loss of effect can proceed further than the zero point, and the "extinguished" stimulus will have an inhibiting effect on the response.

5. Temporary extinction may disappear after a period of rest, or after disturbance from a new irrelevant stimulus.

6. When extinction is carried out repeatedly, recovery is progressively diminished, until it fails to take place.

7. When S_1 has been conditioned to a response, S_2 may be conditioned by being presented with S_1, S_3 by being presented with S_2, and so on. In my opinion this is not an important generalization, since the essential condition of associative learning is the association of the new stimulus *with the response, not with the original stimulus.*

8. A response involving widespread bodily action is more readily conditioned than a response confined to a few local effectors.

9. There seems to be evidence that among children conditioned responses are formed more readily as age advances, and more readily in the more intelligent.

10. The certainty of conditioning seems to depend on the number of pairings of substitute stimulus and response.

11. Negative or inhibitory conditioning is possible, achieved by presenting a stimulus and not insuring the response, or by distracting the response, or by inhibiting the response, or by presenting the substitute stimulus after the original stimulus. The signal has a positive inhibiting effect on the response. In many cases such inhibition is clearly accompanied by conflicting responses.

12. Retention of conditioned responses over a period of years has been reported.

13. A conditioned inhibiting stimulus has an aftereffect which may last as long as fifteen minutes. Such aftereffects are in some cases additive.

14. When a substitute stimulus has been conditioned, other

stimuli to the same class of sense organs may be found to elicit the response. This is called *generalization*.

15. If the substitute stimulus is presented some time before the original stimulus, this delay interval finally characterizes the conditioned response.

16. Similar stimuli (as two tones of about the same frequency) may be discriminated by following one but not the other with the response.

17. A point of resemblance can be reached at which this discrimination will fail and previous conditioning will be lost and a general disturbance of behavior appear.

18. The same disturbances in behavior can be produced by delaying the original stimulus in practice.

19. A stimulus acting separately and the same stimulus acting as an element of a pattern may have radically different effects; the combination may act as a conditioner and the element as an inhibiter, or the element may act as a conditioner and the combination as indifferent. When we refer to a "stimulus" we ordinarily mean a combination of stimuli in which the pattern is essential. Humphrey (1933, page 156) conditioned a response to a tone and found that when the tone was made part of a melodic phrase the conditioning effect was absent. Josiah Royce illustrated this point many years ago by pointing out that a man's response if we step on his foot and then apologize will be quite different from the response we elicit if we apologize and then step on his foot.

The last item on this list, pointing out that the pattern in which stimuli occur must be considered in speaking of stimuli as a cue or signal for a response, and that the stimuli in this pattern may act without reference to their effects when the elements are separate or arranged in different patterns, is not meant as an endorsement of the Gestalt doctrine that patterns are effective without reference to the particular sense organs they may be acting on. This will be considered later.

Pavlov's experiments required an original stimulus to elicit the response. This was the presentation of food or the introduction of acid into the dog's mouth, and the response was the secretion and discharge of saliva. This stimulus Pavlov called the unconditioned stimulus. Razran has suggested calling it the conditioning stimulus to indicate its active role in bringing about the conditioned response. This name is quite misleading, because the conditioning stimulus is not an essential to the effect. We shall here use the term "original stimulus" to name this already established stimulus when there is occasion to refer to it. The new stimulus which becomes a stimulus for a response through conditioning we shall call the *substitute stimulus*. The essential thing is that the response occur, whether we know just what stimuli are responsible for it or not. If the response occurs, such stimuli as accompany it tend to become substitute stimuli for it.

In many cases the response is dependent not on any one known original stimulus but on a complex situation in which the most important features are internal to the animal. Skinner (1938) chooses to class responses for which eliciting stimuli are not a matter of record as operant behavior, and to distinguish such responses from respondent behavior for which the eliciting stimuli are in evidence. The position here taken is that there are no basic differences in the response mechanisms involved and that eliciting stimuli are presumably present even in operant behavior.

Weiss' students at Ohio State University found (Pratt, Nelson, and Sun, 1930) that in newborn infants the specific nature of the response could not be predicted from the specific nature of the stimulus. The response which was occasioned by a light, a noise, a touch, was often some recently practiced response, for which the infant was presumably "set." The infant that had been fanning its toes was apt to respond to any of the stimuli offered it by reacting in this manner.

The view which a number of psychologists (including myself) held for a time, that the newborn infant is equipped with very definite reactions which can be set off by a limited group of definite stimuli, must be given up as the result of work on the development of behavior in animals and man. We can not go the whole distance with Holt (1931) and say that all stimulus-response associations are dependent on conditioning. Maturation of the nervous system appears to be the principal determiner of many classes of acts. McGraw (1933) found, in giving one of two twins elaborate training and comparing results with the untrained twin, that reaching for toys, crawling and standing up alone, sitting erect, grasping and the disappearance of grasping, using a tricycle, all appeared in the two children at the same time without regard to training, whereas climbing, roller skating, and other activities could be developed by training. Gesell (1929) has done similar work with twins; he reports a number of activities that seem to depend on maturity rather than on practice.

Even if we grant that much behavior must wait for the normal growth of the nervous system and that some cues for action are in this sense determined congenitally, conditioning remains the principal way in which the behavior of a person is adjusted to the peculiarities of his environment. If environments were all alike, maturation alone might care for the preservation of life and for propagation. But environments are not alike, and only through developing differential behavior can individuals be adjusted to different or to changing environments.

There are some reasons for thinking that the phenomenon of conditioning is part of a more inclusive rule. The clasping reflex of a frog is only intensified when stimuli which would cause a resting frog to jump are applied. Fighting dogs fight all the harder for the blows that would ordinarily send them howling away. We are forced to believe that new stimuli, unless they cause responses that break up an activity in progress, contribute to that activity and that this fact is intimately connected with their later tendency to evoke that activity. The conditioning effect, the contribution of new stimuli to an activity, is present on the first occasion as well as on the second. On the first occasion its presence is demonstrable only through the added energy of the response. On the second occasion the new stimuli may call out the response without the original stimuli which were necessary on the first occasion.

This has a bearing on the notion of dominance. When stimuli are present which would, if there were no competition, call out incompatible movements or movements of opposed muscle groups the results are complex. In some cases, or to some extent, the opposed muscle systems may be both thrown into contraction, and each group maintain its contraction. We know that a single muscle will respond to stretching or to resistance by heightening its own contraction through circular pathways. The resultant condition is conflict and excitement. But the competition of the opposed movements is not all on this tug-of-war basis. The contraction of one muscle group may result in the relaxation of opposed muscles through central inhibition. Sherrington has demonstrated this phenomenon, but there is after many years still not much agreement over the nature of the central mechanism by which it is achieved.

In this case, one of the two incompatible movements may inhibit the other and so dominate the other. The dominant response will then enlist the stimuli for the other competing response as its own conditioners. The pinprick will become a signal for saliva flow and eating movements; or the food will become a signal for protective withdrawal. Which of these will occur depends on the relative intensity of the competing stimuli, and on facilitation and inhibition from the remainder of the situation. There may result mutual inhibition and blocking without dominance. For this reason I hesitate to burden the theory of conditioning with a principle of dominance, although the principle as stated by Rexroad (1932) describes a common sequence of events, and it may be profitable to use the term "dominance" to describe this. The fact underlying dominance is that the response which occurs is the response that will be conditioned, even if this response is (as it always is to some degree) a compromise movement. The Russian laboratory dog on being pricked and offered food at the same time may eat, but he will eat with a difference. Some movement of avoidance disturbs eating; or he may avoid the pinprick, but with a backward glance at the food.

The principle of conditioning emerges from all these qualifications in a battered but recognizable form. The behavior we would predict or control, the habit we would modify, the name we wish to remember, the fear we wish to avoid, are not generally clear and definite acts. They are never twice just the same. But they are enough the same to be recognizable, and any light on the conditions under which they occur or fail to occur will be well worth while.

The reader is reminded that the views here presented are to be sharply distinguished from the theory that behavior is a composite of the conditioning of stereotyped reflexes. There are no stereotyped reflexes to begin with. The evidence now available would indicate that the first movements of the young animal are best described as general or massive, and that highly specific responses are, with possible exceptions, developed through conditioning in a manner that will be considered in the chapter on habits. E. B. Holt's book, *Animal Drive and the Learning Process*, is a clear and thorough exposition of the possibilities of conditioning as the process through which behavior develops. I do not go the whole way with Holt in his assertion that all the behavior currently attributed to maturation is the result of conditioning, nor do I agree that the physiological basis of conditioning is the growth of neurons in the direction of closer contact between active pathways. I am indulging in no physiological theories whatever, and am restricting myself to an effort to describe the phenomena of learning as they can be observed. Holt believes, for instance, that walking is purely the result of conditioning. I do not agree that we can yet give up the distinction between learning and the behavior that depends on growth and metabolism.

Holt's views and my own agree in being radically different from the notion of behavior as composed of unit reflexes. The statement of conditioning here offered, namely, that stimuli acting with a response tend later to elicit that response, says nothing of elementary reflexes. That which is conditioned is whatever complex of movements was in process, not isolated movements or glandular secretion. Pavlov kept his record of the salivary discharge, but recognized that this was only a small part of the total response which proved conditionable. The term "conditioning" is here preferred to Hollingworth's suggested "redintegration" because the integration of the response, the tendency for behavior to take on stereotyped habit patterns can be understood in terms of conditioning. When a response has once occurred its parts tend to condition each other. Redintegration better describes the total effect, but conditioning is the fundamental event.

Many of the objections to a theory of learning stated in terms of conditioning have been directed at the notion that the conditioned reflex of the Russian experiments is the fundamental type of all learning. The conditioned reflex, as developed in the Russian dogs, is not subject to forgetting to the extent that ordinary learning obviously is. Another objection lies in the susceptibility of the Pavlovian conditioned reflex to temporary extinction; a third objection is that practice seems necessary to establish the conditioned reflex, whereas many associations are established by a single conjunction. These objections are dealt with in succeeding chapters. In my opinion they are valid objections to the notion that the Pavlovian conditioned reflex is the elementary form of all learning; but they are not valid objections to the conception of conditioning here being described. The Pavlovian reflex is not an elementary form of learning, but a complex form. Its peculiarities and its differences from other forms of associative learning derive from the peculiar circumstances of the Russian experiments.

In the laboratory, for instance, the dog is exposed to stimuli which are very different from those he encounters in the kennel. If the kennel were equipped with bells and buzzers, negative adaptation and hence "forgetting" of the conditioned response to these noises would soon take place. As for the need for practice, Pavlov reported (1932) that in the earlier years fifty to one hundred repetitions were necessary to establish the conditioning, whereas improved methods made only ten to twenty necessary. If it were possible to control the dog's posture and movements or if reactions involving intense stimuli could be used, one pairing would undoubtedly be enough. Concerning temporary extinction it may be here remarked that such extinction is not a fundamental law of the conditioned response, but depends on the circumstances of the experiment, as will be explained in the chapter on inhibitory conditioning.

A more serious objection to conditioning as a fundamental principle of learning has come out of some of the experimental work on conditioning. Schlosberg (1932) found that the conditioning of the knee jerk to the sound of a bell failed to occur in some of his subjects in spite of indefinite repetitions, and this is an experience like several reported in our own laboratory. One spoken request to the subject would, of course, have led him to jerk his leg at the signal. This appears to make a sharp distinction between conditioning and voluntary action, and will undoubtedly lead those writers who have a strong prejudice for explaining the simple in terms of the complex to make voluntary action the more fundamental form of behavior and assert that conditioning depends on it.

Further research into the circumstances which favor or discourage conditioning is needed. Failure to elicit the knee jerk to the sound of a bell even after hundreds of pairings may lead to the discovery that the substitute stimulus must be responded to on its own account in order to establish conditioning. Reasons will be given in the following chapter for believing that it is not the bell but the movement-produced stimuli of the response (such as listening) to the bell that are the effective conditioners of the conditioned response.

The outstanding result of conditioning is the anticipation of natural events which have been experienced before. The sight of the bitter caterpillar first moved the chick to peck it. The bitter taste (for which we have the word of the entomologists) causes a vigorous rejection. On a second encounter the rejection takes place before the peck; the chick has what Lloyd Morgan has called a foretaste of the caterpillar and now does its rejecting in time to avoid embarrassment.

What does the principle of conditioning mean in the form of practical advice? Largely this, that if we wish to have any act of our own or of another under our control so that we can elicit it on occasion, we must go through the following procedure: First the act must be somehow or other elicited or simply awaited. If we know an effective stimulus for this, well and good. We must at least know that the act is within the animal's or the person's repertoire. We can not teach cows to retrieve a stick because this is one of the things that cows do not do. It is because dogs' behavior includes chasing sticks, taking objects into the mouth, walking and running, that we can build these into a conditioned response to a signal. At the beginning of the act we may speak a word or make a movement which will in time become the cue for the act.

If we wish to teach a dog to come when he is called, our method will be to get him to come to us by hook or crook. There are no rules for this except what we know of dogs in general. We may hold up a bone, start running away from the dog, pull him toward us with a check line, or use any device which experience has suggested. While he is coming we speak the dog's name. If we take care not to speak the name on any occasion when we foresee that he will not come—when he is, for instance, chasing a cat or gnawing a bone (when we believe an unwanted response is dominant)—we can readily establish a stable conditioned response. We say that the dog "knows" his name. If we are so misguided as to try to call him back from the pursuit of a passing car before we have insured the effectiveness of calling, we have reconditioned the dog and made his name a signal for chasing cars, not for coming to us.

The skilled trainer uses his dog's name only when the prompt response is highly certain. If the response fails, he does not repeat the name, but uses his practical knowledge to remove the cause of failure or waits until the cause is removed. The dog may have been occupied in looking at another dog or watching a passer-by. The trainer waits until he has the dog's attention before he repeats the name. Otherwise the name tends to become a cue for looking at the passer-by or noticing other dogs.

It is on exactly the same ground that the student officer is cautioned never to give a command that he is not confident will be obeyed. If the command is followed by acts other than those commanded, the command becomes merely a cue for disobedience and the officer loses his authority.

If we are ourselves concerned to learn to address a new acquaintance by name we can achieve that result by following a simple rule: Speak his name while looking at him. Social convention prevents our using a method which would insure remembering. This method consists in shouting his name at the top of our voice while looking at him.

A memory for names consists in very simple habits of using the rule of conditioning. The person who excels at it has a settled habit of using names in conservation while looking at his victims, or of rehearsing them subvocally under the same circumstances. The reason most of us fail is that we do not look at the man while naming him. The person with the memory for names takes occasion to do this as often as he can manage: "Yes, Mr. Walker. . . . No, Mr. Walker. . . . Don't you think so, Mr. Walker?"

An examination of the methods of the successful animal trainer or of the well-written practical book on training will find that these can be translated into terms of conditioning with astonishing ease.

CHAPTER IV

Time Factors in Conditioning

Two small country boys who lived before the day of the rural use of motor cars had their Friday afternoons made dreary by the regular visit of their pastor, whose horse they were supposed to unharness, groom, feed and water and then harness again on the departure. Their gloom was lightened finally by a course of action which one of them conceived. They took to spending the afternoon of the visit retraining the horse. One of them stood behind the horse with a hayfork, periodically shouted "Whoa," and followed this with a sharp jab with the fork. Unfortunately no exact records of this experiment were preserved, save that the boys were quite satisfied with the results. The experiment, if it could be repeated on a large scale with many horses, could have been so managed as to throw a considerable amount of light on a very important problem in conditioning. What interval between the shout and the jab would result in the most efficient learning of the association? How great an interval could there be and association still occur? Could the shout have been given after the prodding and have the sound become a conditioner of the vigorous lunge that the boys actually succeeded in attaching to the word?

Will we learn the French equivalents of English words more rapidly if we first read the French and then the English, or the other way about? How long can punishment be delayed after the crime and still have a deterrent effect? Will we have to induce the burglar to reënact the crime and punish him just as he performs, or even a bit before he begins his burglary?

43

These questions all concern the time relations between cue and act. The answers to these questions have been made very difficult by an accidental bad start on the method of studying the conditioned response in the laboratory. Most of the textbooks of general psychology give the answer thus: Conditioning will be most certain if the cue is given along with the original stimulus; the cue can be given somewhat before the original stimulus and still have some effect; but the cue can not be given after the original stimulus and have any conditioning effect.

The essential mistake of this description and of the experimental work based upon it lies in viewing the two stimuli, the original stimulus and the substitute stimulus, as the associated items. It is the time relations between these stimuli that are observed and recorded. But the time relations between the original stimulus and the substitute stimulus are of no particular importance except that they are fairly easy to record. *It is the time relations between the substitute stimulus and the response that count.* It is not the two stimuli that are associated, but the substitute cue and the resultant act.

Like sleep, fatigue also has the effect of diminishing or eliminating the conditioned response. (Cf. Bykow, 1927.) Not the original stimulus, but the response, is the essential of conditioning. If the response fails, conditioning does not occur.

Pavlov used for the original or unconditioned stimulus food or acid introduced into the mouth. There is some evidence that in human beings the movements of chewing cause salivary secretion. In case this is also true of dogs, the original stimulus of food becomes somewhat questionable as the true occasion for salivary flow. Food might start chewing, and chewing start secretion. If we have measured or recorded the instant at which food is offered, this may have been separated from the actual stimuli for saliva by a series of events and one of the later parts of this series is the real occasion for secretion.

Hollingworth has pointed out that for most responses there

is no one original stimulus. The response is the outcome of a large complex of stimuli acting on the animal. He discarded the term "conditioning" as too much committed to definition in terms of an original stimulus. His principle, which he calls the principle of redintegration, is to the effect that after a response has occurred, a part of the original situation present may re-establish the total response. The writer's formula is very similar to this: Stimuli acting at the time of a response tend on their recurrence to evoke that response. But this formula implies definite simultaneity, whereas Hollingworth is noncommittal on that point. There is good reason to believe that in the time relations of cue and act, definite simultaneity is essential for conditioning. The cue must accompany the act if the association is to be formed.

If we follow the method of most of the experimenters and observe the time relations of original and substitute stimuli, there is clear evidence that the two can be separated in time by a considerable interval and association result. Pavlov reported such separation effective for intervals as long as thirty minutes.

If a bell is rung and then, after an interval of, say, two minutes, food is presented, with resultant secretion of saliva, and if this sequence is practiced over and over, the result will be that the cue can be sounded and, after a two-minute interval, saliva will flow whether food is presented or not. Pavlov called this a trace reflex. If the signal is continued throughout the interval he called it a delayed reflex, though the difference between the two is not fundamental.

Even backward conditioning can occur. The signal can be given after the original stimulus and still become an effective conditioner. Whether the boys with the preacher's horse could have achieved this with the sequence, first prod and then "Whoa," we unfortunately do not know. But Wolfle (1932) found something very like this to work. She had an apparatus which gave the fingers a shock; on receiving this the hand would be jerked away from the contact. Sounding a buzzer before the shock or after the shock (backward conditioning) both gave some conditioning. The most effective method was to sound the buzzer three-tenths of a second before the shock, which resulted in conditioning in 58 percent of the cases. Giving the sound just with the shock at short intervals through a forty-minute period resulted in 10 percent of conditioned responses when the sound was given alone. Giving the sound one second after the shock (backward conditioning) resulted in an occasional conditioned response to the noise. Similar results are reported by Spooner and Kellogg (1947).

Experiments with association also show that the cue and the original stimulus can be separated by long intervals and the association still be effective. In one experiment in the association of a nonsense syllable and a nonsense figure (Guthrie, 1933; see also Spooner and Kellogg, 1947) the syllable is thrown on a screen by an automatic projector; there is then an interval of darkened screen and this is followed by the projection of the shape. The intervals between stimuli can be varied. The object is to make the odd figure the cue for pronouncing the syllable with which it is associated. This is backward association, since the original stimulus is shown first and the stimulus that is to become the cue is shown later. The associative strength as shown by the percentage of the list of syllables correctly named when the figures alone were displayed proved to be greater at an interval of 4.9 seconds than for 2.5 seconds.

Forward association, curiously enough, was of almost the same effectiveness as backward at corresponding intervals, and had no advantage. In Pavlov's experiments when maximum conditioning effect was wanted, an interval of about two seconds was used and the substitute cue given first.

How can it be maintained, in the light of such results, that conditioning and association are actually simultaneous? My own answer to this is that the substitute stimulus which is made a matter of record is very seldom the actual immediate stimulus for the conditioning. If it were, Cason (1924) would probably be right in claiming backward association to be an impossible sort of event. How could a stimulus become attached to a response that is over and gone? Or how could a stimulus become attached to a response that is not to take place for five minutes? But if the bell, or the light, or whatever is used as the substitute cue is not the true conditioning stimulus, what is?

The answer is that there are other stimuli in plenty to take that role. When a bell is rung or a light is flashed or any new and emphatic stimulus is applied to an animal, the animal will respond to that stimulus. It will listen to the bell; in response to the light it will move its head and eyes; at a pinprick it will move away its body or its leg; at a smell it will sniff and turn its head. Every such motion is a stimulus to many sense organs in muscles, tendons, and joints, as well as the occasion for changing stimuli to eyes, ears, etc. We may call them *movement-produced* stimuli, for the reason that they are produced by our own movements.

Such a movement as listening or looking is not over like a flash or an explosion. It takes time. The movement, once started, maintains itself by the stimuli it furnishes. When the telephone bell rings we rise and make our way to the instrument. Long before we have reached the telephone the sound has ceased to act as a stimulus. We are kept in action by stimuli from our own movements toward the telephone. One movement starts another, that a third, the third a fourth, and so on. Our movements form series, very often stereotyped in the form of habit. *These movements and their movement-produced stimuli make possible a far-reaching extension of association or conditioning.* They make possible remote association in which the remoteness is limited only by the length of such a regular series of movements. The nervous impulses directly resulting from the sound of a bell are over in a fraction of a second. They travel in nerve trunks as fast as 400 feet in one second, and in a very tall man they have a comparatively short distance to go to any muscle. Strictly speaking, we are answering the bell only for the first half second or so; after that we are answering our own actions. In this case, of course, the series of movements set up is not perfectly stereotyped. We avoid the edge of the table, reach for a pencil, pick up the telephone in response to new "outside" stimuli, but not only in response to these outer stimuli. Our own movements are our chief guides. The effects of the bell may reverberate through our whole future; but the direct impulses from the sound are soon over.

To return to the delayed or trace reflex—here the real direct conditioner of the salivary flow was not the signal given by the experimenter, but the movement pattern of the resulting series of listening movements which happened to be simultaneous with the discharge of the salivary gland.

Pavlov reported that during the waiting period of a delayed reflex new stimuli may either prevent the expected response or lead to its premature release. How are we to account for this unless we assume that the new stimulus has broken in on the serial response initiated by the cue, and may either prevent the actual movement-produced conditioner from appearing, or, in rare instances, hasten it?

It is only fair to the reader to warn him that Pavlov, the pioneer experimenter in this field and the scientist who undoubtedly had the most extended acquaintance with the phenomena of conditioning, sharply disagreed with me concerning the role of these movement-produced stimuli in producing delayed and backward conditioning. One of the experiments which he cited (1932) in his argument furnishes, to my notion, a beautiful illustration of the possible role of movement-produced stimuli in timing the response.

The experiment is this: A conditioned reflex is formed by giving a signal, such as a buzzer. There is then a short interval of waiting, followed by the administering of food. After this sequence has been practiced a number of times there appears the ordinary conditioned reflex; the dog on hearing the buzzer secretes saliva.

Then the program is changed. The interval is lengthened to a few minutes instead of a few seconds. The conditioned reflex quickly disappears when the food no longer follows at the practiced short interval. As the changed program is repeated there is gradually formed a new conditioned reflex with a latent period of minutes instead of seconds. Pavlov did not say that a new reflex is formed, but that the reflex "reappears." It is my belief that the two-second reflex was conditioned to some movement pattern that followed the buzzer, not directly to the buzzer. When the method is changed this conditioned reflex disappears, as such reflexes will if not reinforced with food, and another reflex conditioned on a later movement pattern, the one coinciding with the belated food, is established.

These delayed and trace conditionings are familiar in everyday experience. A good drillmaster always gives his commands in the same tempo. After his preparatory command the command of execution must follow at just the practiced instant or there will be conditioned and premature movements of execution. Where traffic is changed by a double bell signal, a delay of the second signal will find many drivers starting without it. Keeping time with the world is so familiar that our illustrations are striking only when something has gone wrong. The sound of a footstep leads us to expect a visitor after an interval; the musician resumes playing after a musical rest without disturbing the rhythm; Mark Twain describes the tense anxiety produced by the failure of the hotel guest retiring in the room above to throw his second shoe on the floor; we have all waited breathlessly for the inexpert pianist next door to play the delayed chord.

The timing of a delayed response to a stimulus may be

astonishingly exact. The clock mechanism by which this timing is done is not to be looked for where Pavlov sought it, in obscure delays in the cerebral impulses. It is not necessary to suppose that brain nerve cells can hold up impulses and release them when ready, possibly two minutes later. There is a much more obvious method by which this timing can be accomplished. It can depend on peripheral movements and the sensory impulses caused by these movements.

There may exist some cerebral rhythms. Sherrington believes that the rhythm of a dog's scratch reflex is centrally determined and is independent of the return impulses from the muscles. I am not at all sure that the same results would be found for such a movement as tail wagging. Do dogs that have been relieved of the mass and length of a long tail by early operation wag faster than dogs that carry this burden? If they do it is probably because movement to the right has to wait until movement to the left has given the cue.

A generation ago there were many experiments comparing the relative effectiveness of simultaneous and successive association. The experiments were a no-decision affair as they should have been, because the results depended on the opportunity for simultaneous conditioning offered by the particular activity studied. Pavlov and many others (Borovski, 1927) reported that maximum conditioning occurs when the cue is given from 0.2 to 2 seconds before the original stimulus. In less than two-tenths of a second the sensory nerve impulses have probably had all the direct effect that they ever will have; and it is not their direct effect on the brain, but the effects of their effects, the movement-produced stimuli from the movements they start, that serve as the release of the conditioned response when it comes.

Backward conditioning is probably like forward conditioning in depending on the actual coincidence of the real cue and the response. It is ordinarily harder to establish in simple reflexes than is forward conditioning. That it can be established at all probably depends on the fact that no normal contraction of muscle in behavior is instantaneous, and the substitute stimulus for contraction can be established as long as the contraction is taking place. This often lasts for some time after the original stimulus has stopped.

When the contraction is over, the chance for conditioning is lost. Cason (1922) found it impossible to condition a wink to a cue given after the wink was over. Krasnogorski is quoted by Pavlov to the effect that giving the cue two to ten seconds after administering food brought no conditioning even when repeated a thousand times. There was in Krasnogorski's experiment no record of the time relation of the cue to the actual response, however.

Most movements are not so episodic as the wink, and hence are more susceptible to backward conditioning. And some behavior involves the repetition of movements, so that conditioning can take place long after the original stimulus. This is true in experiments on association which use speech. In our own laboratory (Guthrie, 1933) we found that a nonsense figure exposed on a screen 4.9 seconds after a name had been exposed became, after some practice, a cue for the name. It became a more effective cue than when the interval was only 2.5 seconds. None of the experiments on backward conditioning of simple movements found conditioning at such long intervals. I am convinced that this remote association was possible because the name was still being responded to when the figure was shown. The syllable was being "held" or in some cases being repeated as the figure appeared on the screen. Most of the subjects reported that they could thus "hold in mind" the figure or the syllable for some seconds. Of course they were holding it in their muscles as well as in their quite problematic minds, but their report was substantially correct.

In associative learning involving speech or thought, conditioning loses its clear time relationships. It is so difficult to observe the movements that accompany thinking that we can not know just when the response is present and when not. Original stimulus and substitute stimulus may be separated for days, and their association depend on mediating associations. This is true in cases where delayed punishment is effective. When a parent spanks a child for writing on the living-room walls an hour after the offense and in a different room, the only possibility that the punishment will establish a new response to walls and pencil in hand is that speech is so well established in the child that it can conjure up the tempting situation by its associations. Through language the child is stood again before the wall with a pencil, and by the spanking the original tendency to write is displaced by other tendencies.

We may be told that the name of the man we met yesterday is Wilberforce, and remember this when we next see him. The phrase, "the man you met yesterday," serves to reinstate our perceptual response to the man, and with this is associated the name. When we come across him the perceptual response occurs and now serves as a cue for the name.

Robinson has suggested (1931) that the law of association by contiguity should state associative strength as a function of the interval between the cue stimulus and the original stimulus. This function would be graphically represented by a curve rising from the very low values for backward association to a maximum for simultaneous association. It would fall off more gradually as the interval increases in forward association.

This curve of Robinson's fits very well the experimental results of conditioning simple movements, except that maximum associative strength is found when the substitute cue is given a fraction of a second before the original stimulus, and not when the two stimuli are given together. But Robinson's curve does not at all fit the results of experiments in word association like the experiment of my own described above. The type of curve depends on the nature of the material used in the experiment, and ultimately on the chances for overlapping of cue and response.

The reason why forward association is so much more effective in experiments with animals and with simple movement in human beings is that the cue or signal used in the experiment may start its own movement series of indefinite length, and any phase of this movement series may act as a simultaneous conditioner when the response takes place. We get better results with short intervals because we can depend on the movement series to be more stereotyped for a short interval.

Backward association, on the other hand, usually depends on the prolongation of the movement conditioned, and so the cue must often occur within the space of a second. If we wait longer, the response is no longer there to be conditioned. In experiments with word association we have to deal with very complicated learning. Attention is more precarious. We can not be as sure that a subject really "looks at" a word or a figure on a projection screen as we are that he jerks his hand away from a shock or hears the sudden noise of a buzzer. And in word material the subject may continue to form the word soundlessly, or continue to perceive the figure after the word and figure are gone. He may be rehearsing inner speech without our knowledge. We find the curve of relationship between associative strength and associative interval in this case quite different. There is no general curve for the relationship between associative strength and associative interval because different activities offer differing opportunities for simultaneous conditioning.

We may summarize our findings on the question of the time relation between a conditioned signal and its response. The actual associative process is probably always dependent on a precise coincidence of the cue and the response for which it becomes a cue. This, however, requires the assumption that the actual cue is seldom the observed and recorded one. The recorded cue has started a series of events, and one of these unrecorded and usually unnoticed events is the signal directly responsible for the nerve impulses that begin the movement.

Our theory, then, can not give clear advice about such questions as were asked at the beginning of the chapter. It becomes necessary to know something about the nature of the activity before we can say whether a long or a short interval between the signal and the desired response will be more effective, or before we can say whether the signal should be practiced before or after the original stimulus. It is possible to say that in a simple movement like the flexing of an arm, signals have a maximum effect when given a fraction of a second before the response. The length of this time interval would indicate that the effective conditioner is not the signal given, but the response to that signal. In our illustration at the beginning of the chapter the farm boys in their sinister training of the pastor's horse undoubtedly followed this procedure and shouted "Whoa" an appreciable time before applying the fork. It is to the horse's perceptual response to "Whoa" and not directly to the word that the response is attached. In human behavior, many of our acts are conditioned, not directly on the external cues, but on the perceptual response to these cues. In verbal association, these perceptual responses can be so maintained and repeated that the underlying simultaneity of the actual conditioning is effectively hidden from observation.

CHAPTER V

Inhibitory Conditioning

WE BREAK habits as well as form habits. Under what circumstances does a conditioned stimulus cease to call out its response? Learning any skill depends as much on getting rid of awkward movements and useless movements as it does on acquiring the proper movements to the proper cues. How do we lose hates and loves, fears and indignations, our memory of friends' names, our typing errors, our enthusiasms? What rules can we follow to rid ourselves of annoying habits? Can such rules as are offered us fit into our general theory of learning?

The fact is that a stimulus which has, to use Pavlov's language, been conditioned to a response may become not only "unconditioned" or "deconditioned" but an actual discourager or inhibiter of a response. We shall use the term *distraction* to describe the effect of diminishing or partially impeding a response; for the prevention of a response, or of its overt expression, the term *inhibition* is to be used. Inhibition is almost never complete. Even when overt expression is prevented there is usually discernible some minimal expression of any response for which cues have been received.

How do stimuli become distracters or inhibiters of an action? We may recall that in the case of the pastor's horse the sound of the word "Whoa" had previously been a signal for stopping. This had been in turn the effect of training in which the horse had been checked by the rein and the sound uttered a second or so before. The boys' efforts had substituted another reaction for the conventional one and in effecting this substitution the word became an inhibiter of the first response.

A stimulus which has become a conditioner of such an act as turning the head to the right or dilating the pupil of the eye, or of any movement whatever, will necessarily inhibit turning the head to the left, or contracting the pupil, or performing movements incompatible with its conditioned response. Turning the head to the right physically prevents turning it to the left, but that is not all. Physiologists, notably Sherrington, have demonstrated in many instances the existence of a reciprocal innervation which brings it about that the contraction of one set of allied muscles tends to relax the muscles opposed. This interference is accomplished through central connections which allow flexor muscles, through their muscle sense organs and central nervous system connections, to deprive the extensor muscles of impulses or allow the extensors to have the corresponding effect on the flexors.

When rival movements are both in process, the outcome of the rivalry is in some cases undoubtedly a matter of the relative strength of the opposed movements, but in most cases it is also a question of priority, much as at a grade crossing the train which reaches the crossing first sets a derailing switch against any competing train.

A stimulus may thus be unconditioned by the very simple means of becoming a conditioner for an incompatible movement. Unlearning becomes merely a case of learning something else. And the rule which states whether conditioning or unconditioning will occur becomes simply the familiar principle of conditioning: Stimuli which are acting at the time of a response become conditioners of that response. In this case, *the response referred to in the rule is a response incompatible with the former response.* The horse can not lunge forward and stop at the same time. This is physically and neurologically impossible. The signal inhibits stopping because it has become alienated from that response by a later association with the incompatible response.

In his typical experiment Pavlov accustomed the dog to the experimental room and apparatus. When the experiment begins after several days of this introductory training the dog is stimulated by the ringing of a bell, and this is followed in perhaps two seconds by the presentation of food. When the bell rings the dog pricks up his ears and turns his head or makes other movements which we may describe as listening. The presentation of food interrupts these movements and causes the dog to turn to the food and eat. We have been in the habit of describing these responses as (1) listening and (2) eating, and of speaking as though the responses both maintained their original character after they had occurred together. This is a misleading description, because it attributes a false simplicity to the event. In reality, after their conjunction, neither response is the same. The two responses can not take place in the same dog and fail to affect each other. Eating may supplant listening when the food is administered, but some traces of listening behavior persist. The resultant response is not an exact reinstatement of either listening or eating. And it is the resultant that is conditioned.

Pavlov stated (1932) that the listening movements gradually disappear, so that no trace of them finally remains after a number of practice periods, and the bell causes the dog to lick his chops and stand ready to eat. This statement calls for a little skepticism. The gradual disappearance of listening may leave many traces in the final behavior of eating which are not conspicuous but still are present.

Why should listening tend gradually to disappear? What parts of listening disappear first? Razran and Rexroad would answer this in terms of a principle of dominance. In Rexroad's words, "A stimulus gains effectiveness for a given response when the stimulus is followed by that response as a dominant response." I believe the words, "as a dominant response," are here unnecessary. The stimulus gains effectiveness for whatever response or mixture of response it is that follows.

The answer to the question why listening tends gradually to disappear is that some of the movements of listening and of eating are incompatible. Food and the dog's hunger in causing him to eat cause him to stop listening—at least to end such motions of listening as are incompatible with eating. Listening becomes a cue for eating plus such traces of listening as have not been inhibited by eating. In so far as the two acts are incompatible, eating has won. The outcome might have been very different. If the noise of the signal had been so loud as to inhibit the movements of eating and cause the animal to struggle in the apparatus, the administering of food would have become a cue for fright and struggle.

The response that prevails has the advantage. Tensions in the opposing muscles of the submerged response were overcome, some of them physically, by superior force, and some of them through neural inhibition. On the next occasion such inhibition tends to occur earlier, to be anticipated, for this is a normal result of conditioning. The result is that one response or the other, in so far as they are incompatible, finally prevails more and more thoroughly and enlists the stimuli for the submerged response as cues for the prevailing response. But the final conditioned act is not a replica of either original response.

It will be seen from this account that the Pavlovian conditioned reflex is by no means an instance of simple conditioning in the sense in which that word is used in this book. Pavlov's conditioned salivary reflexes are to be explained in terms of conditioning, but they are not the elementary forms of conditioning on which to base a theory. There are no such elementary cases of conditioning in an animal of any complexity because its behavior is not to be described in terms of a limited number of elementary responses or reflexes which can be named and numbered and easily identified. The very process of conditioning confuses and mingles responses into new combinations. The behavior of any animal is a total integration in which we recognize and name occasional familiar details. Our only hope of predicting behavior, and hence our only hope of a theory of learning lies in describing the approximate circumstances in which such recognizable details will occur. It is our present contention that the circumstances under which responses recur include stimuli present when the response last occurred.

It is quite consistent with this conception of conditioning to describe *inhibitory conditioning* as the conditioning of some inhibitory response. A stimulus which has in the past contributed to one set of movements may cease to do this and may act as an inhibiter of such movements when it has been associated with another response. The loss of an associative connection with a response was called *negative adaptation* by Stevenson Smith and me in our *General Psychology*. At that time we suggested three ways in which inhibitory conditioning could be brought about. *The three ways all involved the presence of the cue and the prevention of the response.*

A conditioned stimulus may be acting and the response fail simply because the stimulus is below the threshold; or the response may be eliminated through exhaustion or fatigue; or the response may be inhibited by the action of incompatible responses. In any one of these three cases a stimulus is present and a certain response fails to occur. Other responses do always occur. The result is that the stimulus conditions the other responses and is thus an inhibiter of the response in which we were interested.

To these three methods of establishing inhibitory conditioning by insuring the failure of the response there may be added a fourth, to which Dodge has called attention: The substitute stimulus may be applied again so soon after its response that the response is still in what is called its refractory period. The evidence is that most responses have such a refractory period. Immediately after the movement has taken place there is an interval during which the movement can not be elicited; following this there is a period during which the stimulus must be of greater than normal intensity in order to elicit the response. This is called the relative refractory period and may also show itself by a diminished response to a normal stimulus. This method of establishing inhibitory conditioning is, like the others, the result of applying the stimulus under circumstances which prevent the response. The conditioned stimulus loses its connection with the former response because it has become attached to other behavior.

A bitter taste may be so slight that it fails to cause ejection of food. Such a taste may be introduced into food very gradually and the result be a toleration of a degree of bitterness which at first would have been out of the question. This is an instance of the first method of negative adaptation. The bitter taste has been present in increasing degree. It becomes a conditioner of appetite and eating, and may eventually be necessary to the enjoyment of some foods. In the same manner we may become adapted to the pain of fatigue or late hours, or to cold temperatures, new diets, changing conditions of life, without once having been disturbed if the changes are gradual enough.

Whitford's *Training the Bird Dog* suggests how the trainer may bring about negative adaptation to the noise of the gun. Training should commence with the discharge of a cap pistol at a great distance from the dog, and without any unusual movements on the trainer's part. Later a louder pistol may be used, and a shorter distance. This may be followed by light loads discharged from a gun (pages 76–79). If by bad training or unfortunate combination of circumstances a dog has been made gun-shy, retraining is a long and tedious affair, and not ordinarily worth the trouble.

I once asked an old cavalry sergeant who "broke" the new

horses furnished the regiment. His language cannot be repeated here, but it was to the effect that no horsebreakers were used in the army. The method used is the first method of negative adaptation described. The trainer keeps always within the threshold of tolerance of the animal. First a light blanket, and then possibly a sack with a little grain are put on the horse's back. At no time is the horse so startled that it plunges or struggles. In time new burdens and harness are added until the horse is accustomed to the weight of a rider and to the bridle without ever having been stirred to excited resistance. The method used on the western ranches was often very different. The wild horse was forcibly saddled, bridled, and mounted. The rider "stuck out" the resultant struggles until the horse was too exhausted to struggle more. At this stage the disturbing stimuli are present but are not reacted to, and negative adaptation is taking place. The disadvantage of this method is that traces of the first learning in which the rider and equipment are responded to with struggle are apt to survive the breaking. Reconditioning is not complete.

Thus inhibitory conditioning may be brought about by furnishing the stimulus situation when fatigue or exhaustion has stopped the response as well as by increasing the stimulus and keeping it always under the threshold or within the tolerance of the individual. In both cases the stimulus becomes the conditioner of other responses and so an inhibiter of the undesired response. Many a speaker has never suffered from stage fright because his introduction to public appearance has been so gradual that excitement has never appeared. Others, perhaps the majority, recover from stage fright only through being forced to go through with their performance and to continue after the excitement has passed. If they give way during the excitement, positive adaptation occurs and they become incapable of composure before an audience. If they continue on many occasions through the excitement and after it has ceased, the sight of the audience no longer disorganizes their behavior. It is during this period that negative adaptation is taking place. The stimulus situation which had caused excitement is present, but the excitement has been replaced by other behavior. The stimulus situation now conditions the new behavior.

The third way in which inhibitory conditioning or negative adaptation may be brought about is through the presentation of a stimulus at a time when its response is inhibited by other elements in the situation. Here also the stimulus is present, but other responses are present shutting out the former response, and the stimulus becomes a conditioner of these and an inhibiter of its former response. Whether or not the child comes at his mother's call depends on what he is doing as well as on the loudness of her call. By calling him only when he is occupied any child can promptly be negatively adapted to his mother's voice.

Whether a student will be able to read in the bustle of a library room depends on his early experiences there. If he begins with an engrossing book he will attain quick adaptation to the noise about him. If he begins by noticing what is going on in the room, the open book will eventually be a mere cue for looking about. The city dweller when he visits the country finds that he was dependent on the city traffic noises for his sleep and lies awake through a quiet night. One wakeful night or two, however, and his trouble is over. Fatigue makes sleep more imperative; and while sleeping in country surroundings, these surroundings become the new conditioners of a good night's rest. Bachelors often enjoy negative adaptation to rattling windows and dripping faucets and sleep peacefully through such disturbances; after marriage and enforced nocturnal investigations of house noises they find that sleep is impossible while the noise continues.

Dodge is responsible for pointing out (1927) that inhibitory conditioning may be achieved by presenting the cue during that brief refractory period after a response when the response can not be elicited. This also comes under the rule that when the cue occurs but the response *is prevented by any means,* negative adaptation of the response to that cue takes place. After the knee jerk, Dodge reports (1931) that a second stimulus of the same intensity elicits a second reaction averaging two-thirds the amplitude of the first. The refractoriness of the lid reflex lasts two or more seconds. "Direct experimental evidence," he says (1931, page 18), "for refractory phase in neural systematizations higher than the reflexes has hitherto been conspicuously inconclusive. This is especially true of cerebral systems. There is, however, a strong theoretical presumption that some barrier to repetition analogous to refractory phase is a post-stimulation phenomenon of all neural tissue. Such a presumption is congruent with many observed facts in behavior and consciousness, but there are few experimental techniques for demonstrating it." "It is," he suggests, "apparently combined in some unknown way with a longer process of negative adaptation." Whether this refractory phase, demonstrable in nerve and in simple reflexes, has any bearing on our disinclination to repeat more complicated behavior immediately is not, of course, at all clear. It would be somewhat absurd to account for a small boy's unwillingness to respond to an immediate second request for his name by calling this a refractory period. This may be a very different brand of refractoriness. Since the work of Dodge there has been remarkably little research into the role of refractory phase and learning.

Many psychoanalytic cures are undoubtedly instances of the third form of inhibitory conditioning. Pathological fear or disgust is felt on speaking or thinking of some situation. The psychoanalyst leads the patient to speak of the critical event under carefully controlled conditions which, through the prepared response of the patient to the analyst, tend to inhibit the obnoxious emotional response and to condition the situation to such substitute responses as prevail in frank conversation. The prominence of the erotic in psychoanalytic method does not indicate that the causes of the neurosis are uniformly erotic in nature, but that sex is a topic of rather universal interest and hence an easy and practical general approach to the establishment of the responses and attitudes which are to be substituted for the neurosis. The occasions for the neurosis may be rather remote from sex and peculiar to the patient. In a country where food is scarce it is probable that the approach to the cure could be as readily established through conversation about food as through conversation about sex.

In other words, the analyst uses erotic conversation for its distracting and finally inhibiting effect on the neurotic behavior, and in many cases achieves the reconditioning of the disturbing topics and incidents to harmless response. The same process is involved when we recount an embarrassing incident to our friends and their laughter at our discomfiture causes us to laugh and the memory of the experience loses its power to shame us. A case still more elementary is the effect of a lollypop on a crying child. In psychoanalytic practice, erotic conversation serves in place of the lollypop for the distraction and inhibition of the undesired response and furnishes a chance for retraining. Dollard and Miller (1950) have spelled out many very convincing applications of conditioning to psychotherapy and psychoanalysis.

We choose our final illustration from the laboratory. Razran (1933, page 86) quotes an experiment by Slutskaya in which children were pricked with a needle and formed a voci-motor avoiding conditioned response to the sight of the needle. This was followed immediately by feeding. In three out of five cases in normal children the conditioned stimulus for avoidance became a conditioned stimulus for swallowing or eating movements. The needle had become an appetizer.

Unmaking a bad habit is thus essentially the same process as establishing a good habit. Bad habits are broken by substituting

for them good habits or innocuous habits. The rule for breaking an undesired conditioned response becomes this: So control
the situation that the undesired response is absent and the cue
which has been responsible for it is present. This can be accomplished by fatiguing the response, or by keeping the intensity
of the cue below the threshold, or by stimulating behavior that
inhibits the undesired response. If the cue or signal is present
and other behavior prevails, the cue loses its attachment to the
obnoxious response and becomes an actual conditioner of the
inhibiting action.

Many an adult who suffers from "cat fear" has been thus re-
trained by tolerating in the house a kitten so small and helpless
that the fear is not called out. The kitten's growth is so gradual
that habits of caring for it and tolerating it, petting it, persist
even when it has reached maturity, and the patient finds that cats
no longer call out panic. A psychoanalytic treatment involves
essentially the same process. An effort is made to recall the circumstances under which the original conditioning of panic occurred. The circumstances recalled—or reënacted, which is
much the same thing—include many of the conditioners for the
panic which are also called up by the actual presence of cats,
and which are a necessary condition for the production of the
fear. To these, under the careful management of the analyst,
the patient responds without fear. As a result, the sight of a cat
or mention of a cat may become merely cues for talking about
cats or about the original incident.

Our embarrassing moments continue to embarrass us in
retrospect until we have recounted them to ribald or unsympa-
thetic friends whose laughter helps to make us laugh. From
that time on, they become not occasions for shame and humilia-
tion, but conversational anecdotes. Our dining mishaps, our unfortunate remarks to the hostess, our encounters with the highway patrol in which we played so meek a part, are turned to
assets instead of liabilities by being "made light of." Emergen-

cies that require action drown our griefs, soften our humiliations, wipe out depressing memories. Laughter has an important part in social adjustment, in substituting for tension and anger, irritation or embarrassment. And laughter plays this part because it alienates from stimuli their unhappy responses and enlists them as conditioners for laughter. Unfortunately, our ambitions as well as our troubles can be "laughed off."

This ends, for the time being, our account of conditioned inhibition and negative adaptation, which are two names for the same phenomenon. There is another characteristic of the conditioned response which resembles conditioned inhibition, but with a difference. For the description of it we are indebted to Pavlov. A substitute stimulus may be detached from its response *temporarily*. If the salivary secretion of a dog has been conditioned on the sound of a bell, the repetition of the ringing at short intervals causes less and less reaction until secretion no longer takes place. But the extinction of the response, unlike the conditioned inhibition described above, is not a lasting extinction. After an interval, the conditioned secretion again appears. If the process of extinction is repeated, the recovery is less and less complete until finally complete negative adaptation is present. Moreover, the extinction may be carried beyond the zero point. If the cue is sounded after secretion has ceased to occur, the cue becomes an active inhibiter of secretion and will prevent or retard secretion when another stimulus for secretion is applied.

Pavlov and his followers established that this temporary extinction is not a result of fatigue of the gland because the gland will still respond to other conditioners as before. Pavlov and several Russian writers look upon temporary extinction as quite distinct from inhibitory conditioning. Several American writers have regarded it as evidence that the conditioned reflex is a very special and peculiar form of learning and not, therefore, to be accepted as the basic form of all learning. Other associative learning, they argue, can not thus be temporarily extinguished.

I do not agree with either of these opinions. I believe that temporary extinction is not a fundamental characteristic of conditioning, but a characteristic determined by the special conditions of Pavlov's experiments, and that it is an instance of inhibitory conditioning, hence of the conditioned response.

In the special case of Pavlov's experiments in extinction the explanation may be that a temporary attitude was established, like that in a balky horse or an obstinate person, the secretion falling off because the primary cause of it, the food or the chewing, was missing, and stray distractions have a cumulative effect in inhibiting the response. But this inhibition is conditioned upon the particular circumstances of this particular sitting, and may not be revived when the experiment is renewed. The inhibition may depend upon a particular posture maintained throughout a special occasion, just as a fit of obstinacy in a human being may be self-maintained and dependent on the general set of the moment.

If you strike a person on the forehead with a rolled paper, blinking is the normal result. If you continue, blinking at first occasionally fails, and then, as you continue, frequently does not occur. If you now allow a few minutes to elapse, or introduce a sudden diversion such as a slap on the back or a loud noise, blinking will again follow the blow. This suggests that something resembling the attitude which I described has been built up, a set which inhibits blinking, and which is gone after the sudden interruption of the slap on the back or the noise, or after the lapse of a short interval.

Humphrey, in his book, *The Nature of Learning in Relation to the Living System*, regards "learning not to do," which he calls *habituation*, and associative inhibition as different phenomena. In his opinion habituation is a primitive characteristic of behavior; the gradual diminution of response to a repeated stimulus is, for him, "an instance of the process whereby a living system reëstablishes a conservative mechanical equilibrium with the environment when equilibrium has been disturbed. It is found at all grades of life, and in the higher living forms it may be effected by specialized structures such as the receptors and, apparently, the central nervous system, when it is known as sensory adaptation and negative adaptation respectively. There is no rule which will determine whether it will take place in a given organism for stimuli of a given intensity, quality, or temporal interval. Teleological considerations do not seem to apply."

One of Humphrey's illustrations of this primitive habituation is taken from an experiment of his own in which land snails were placed on an oaken platform which was jerked at regular intervals of two seconds by an electrical attachment. At first the snails retracted their horns at each jerk of the platform; gradually this response diminished and disappeared. The phenomenon can not be classed as fatigue, he argues, because several snails retracted their horns only to the first jerk, and because a more intense stimulus restored the response. "A fatigue," he says (1933, page 137), "that is diminished by more intense stimulation of the same kind seems self-contradictory." The contradiction is not at all evident to me, since I am under the impression that this is a characteristic of all fatigue.

In the term "habituation" Humphrey includes the diminution of response that may result from sense-organ adaptation which Adrian has directly observed, or diminution from a "central" adaptation which Humphrey calls negative adaptation, or diminution from effector fatigue (1933, page 147, note).

The present account differs materially from Humphrey's. We have left no room for the phenomenon which he calls negative adaptation, classifying those instances of diminution of response to repeated stimulation in which rest brings recovery as fatigue, not as learning. It seems preferable to reserve the term "learning" for the more lasting changes in behavior tendencies.

And we have suggested that there is a rule which will determine whether or not a response will follow a given stimulus more certainly or less certainly. The rule is: If the response has followed a given stimulus on one occasion, it will more probably follow that stimulus on the next occasion; if the response has not followed the given stimulus on the first occasion, it is less likely to follow it on the second. The exceptions to this rule we have assumed to be instances of fatigue, or of stimulation within the relative refractory period of a response, or of sense-organ adaptation.

We find it hard to rise in time for breakfast. We buy an alarm clock. Is there any rule by which we can predict whether we will rise more and more promptly under the stimulus of the alarm or will relapse into that too common state of entire disregard of its summons? There is such a rule, and it is this: If, on the first morning, we rise promptly, there is an increased chance that this will happen on the next morning. If on the first morning we hear the bell and reflect that there is time for another minute or two of precious sleep and as a result merely turn over and bury our head deeper in the pillow, this is what is probably going to happen on the second morning. By not answering the alarm we may eventually be able to sleep through it without discomfort. By answering it we insure that it will be answered in the future.

The issue that Humphrey raises is this: Is it necessary to have, in addition to association or conditioning, a descriptive category of habituation, defined as a diminution of response resulting from repeated stimulation? For my own part I believe that the phenomena of diminishing response to repeated stimulation are adequately described by the terms sense-organ adaptation, fatigue, and refractory period, and, besides these, associative inhibition or inhibitory conditioning, which, unlike the others, is not temporary in effect.

My conviction on this point, however, is not so firm that I am unprepared for a shift to Humphrey's opinion on very slight additional evidence. More detailed analysis of the phenomena may demand recognition for a primitive form of learning consisting of a tendency for reaction to repeated stimuli to diminish and disappear. In the experimental work so far reported this phenomenon is transient, and the reaction recovers with lapse of time.

In the two chapters preceding this we have discussed the conditions under which a response becomes attached to a new cue. In the present chapter we have considered the circumstances under which responses become detached from their former cues, and the former cues acquire an actual inhibitory effect on their original response. This has been explained as the attachment of the former cue by association to new behavior which inhibits the original response. Whether the response is prevented by fatigue, by inhibition, or by the fact that the stimuli are below the threshold, the result is the same. The cue becomes a cue for other behavior and is alienated from its response. Temporary extinction has been explained as depending on the building up of a temporary state such as excitement which inhibits the response but is dependent on certain transient elements in the situation. Humphrey's suggestion that the diminution and disappearance of response to a cue are a primitive form of learning distinct from conditioning has been rejected on the ground that the phenomena he cites are adequately described by the concepts of fatigue, sense-organ adaptation, and refractory period, which are temporary effects and from which recovery is a matter of physiological process, and, in addition to these, inhibitory conditioning, which is merely an aspect of conditioning, namely, the conditioning of an inhibitory response.

CHAPTER VI

Generalization

ONE very startling feature of the conditioned reflex as it appears in many experiments is the tendency for the reflex to respond to stimuli *which have not previously accompanied it*. In Pavlov's laboratory a tone might be used as the substitute stimulus and after several pairings of tone and food the reflex will be in evidence as a conditioned response to another tone. If a touch on the flank is the practiced signal, then, after some practice, a touch on some other part of the dog's body will occasion the flow of saliva. This tendency for unpracticed stimuli to elicit the reflex Pavlov referred to as irradiation. It has been also called generalization.

Generalization has a number of characteristics. It appears soon after the beginning of practice and disappears as practice continues. It is usually confined to unpracticed stimuli from the same class of sense organs, although this rule has exceptions. And Pavlov asserted that when the conditioning employs a touch as the signal, touches on other parts of the dog's skin are effective in proportion to their nearness to the original practiced spot. Touches on distant areas start only a few drops of saliva, whereas a touch in the immediate neighborhood of the practiced area is almost as effective as this area itself. The experiments on which this generalization is based are rather sketchily described in Pavlov's *Conditioned Reflexes,* and the reliability of the correlation between distance from the original site and effectiveness in eliciting salivary secretion is not determined.

Pavlov believed that this phenomenon is to be explained by

the spread of a state or condition in the brain from the projection area of the sense organ, the part of the cortex to which sensory nerves are relayed from the midbrain. This state is supposed to be a state of excitation that spreads from the point corresponding to the sense organ used as the signal to neighboring centers and ultimately to more remote areas. The spreading of this unknown brain state is supposed to stop eventually if practice is continued and the areas affected by it again grow smaller until the reflex is finally elicitable only through the sense organs used as substitute stimuli in practice.

Something of the nature of this generalization undoubtedly occurs in the laboratory and in ordinary experience. Are we to accept Pavlov's view that this generalization is one of the primary characteristics of conditioning and is to be explained by his speculative and remarkable brain state, or can generalization be accounted for in terms of ordinary conditioning without invoking a new and otherwise unknown physiological process?

Taken at its face value this phenomenon is not conditioning in the sense of associative learning. *The new stimuli are effective without ever having accompanied the response.*

We may, in the first place, be allowed to express some skepticism concerning Pavlov's explanation in terms of the spread of an excitatory state to neighboring brain areas across the usual pathways of conduction. Pavlov believed that both excitatory and inhibitory states can thus spread in the cerebrum. The spread of excitatory states accounts for generalization and the spread of inhibitory states for temporary extinction, which is the result of applying the signal repeatedly without following it with food. Both these supposed states, excitatory and inhibitory, are like no phenomena yet observed in nervous tissue by the physiologists. They are of no use in the explanation of generalization and temporary extinction because they are beyond any present means of observation.

We have excellent reasons for believing that the conditions

determining these two phenomena are not the obscure and speculative brain changes suggested by Pavlov, and that they will be found to depend on certain conditions more open to observation. We may first remark that the substitute stimulus of the laboratory record is probably not the actual conditioner. The tone or the touch is habitually presented in Pavlov's laboratory some two seconds before the food. In two seconds impulses from these sources would have had time to travel some eight hundred feet if there were available pathways. It is quite probable that the direct impulses from ear and skin sense organs are finished before the end of the two-second interval, and that the actual stimuli which accompany the salivary secretion and eating movements are movement-produced stimuli attending on listening to the tone or on shifting position in response to touch. The fact that cue and reflex can be separated by several minutes makes this even more probable.

If these movement-produced stimuli are the actual conditioners, the stimuli actually contiguous in time with the response, the phenomenon of generalization or irradiation is very simply explained. Listening to a different tone may involve listening movements so much like those called out by the practiced cue that these similar movements furnish the real conditioners of the action.

The inverse correlation between the distance of the point stimulated from the point used in practice and the strength of the response becomes, to my notion, an excellent reason for the view of the nature of generalization here presented. Touches on neighboring areas of the animal cause similar protective movements. Touches on distant areas elicit movements that have less in common. Touched on the right flank, the dog may withdraw somewhat to the left and turn his head to the right. Some phase of this action may be the actual conditioner of the response, the stimulus combination associated with the response. When the dog is later touched on a spot ten centimeters from this point, the touch stimuli are new. They have not been associated with the response. But the resulting movement will be almost a repetition of the first movement, and may hence serve to call out the response in almost its original strength.

Pavlov himself did not accept this explanation and offered (1932) a number of reasons. He did not believe that impulses from proprioceptive stimuli ordinarily reach the cerebral cortex or can act as conditioners. How any motor skills or motor habits could be acquired if this were true is very difficult to understand. Furthermore—and this is the more serious objection because it was made by an experimenter much more familiar with actual experiments in conditioning than I am—Pavlov stated that the movements of listening or the movements made in response to the substitute stimulus may disappear in the course of the experiment. The dog may eventually, when the tone is sounded, go through the motions of eating without showing any evidence of the listening that first occurred.

Pavlov's observations on this point are entitled to much more respect than my own very cursory ones, and only future experiment and observation can decide whether the role of movement-produced stimuli is as important as here represented. I remain convinced that it is. Listening movements do normally become less and less conspicuous, unless, of course, the noise is so intense that eating and secretion are inhibited and listening prevails. In that case, the presentation of food will probably become a cue for listening. It is quite possible that this diminution of listening movements accounts for the observed loss of generalization as practice continues. Listening to the practiced tone is gradually inhibited through anticipation of food and listening may be so reduced and *altered* that only the altered response to the practiced tone, and not the uninhibited response to the unpracticed tone, will serve as a cue for secretion and eating movements.

In this explanation certain familiar events serve instead of the highly supposititious spread and retreat of an excitatory brain state proposed by Pavlov. The fact that listening movements are normally present at the beginning of practice, and that these are altered and diminished as practice goes on was reported by Pavlov himself.

Human behavior has many parallels to this phenomenon of generalization. That recently practiced acts for which the person is still "set" may be released by a wide variety of stimuli was illustrated by Jensen's experiment showing the resumption of nursing when an infant is stimulated in almost any sudden manner. Practice narrows the field of eliciting stimuli to the regular attendants of the movement. The infant ceases to accept any nurse and responds only to its mother or its regular nurse. Puppies lose their general friendliness and become devoted to their masters, unless they have been made neighborhood pets. The child becomes shy in the presence of strangers unless hotel life has accustomed him to a variety of persons. The young man finds himself interested in one girl to the exclusion of others unless a number of previous shifts of attention induced by external circumstance has prevented such fixation. Pavlov's dogs fed exclusively on milk later showed no interest in meat. Probably only mild starvation would develop such an interest. As infants we all attempted to be omnivorous, but sand and soap have lost their attraction and we have all moved toward an addiction to our national dishes, unless travel has given us practice in variety. In each of these cases certain acts could, soon after they were begun, be occasioned by a large variety of situations, but after long practice they are gradually limited to the situations which have regularly accompanied them. Our behavior becomes increasingly specific in its adjustment to recurring stimulus patterns. A child rides on broomsticks, chairs, the banister rail, his father's back, or the St. Bernard. When he grows up he has specific forms of behavior for all of these and riding is confined to the range of his practice.

At first we give the same response to similar stimuli. A child frightened by an animal will show distress on being confronted with other animals of different shape, or even with bits of fur, or cloth with a long nap. These generalized stimuli are not the same that accompanied the first fright, but they have some common feature to which we have given an identical response, or a response identical in some respect. The movement-produced stimuli of the response serve as the conditioners for the generalized behavior. Out of many experiences with the family dog the child eventually has a perceptual response to the bark, the footsteps, the sight of the dog in many positions and distances because these have been present when the perceptual behavior was in progress. When this has been achieved, one unfortunate experience with the dog resulting in fright will be found to be generalized. The child is frightened at the sound of the footsteps, at the bark of the dog when it is out of sight, at any of the visual patterns which have previously been associated with the perception. Very few of these have been directly conditioned or associated with the fright, but they are all able to evoke it. They have the power to evoke fright because they evoke the perception of the dog, which has become a signal for fright. In Pavlov's dog listening was conditioned to salivary secretion. Any response, then, that provokes listening will occasion secretion. The nature of the stimulus by which listening is called out is at first unimportant. But with the repetition of the experiment, listening is altered by eating, and eventually only the stimulus which has regularly preceded that particular, modified form of listening will be effective. The bell has been made the specific stimulus for eating because a specific response to the bell has been developed by the practice. Only the bell has preceded this modified response, not the other sounds.

A dish eaten on shipboard while on the verge of seasickness has a strong flavor of orange. Weeks later the sight of an orange brings on a slight qualm and a memory of the ship's dining saloon. The sight of an orange has not been associated with qualms and has no direct connection with its present response. The connection lies in the fact that the sight of the orange has often accompanied the taste of an orange, and the foretaste called up by the orange is a perceptual response which undoubtedly includes behavior and stimulation from this behavior. But this perceptual response has been present on shipboard as a consequence of the taste. It has become a cue for the associated distress.

CHAPTER VII

The Effects of Repetition

ONE of the oldest laws of association has been the law that the strength of an association depends directly on the frequency with which it has occurred. Aristotle speaks of "the rapidity with which we recollect what we frequently think about" (*De Anima*, 452a). Aristotle also noted exceptions. "But," he says, "it is a fact that there are some movements, by a single experience of which persons take the impress of custom more deeply than they do by experiencing others many times; hence upon seeing some things but once we remember them better than others which we may have seen frequently" (*ibid.*, 451b). The rule and its exceptions have puzzled psychologists ever since.

It is an undeniable fact that frequency of connection of substitute stimulus and response or of memory and cue normally influences the associative strength or the degree of probability that the response will follow its signal. Pavlov said in an article (1932), "During our first experiments often fifty to one hundred or more repetitions of the procedure were required in order to develop a complete conditioned reflex, but now ten to twenty times are sufficient, and often much fewer." Ebbinghaus found that the memorizing of series of nonsense syllables tested the next day by the amount of time necessary to relearn (the so-called "savings method") showed associative strength directly proportional to the number of times the series was repeated. A mass of laboratory evidence as well as common experience would seem to indicate that the more often a response has followed a stimulus cue the more apt it is to follow that cue. Aristotle speaks of words, tunes, or sayings which become inveterate on the lips. "People give them up and resolve to avoid them; yet again and again they find themselves humming the forbidden air or using the prohibited word" (*De Anima,* 453a). Our habits become notoriously predictable with exercise. Habits of long standing are beyond our control, by which is meant that they are so automatic and predictable that they march on in spite of social deterrents, advice, or good resolutions. We are slaves to a habit when the habit takes precedence over our other habits of polite behavior or morals, and such slavery seems obviously the result of long usage.

Close examination, however, makes the law of frequency less certainly true. We have first those instances in which a habit is established with one repetition, a name recalled with one introduction, a terror founded on one incident, a childhood memory restored in middle age without intervening practice. These are admittedly exceptions to a rule, but a proper rule will provide for its exceptions. To cover such exceptions another law has been formulated, the law of "vividness" or of "intensity." It is explained that, other things being equal, of two associations with the same cue, that one will prevail which was formed under circumstances that made the experience more vivid, or under circumstances which included greater excitement. In the latter form this law requires separate examination and will be the subject of a separate chapter.

Another class of exceptions is furnished by instances in which a habit of many years is supplanted by one just acquired. We may on thousands of occasions have raised our hat to our female acquaintances, reached to the left side for the emergency brake, made a certain turn on the way from office to home, waked at seven-thirty, until these acts are stereotyped and dependable. If we don a straw hat we find ourselves clawing vainly at its flat crown when we try to remove it; or, on buying another car, thrusting the left foot where the clutch pedal had been; or taking the old turn after we have changed our residence; or still waking at seven-thirty though we need not rise until eight. But the new adjustment seldom requires practice equivalent to the practice of the discarded act. Very often only a few awkward blunderings, and we have changed a habit of years. If the law of frequency were taken literally it would take years to undo the habits of years. This is obviously not so.

Another qualification of the law of frequency is made to cover such cases. This is the law of "recency." Of two associations which have had equal practice, the more recent will prevail. This law we shall now examine.

We may first note that it is not absolute recency but relative recency that will be effective, assuming the rule of association to be dependent on contiguity. It will be the last association that prevails over earlier associations and without reference to the number of pairings or reinforcements of the earlier associations. Voeks has suggested (1948) that the word *postremity* be substituted for recency in this connection, and there is no doubt that this would make for less ambiguity.

Apparent exceptions to the rule of postremity, which is a corollary of the principle of association by contiguity, would depend on unreconditioned stimulus complexes. An illustration is a familiar experience among men who have stopped smoking after having maintained an addiction for years. This familiar experience is to discover an occasional strong impulsion to smoke in "unreconstructed" or unreconditioned situations. Thus, listening to papers at an association meeting once a year or doing work of a sort that was accompanied by smoking and has not been undertaken since swearing off may provide such unreconditioned situations.

It has been the custom in textbooks of psychology to state that the law of frequency is based on the physiological events at the synapse. Conditioning clearly implies a change in the course of nervous impulses through the nervous system. It has been assumed that impulses are "drained" into active motor pathways, and that each passage of an impulse over a new path so established "weakens the resistance" of that path and so makes it more certain that the next occasion will find the impulse going that way. This has been held to be a fundamental characteristic of conditioning. The more times the cue occurs with the response, the more certain is the cue to bring about the response. Pathways are "worn" with use and become easier to traverse.

This account of the basis of the law of frequency has been so taken for granted that it is quite astonishing to find that there are serious reasons for doubting its accuracy. Peterson (1922) called attention to this, having found that with human subjects learning the "mental maze" the effects of recency and of frequency could be negative instead of positive. Many other experiments have thrown doubt on the generality of the law of frequency. And there is no direct physiological evidence that pathways through the nervous system are thus established by "wear." The resistance at the synapse or functional connection between successive neurons can not be directly observed; hence explanation of the law of frequency in terms of such resistance is pure speculation. If experiments tending to demonstrate associative learning in animals without a synaptic nervous system are confirmed, the synapse will be still less able to support the burden of explaining learning. So far as the facts are concerned it is equally probable that conditioning is an all-or-nothing affair, like the setting of a switch rather than like the wearing of a path. In other words, it may be that the law of recency or postremity describes one of the fundamental characteristics of associative learning and that the results of frequent repetition depend on the enlistment of more conditioning situations, not on the strengthening of the association of any single conditioner.

I believe that the hypothesis that conditioning involves a definite rerouting of impulses from sense organs, and that this rerouting persists until further conditioning alters it, is sounder than the hypothesis that associative strength varies directly with the number of pairings. It can be reasonably argued that of two responses associated with a given substitute stimulus the second is always the one conditioned by that stimulus. The second will not always follow its cue, obviously, because other cues may elicit the first. But if any cue has been acting at the time of a response different from the associated response, that cue will become a conditioner of the new response, and whatever effect it has will be to further the new response. If it is not immediately effective in bringing about the new response, it will again serve to energize whatever response is prevailing and will again be alienated as a conditioner.

If this is the case there is much to be explained. The facts seem directly to contradict this view. Practice of a response with a cue has generally an increasing effect on associative strength. How can this undeniable fact be reconciled with the view that practice of a response with a cue does not have an increasing effect on associative strength?

Some light on the nature of the answer is thrown by Pavlov's remarks quoted at the beginning of this chapter. He said: "During our first experiments often fifty to one hundred or more repetitions of the procedure were required in order to develop a complete conditioned reflex, but now ten to twenty times are sufficient, and often much fewer." What change took place in the methods of the Leningrad Laboratory which would make less practice necessary? It is my belief that the improvement has been in the control of the conditions under which the experiment was taking place. There has been achieved more uniformity of procedure. More practice was formerly necessary because, in spite of the soundproof experimental room and the removal of the experimenter from the room in which the dog was placed for the experiment, in spite of all these precautions a great part of the stimuli affecting the dog were not controlled successfully.

Standing in the loose harness the dog could shift his weight from one leg to another, turn his head, prick up his ears, yawn, stretch —in fact alter his whole pattern of proprioceptive stimulation, and a certain amount of his exteroceptive situation. It is my belief that if all these features of the dog's situation could be made uniform from day to day, not fifty or one hundred, not even ten or twenty practice periods would be necessary for establishing the certainty of conditioning, but only one.

The dog is responding not only to the food and to the bell, not only to his state of hunger with its attendant stomach contractions and general muscular tension, but to his own posture, to his own movements through the movement-produced stimuli in which they result. These are subject to variation. Improved laboratory practice reduces that variation. Pavlov mentioned that some preliminary practice is necessary to accustom the dog to the apparatus before starting experimentation. This practice is needed to eliminate the restless movements by which the dog would so vary his situation that conditioning would take more time.

On the first occasion on which the substitute stimulus is presented the dog may be found responding to some minor skin stimulation, turning his head to the right, easing muscular fatigue by shifting his position. These bring movement-produced stimuli which accompany his response to the food in a much truer sense than the substitute stimulus which occupies the experimenter's attention and record. The bell, if it is used as the substitute stimulus, may have ceased to ring many seconds before, so that only the movement-produced disturbance which it has left remains to serve as the conditioner of the response.

In Pavlov's own laboratory it was established that under some circumstances substitute stimuli have an additive effect. A response conditioned upon two separate stimuli on separate occasions will be stronger and more certain if the two conditioners are presented together. Two conditioners generally are more effective than one, just as a conditioner presented with a conditioned inhibiter results in interference and diminished effect. In the first practice period not only the bell and its direct motor effects but other accidental features of posture have all become conditioners. If they could all be reproduced together, the one practice period would very probably prove to be sufficient. It is not ordinarily sufficient because there are uncontrollable differences in the situation on the second presentation of the substitute stimulus.

But why should practice make the effect increasingly certain? Is it not quite possible that in successive practice periods more and more conditioners are enlisted, so that after twenty periods there is a high probability that the cue will have enough support to be effective? Pavlov remarked that any minor disturbance, like that made by a fly in the experimental chamber, will ordinarily prevent the response from appearing. The most reasonable supposition is that this fly has so changed the situation that the supporting cues from movement-produced stimuli are dissipated. The bell has rung, but the usual movements of listening have been disrupted by the fly. No saliva flows because the cues are lacking. If flies were always introduced into the experiment a conditioned response to the bell might eventually be established, but it would probably require several hundred practice periods and not even then reach the point of dependability usually attained.

"Practice makes perfect." We do not take this adage too seriously because we know too many exceptions, but there is some truth in it. We should probably say, if we are to be exact, not that practice makes perfect but that perfection is seldom approached without practice. Many writers have confused this fact with the facts covered by the law of frequency or use. They are, however, quite distinct. Perfection, or progress in the direction of perfection, is not at all the same thing as increased certainty of response to a cue.

The attainment of perfection demands that awkward and useless movements be detached from their cues as well as that useful movements be attached to cues. The increase in skill that so commonly results from practice is thus no evidence for a fundamental law of frequency in describing the nature of the conditioned response. How skills are attained must be left for another chapter, since it is a very distinct problem.

Our proposed explanation of the law of frequency and its exceptions is then as follows: The law of frequency is not a fundamental characteristic of conditioning. The observed effects of frequent repetition are to be explained not in terms of increased associative strength with added repetitions, but in terms of the enlistment of added conditioners which is normally the result of repetition. The exceptions to the law of frequency are not exceptions to the general principle of conditioning, but illustrations of that principle. Those exceptions which have been classed under the law of "intensity" can be explained in terms of the nature of motor excitement; this will be done in another chapter. Those exceptions which have been classed under the law of "recency" are merely illustrations of simple conditioning, in which the last conditioning probably always prevails.

The reason that one occasion is not enough to rid us of an annoying habit, though the cue is present and we have succeeded in inhibiting the response, is that not all the cues were present, and not all the possible conditioners were alienated. On each successful inhibition some of these cues may be attached to the inhibiting response and eventually we may have enlisted such a proportion of cues for our inhibiting behavior that the annoying habit will appear only occasionally, when some one of the rarer stimulus patterns which have not been reconditioned happens to be present. The habit of smoking is in reality made up of thousands of habits. The sight of tobacco, the smell of it, the mention of it, finishing a meal, finishing an office task, looking at the clock, and innumerable other situations have all become signals for smoking. We resolve to stop smoking. We substitute for a few of our conditioned responses inhibitory responses—a grim closing of the mouth, a tendency to push away the pipe, groping movements ending in substituting chewing gum, or nails, or pencil. We suddenly find ourselves smoking. Some cue which we have not alienated has taken us unawares and had its usual response. As a result we find it necessary to practice not-smoking on numerous occasions before our rejection is a settled habit. The apparent exceptions to the rule that the most recently practiced stimulus-response sequence will prevail turn out not to be exceptions in fact.

CHAPTER VIII

Emotional Reinforcement

THE most startling exceptions to the rule of frequency are those incidents in the experience of all of us in which a memory or a motor habit is so impressed with one occurrence that it is beyond our control. Once the cue is encountered, the response is inevitable—as inevitable, to use Aristotle's simile, as the course of a thrown ball that has left the hand. The proper appreciation of the role that such events play in human life was left to Freud and the psychoanalysts to uncover. The psychoanalytic literature expresses a lofty disregard of the law of practice and leaves it to the academic psychologists as a harmless laboratory subject. The psychoanalyst is interested in the experiences that rise above practice and impose patterns on behavior which alter lives and fortunes without need for humdrum repetition. Our memories for names are explained not in terms of the number of rehearsals we give them, but in terms of the wish to remember or the wish to forget. Perverse tendencies in behavior are the result not of habit but of one tense experience. Tics, those maverick habits which distress us because they are actions out of place, may, it is true, be somewhat harder to eradicate if they are of long standing, but they are said to be established beyond control because they attended some strong repression, and they are said to be removable by one experience, the consciousness of their origin.

Suppressed behavior does not, in the Freudian accounts, lead to inhibitory conditioning as our present theory would lead us to expect. It continues to affect behavior in the form of unconscious wishes and repressed desires.

Every person's experience holds instances of fears based on one terrifying event, of strong distastes founded on one incident, of embarrassment dating from one unfortunate encounter, of names remembered with one saying.

Under what circumstances does this super-learning occur? Why will one telling experience sometimes take the place of twenty practice periods? The psychoanalysts have suggested the answer and there is reason to believe that it is substantially right. All these cases of phenomenal learning seem to take place under strong emotion. The behavior that is attended by strong emotion seems to undergo fixation. What leads to excitement tends to become a strong interest. The acts we perform when depressed or relaxed leave less impression.

If exciting emotion is the common circumstance that explains our instances of accelerated learning, how is this accomplished? Laboratory experiment has offered some faint evidence that there may be direct effects on the nervous system of the hormones known to be or suspected to be in the blood stream in increased quantity in exciting emotion. Strychnine and caffeine seem to have such effects. But it has not been established that the accelerated learning brought about by substances in the blood stream is to be explained by their action on nervous tissue. There is another possible source of their effect. In those drugs which exaggerate muscular response the acceleration of learning may be dependent on the extended action of muscles and tendons on sense organs resulting from the increased amplitude of muscular response. Exciting emotion involves the quick relief of fatigue through the direct action of adrenin on muscle tissue. The muscle so affected responds with greater contraction to the same motor impulses and by its greater contraction stimulates new fields of proprioceptor sense organs in the muscle and the joints and tendons. These added stimuli may become conditioners of movement and hence explain the increased certainty of conditioning. Movements during excitement are more complete and vigorous than movements during unexcited states. In excited movement there are new movements to be conditioned as well as added conditioners for movement. The strong tendency for movements executed during excitement to become stereotyped into habits may have this explanation.

Excitement is not the result merely of endocrine action. There are contributing factors in excitement which are better established than are the effects of any endocrine action, with the possible exception of adrenal secretion. When muscles contract they stimulate their own sense organs and the resulting impulses are responsible for an additional contraction of the muscle itself, as well as the contraction of allied muscles. Not only contraction, but stretching, and sudden resistance to contraction have this effect of adding to the original tension of the muscle. The contraction of any muscle thus leads to a sort of reverberation which tends to increase muscular tonus. The main feature of states of excitement is undoubtedly this general increase of muscle tonus which tends to be self-sustaining through the circular reflexes described, and to exaggerate or reinforce whatever action is taking place. There is also evidence reported by Cannon that muscular contraction tends to accumulate general muscular tension through endocrine secretion in the muscle. Cannon has called the presumptive secretion of the tense muscle secretin.

Through muscle-to-muscle pathways action and posture tend to be maintained. Even the knee jerk is a somewhat prolonged tetanic contraction and in no wise a muscle twitch, though it is elicited by a single stimulation.

States of excitement thus tend to maintain themselves or to increase if intense stimulation is present. They also tend to increase if there is recurrent stimulation which results in an accumulation of tension in a muscle. Sherman and Sherman report (1929) that high muscular tension and crying could be produced in infants either by intense stimulation for a short time, or by very mild stimulation repeated at short intervals. For instance, if the edge of a card is drawn lightly along the sole of the infant's foot a Babinski reflex is elicited along with some general activity. When this is done a second time, before the effects of the first stimulation have worn off, more activity is evident. After five or six repetitions the infant will be crying and in a state of general excitement. General tension can be built up not only by intense stimulation and by recurrent stimuli with resultant accumulation of tension, but also by resistance to the action of muscles. Obstacles to action result in building up states of excitement which have an obvious utility.

It has been suggested by Holt in his *Animal Drive and the Learning Process* that these muscle-to-muscle reflexes are themselves the result of conditioning. If the muscle contracts, the contraction is necessarily accompanied by the stimulation of sense organs in the muscle itself. If such pathways are subject to conditioning, muscular contraction will tend to be self-sustaining, or lead to a progression of movements.

Understood as a general condition of increased muscular tension leading to exaggerated action, states of excitement would lend themselves readily to accelerated learning. There is some evidence that such simple tasks as learning a series of nonsense syllables are facilitated by the slight addition to muscular tonus provided by gripping a dynamometer while practicing (Bills, 1927). The improvement in the speed with which one can add figures is much more rapid under the same conditions. Congo schoolmasters speed up the acquisition of associations in their drowsy and relaxed pupils by making them study while standing on one leg. Drowsy husbands at evening lectures remember more of the discourse when occasional conjugal nudgings maintain a state of respectable muscle tonus. At the symphony concert they can often recall only what followed the fortissimo passages. Reclining chairs in the lecture hall would be fatal to the spread of information.

An interesting feature of the emotional reinforcement of memory has been pointed out by Stratton. While his evidence is anecdotal, the experiences are common to all. Not only are the events which accompany excitement subject to unusual fixation in memory or hypermnesia, but the events which *precede* the excitement may be likewise so fixed. The reason for this is probably that such events are recalled or rehearsed during the excitement and so share the reinforcement. We recall what we were doing on the morning of the day of the fire, though the fire took place in the afternoon. We have forgotten what we were doing the morning before or the morning after. The associations tentatively established in the morning would have faded by now if they had not recurred during the excitement of the afternoon and so been fixed.

In his *Progressive Relaxation* Jacobson has reported a number of observations which are very interesting in this connection. When his subjects were taught by long training to relax one muscle group after another, and eventually the muscles of the neck and the external muscles of the eyes (which last could be verified by the absence of the involuntary movements under the lids), they reported that they could not evoke any visual imagery on request until they had developed noticeable tension in the eye muscles. Nor could they "think" a sentence without first developing noticeable tension in the muscles used in speech. Many thought trains are obviously accompanied by appropriate slight movements. It is my belief, though certainly it is not an established fact, that all thought trains depend on movement trains, and that in all instances the association of ideas is an association of successive movements through conditioning. St. Augustine (*De divin. daemon.*) was of this opinion for he explained the fact that the devil, though he was not omniscient, could so well read human intentions and thoughts by the fact that all thoughts are accompanied by slight appropriate movements and the devil's skill was in the recognition of these movements. That this was what Aristotle meant when he wrote the following passage (*De Anima*, 453a) is not impossible: "That the affection (memory) is corporeal, i.e. that recollection is a searching for an 'image' in a corporeal substrate, is proved by the fact that in some persons, when, despite the most strenuous application of thought, they have been unable to recollect, it (viz. the effort at recollection) excites a feeling of discomfort, which, even though they abandon the effort at recollection, persists in them none the less. . . ."

Certainly in states of excitement, thought is more apt to be accompanied by obvious action, and the reinforcing effect of excitement could clearly be the result of the great increase of movement-produced stimuli available as substitute stimuli.

Possibly even more effective in guaranteeing the intact recurrence of excited behavior is the fact that the increased vigor of response more successfully resists distraction and inhibition. In panic, for instance, men become absorbed in the features of the situation to which they are responding and are unlikely to notice, to reflect, to hesitate. Excitement tends to exaggerate the all-or-nothing organization of responses. Indecision is characteristic of fatigue and weakness but is almost lacking in excitement.

Not only is excitement, in the form of increased tonus and consequent increased amplitude of action, an accelerator of learning, it is itself subject to conditioning. Stimuli present during excitement have on later occasions become conditioners of the total behavior pattern; in addition, each part of the behavior pattern tends to condition the rest, and an integrated and stereotyped response may be developed, sometimes of extreme complexity. Hysterical seizures are commonly rehearsals of behavior which included an emotional crisis, a hostile attack, an erotic incident, a fit of rage, or a terrifying accident. The seizure re-enacts the original event. Psychoanalysts make a point of seeking for this reliving of an emotional experience as a step in its cure, though a mere reënactment is of very doubtful value. The hysterical attack is subject to increased fixation through practice.

That overt action leads more readily to the stereotyping of a serial response has confirmation in experiments showing that material read aloud or recited is more quickly learned than material read silently. Barlow, for example (1928), found that lists of words which were whispered while being read were retained better than when read with a pencil held in the teeth.

The importance of conflict in human behavior has been forced on the attention of academic psychologists by the psychoanalytic movement. The essential nature of any conflict is the innervation of opposed action systems, resulting in an increased muscular tonus and the other symptoms of excitement. A situation which includes conditioners for two opposed actions results, in the normal individual, in excitement and a consequent unstable equilibrium. One system gets under way and inhibits the other. In great fatigue, or in illness, or for other causes, the requisite emotional reinforcement may be lacking and the result be a chronic low tension insufficient to resolve the conflict. Many neurotics have learned, according to Janet, that quarrels, risk taking, even the added excitement of committing a theft will bring the necessary emotional reinforcement and resolve the conflict. Behind every neurosis there is a difficult choice, with attendant tension and consequent physical exhaustion. If the outstanding symptom is the difficulty of choice it is customary to call the neurosis psychasthenia; if the symptom that attracts attention is the exhaustion, the name applied to it is neurasthenia; if the conspicuous feature is the chronic (but inadequate) excitement, the disorder is referred to as anxiety neurosis. The situation usually starts a vicious circle; the unresolved conflict or choice results in a state of exhaustion which makes its resolution still less probable. The primary occasion may be a physical lack that makes choices difficult, or it may be a conflict that brings physical inadequacy in its train.

The reinforcing effect of excitement on learning is of immense importance in determining the development of human interests and controlling the nature of human values. Until we are of an age when the physiological reserves of muscular activity are diminished and excitement is difficult to produce, we tend to fix our habits about those activities which induce excitement. Dangerous sports, risks, war, play (which can be defined as activity that furnishes its own reinforcement), noise, bustle, all are interesting and compelling because they have a tremendous advantage in forming habits, in establishing conditioning. As we grow older or become ill, excitement is followed by exhaustion and the activities suffer conditioned inhibition. Sport loses its fascination; we enlist for office duty instead of in the regiment of the line. We no longer sympathize with our children's passion for bedlam.

The young person in good health learns to do what is exciting. He does this because excited action is more readily fixed as habit. It is more energetic and more extensive. In old age and in illness excitement is avoided because the energetic action brings exhaustion, and *the activity ceases while its cues remain*. Inhibitory conditioning occurs. The sights and sounds which in our earlier years stirred us to active response have been present when we failed to respond and so have lost their power to thrill.

Jung has pointed out that our intense interests, our violent loves and hates, our strong moral indignations, all betray traces of their opposites. Violent love is more often changed to violent hate than to a state of indifference. The sin which we condemn most passionately is the one to which we are most apt to succumb. This is a very shrewd observation, and Jung's explanation of it is extremely plausible. Violent emotion appears in us only when we are in a state of conflict. Jung interprets such states of conflict in mental terms, but they can be more clearly understood when we realize that they are states of actual muscular conflict. Only if our habits strongly incline us to the sin we condemn, only if the actual beginnings of the condemned act are present in the form of muscular tensions, and restraint and self-control are also present in the form of tensions of those muscles used in avoiding or withholding, can a high degree of emotional excitement be produced. Muscles in opposition are the primary condition of emotional tension.

In like manner our strong interests and passions are dependent on obstacles which may be external, or the obstacle may be a conflicting habit and so internal. If we mean by "true love" a state of great excitement, its course never could run smooth, because with smooth running and without obstacles or conflicting habits no excitement can appear.

The utility of physiological excitement and of emotional reinforcement of action lies not only in the additional energy of movement which may carry us past the obstacle, but in the effect of excitement on learning. This is twofold. Excitement facilitates learning and the stereotyping of habit, and the conflict which is responsible for the excitement breaks up old habits. The outcome is often an improved adjustment in the form of a new habit routine adequate to the situation.

CHAPTER IX

Forgetting

NOTHING seems more sure than that time erases the effects of learning. The events of the last few minutes are always clearer in memory than the events of yesterday, or of a year ago. Almost always, that is. We can recall the last bridge hand, but not for very long. The mere lapse of time seems to soften grief or hatred and to rob us of our skills and accomplishments. The sophomore engineering student finds on entering college in the fall that the mathematics he was able to use in the spring has deserted him, and that the names of some of his companions must be relearned. In the courtroom a detailed account of a long-past event is looked on with proper suspicion that it has been "refreshed."

Even the law of recency, which holds that of two associations with the same cue the more recent will prevail, seems to state only this same fact, that the older an association is, the less associative strength it has. But this is not what the law of recency means at all if we examine it closely. It does not assert that the mere lapse of time will have any weakening effect on learning. It states that when two different responses have been attached to the same substitute stimulus or cue, the one attached last has the advantage over the other. This makes no reference to elapsed time.

Most psychologists still assume that time, just by virtue of its lapse, accounts for the gradual loss of the effects of learning. It is supposed that the metabolism of nerve cells gradually eradicates the structural changes left in learning. It was on this assumption that Ebbinghaus (1913) made his studies of the rate of loss of memory of nonsense-syllable series and established his curve of forgetting. He practiced a series of given length until he could repeat it once from memory without error, but found that a few minutes afterwards it was impossible to duplicate the performance. But not all the effects of the learning had disappeared. The amount left he undertook to measure by finding out how many repetitions were necessary to regain his ability to reproduce once perfectly from memory. Trying this with different series he found that the loss was very rapid at first, less and less rapid as time went on, and that after the lapse of a day forgetting proceeded at a very slow rate.

After Ebbinghaus the investigation of the "curve of forgetting" became a very popular pastime with psychologists, and many studies have aimed at finding a mathematical formula for it. One of the first eccentricities discovered in the curve was a tendency for it to rise somewhat just twenty-four hours after the practice. This was evident not in all the studies, but in a substantial number. It was also noted that the curves of forgetting for nonsense material and for sensible, or somewhat sensible, material such as doggerel verse were materially different. A sentence of twenty syllables might be remembered for many days after one rehearsal, while the same interval would reduce the ability to recall nonsense syllables almost to the zero point. Strange effects were sometimes evident. Children and prisoners in solitary confinement, for instance, were able to recall better the series they had learned after twenty-four hours than they were after one hour. This phenomenon was given a name, reminiscence, and a place in some of the textbooks, and given the far-fetched explanation that the cell changes which must occur in learning continued active some time after the associations were established.

Freudian psychologists have all along paid scant attention to the role of time in forgetting, or denied it altogether, holding that nothing is ever forgotten, that memories may for a time be submerged in the "unconscious" but from there may be retrieved intact under the proper circumstances. Of late other psychologists have shown some signs of a changed opinion on forgetting. It is interesting to note that the Russians who followed Pavlov in the investigation of the conditioned response, in the years before politics and party line began to dominate psychological research, said very little about forgetting and the effects of the lapse of time on the strength of a conditioned response. They have confined themselves to mentioning that after a conditioned response is established—and by this they mean that it will occur some indefinite number of times in succession—the response has been found present after a lapse of months or, in some cases, years. Nothing like the definite "curve of forgetting" appears with the conditioned reflex.

Attempts to express forgetting as a function of time, to predict the amount of forgetting in terms of the lapse of time, have not discovered any general law. It is true that for some cases of learning, as, for instance, the memorizing of a list of nonsense syllables in the laboratory, a fairly definite relation between time and extent of forgetting seems to hold. The "curves of forgetting" of different investigators have similar shapes. But if poetry, or a skill, or a conditioned reflex is substituted for the nonsense-syllable list, the curves of forgetting have very little family resemblance. The reason for these conflicting results is that the effect of lapse of time on memory depends on what happens during the lapse of time. The evidence from common sense and from scattered reports of experiments in conditioning is that under some circumstances forgetting does not take place. Our question is: What are the circumstances under which conditioning remains unimpaired?

A suggestion of the answer is to be found in the experiments on conditioning. Here ten to fifty pairings of food and a bell in the experimental chamber establish a conditioned response to the bell. Once established, this response is stable and is often found in full strength months later, unless the dog has been subjected to some specific process of unconditioning with the use of the bell. The most probable explanation for the stability of the conditioned response and its freedom from forgetting is that learning does not disappear as the result of a mere lapse of time, but only when that lapse of time includes new learning which erases the old. In the case of the dog in the laboratory the conditioned response has one great protection against forgetting, and this is the fact that the conditioned or substitute stimulus is the sort of thing the dog does not encounter in his daily routine. It is reserved for the laboratory situation. Between experiments the dog is exposed to very few of the stimuli that make up the experimental situation. If bells not followed by the feeding rang in the kennels, negative adaptation would surely occur. Such negative adaptation would be forgetting.

This striking tendency for certain laboratory conditioned responses to be apparently exempt from forgetting has been used by a number of writers to argue that conditioned reflexes differ fundamentally from other forms of learning. This is not the case. Any response whose cues have not been alienated in intervening experience will be thus preserved and protected from forgetting. The reappearance of certain childhood habits and childhood skills may occur in old age, if these have not been disorganized through relearning.

Laboratory studies of the effects of intervening activities on forgetting have used the terms *associative inhibition* to describe the difficulty of forming an association between *A* and *X* because of an earlier association between *A* and *B* (Mueller's law), and *retroactive inhibition* to describe the complementary phenomenon, the loss of an association caused by intervening activities. The discussion of retroactive inhibition has turned about the question: Is retroactive inhibition the result of engaging in a similar activity during the interval? When a list of nonsense syllables has been learned it is better retained at the end of an hour or so when the hour has been spent in some quite unrelated activity than when it has been spent in memorizing another list of nonsense materials (cf. McGeoch, 1929, 1930, and Robinson, 1927). The experimental results have been somewhat conflicting because "similarity" of intervening activity has not been defined. Some similar intervening activities favor recall; some impede it. The probable explanation is that an activity in which some of the cues of the previous learning occur but are followed by different responses, results in the alienation of these cues and hence in interference; whereas if the common cues in the intervening activity have been followed by the same responses there is facilitation rather than inhibition. Because of the failure to distinguish these cases, little enlightenment has resulted from such experiments.

It is very interesting to find that in general a period spent in sleep results in much less forgetting than an equal period spent in waking. Dahl found (1928) that both figures and nonsense syllables were better recognized after six to eight hours' sleep than after a waking period of the same length. After one or two hours of sleep, it is true, less was remembered than after one or two hours of waking, but this has a possible explanation in the circumstances of being wakened after so short a period. Van Ormer (1932) used the savings method in which the practice necessary to relearn was measured. He found no difference in effect on amount retained between one-hour periods of sleep or waking, a slight difference for two-hour periods, and a very reliable difference in favor of sleep for eight-hour periods. This is a substantial confirmation of the original experiment by Jenkins and Dallenbach (1924), who found twice as many syllables retained after a period of one, two, four, or eight hours of sleep as after an equal period of waking. Moreover, they found the amount retained after eight hours practically as large as after two hours. Of the nature of forgetting they say (1924, page

612): "The results of our study as a whole indicate that forgetting is not so much a matter of the decay of old impressions and associations as it is a matter of interference, inhibition, or obliteration of the old by the new." Van Ormer likewise says (1932, page 45): "It is suggested that our results in favor of sleep are brought about by the absence of the inhibition and obliteration of the learned material by the waking activity." McGeoch very ably marshaled the evidence against the dependence of forgetting on lapse of time in an article in the *Psychological Review* (1932). Common experience verifies this. We recall on waking much more detail of the hour just before sleep than we can in the evening recall of the events of a morning hour, provided, of course, that no extraordinary conditions prevailed on either occasion.

If we deny that forgetting is the result of the mere lapse of time, how is the rather regular and predictable disappearance of memory for a list of nonsense syllables to be explained? The answer is that, unlike the laboratory bell, the nonsense syllables, each of which is a cue for its successor, do occur in the interval following the laboratory practice. Syllables of the series occur in word combinations and acquire new attachments during the interval. As time elapses, more and more of the conditioned cues of the original learning are alienated from their responses and their new responses tend to break up the continuity of the memorized series.

This is probably the reason why so many studies have shown forgetting to be very rapid at the start of the interval, and increasingly slower as time goes on. When the response occurs it probably enlists many thousands of conditioning cues from among the stimuli acting. More of these cues are eliminated at the beginning because there are more cues to eliminate. Accompanying postures and movements and tensions are, as time goes on, incidental accompaniments of other situations, and so lose their associative connection with the response we have in mind. Furthermore, the evidence from experiment that in nearly all cases some faint traces of learning are present even if months or years have elapsed is very plausibly explained by the supposition that there are generally some cues which have not occurred in the interval and so have not been alienated.

The reason why we can go from winter through spring, summer, and autumn and find the next winter that our skill in skating is almost what it was when we left off ten months before is that the postures and movements of skating simply do not find a place in our domestic routine or in our summer sport. The associative interconditioning is thus not subject to forgetting because there has been no occasion for reconditioning and inhibitory conditioning. Rowing an ordinary boat during the summer will do more to make a crew man forget his training than will selling insurance, because many of the cues on which his proficiency depends are necessarily followed, in managing a rowboat, by behavior inappropriate in a shell.

Popular tunes heard daily on the radio or in the restaurant lose their power to please. Played while we are conversing, while we are eating, or while we are casting up the amount of the check, they become conditioners of these activities and active inhibiters of the pleased attention they once caused. In the age of the radio and television, popular songs have a life of a few weeks as compared with the occasional period of over a century for songs which before the days of easy mechanical reproduction were heard only on occasions when they could be given undivided attention. It is not time that robs beauty of its charm, but preoccupation with other affairs in its presence.

Grief is recalled to a large extent by the objects and scenes which were associated with it. A change of residence and new scenes will not always do away with it because it has become conditioned on our own behavior. But the demands of practical affairs will be effective even if we remain in the same surroundings. Those who are at leisure to enjoy their grief may preserve it indefinitely. Those who are compelled to an active part in living find that forgetting has taken place. The reminders which conditioned the emotion have become conditioners of other activity.

The home in which a much beloved member of the family has died calls out more poignant memories in the survivor who has lived elsewhere since that event than it does in those who have made it their residence, although those who remained at home may have suffered more than the wayfarer who escaped from the sad reminders of the family's loss. Those who continued to live in the home have had grief more often stirred in the days following the death, but they have become more immune to the home as a reminder of their grief. They have lived in it while occupied with practical affairs and grief has suffered inhibitory conditioning.

CHAPTER X

Habits

THE conditioned response has been spoken of as if it were made up of an isolated, stimulating event and a consequent movement. In reality, stimulus and response are abstractions from a continuous flow of change in the world and in the responding person. We select some outstanding feature of the situation, some easily observed or some readily controlled change that affects sense organs, and some arbitrarily limited feature or section of the organism's movement and call these stimulus and response. We learn in terms of conditioning to predict that this response will or will not follow a given stimulus.

Considering all our handicaps, our inability to control the whole stimulus situation, and the indefinite character of most responses, it is astonishing that we can be right in our predictions as often as we really are. Our anticipatory actions are, of course, much more detailed and much more accurate than our verbal predictions. We learn to be ready for the oncoming behavior of others much more easily than we can predict in words what they will do. Words are so roughly fitted to recurring events, so oblivious of their minor differences, that as psychologists trying to anticipate by verbal formulas we have a great handicap in competing with ourselves as simple men ready for what is to happen in the behavior of our neighbors. We can pull an oar with a friend at the other oar, shift our position in a boat in time to meet his shift, reach for the food that he is about to pass, or yawn at the anecdote he is about to tell, without being able to put this anticipation into a formula. But science is confined to formulas. Science is the formulation of our anticipations of change. If there is one thing in the behavior of our neighbors we can be certain of, it is that it will often escape our verbal rules and surprise us. The most complete psychology will only reduce somewhat the number of occasions when we fail to be prepared for what they do.

Action is the result of stimulation which, in a properly constructed organism, signals a threat to those vital states of equilibrium which Cannon has called homeostasis. These states of internal temperature, water balance, blood salt concentration, acid-alkaline balance in the blood, and many others which are the conditions on which continued life depends are protected by the sense organs and nervous system and effectors. The maintenance of life may be viewed as the maintenance of an indefinite number of these conditions in the body. Sense organs in the body are so placed and so made that they are stimulated by natural events which represent threats to the maintenance of these conditions of bodily equilibrium, and all living activity can be viewed as serving these states.

A single disturbance may be reacted to in such a way that the threatened upset is avoided. This can occur even in mechanical systems or in creatures which are, like plants, without mind. The difference between the reactions of plants and of creatures with mind is that plants continue to react in the same way to a recurring disturbance, whereas the characteristic of mind is to change the form of reaction to repeated disturbance.

One of the outstanding features of the changes that take place in learning is the tendency to form, in answer to a repeated disturbance, a stereotyped response which is adequate to the repeated disturbance and which expends less energy than earlier performances. A recurring problem is solved when a routine and stereotyped habit has been formed that returns the animal to the state of equilibrium from which it has been displaced. Hamilton (1925) placed a variety of animals in confinement from which they could escape only through one of four doors—but which door (excluding the one just used) would on any occasion allow escape was settled by throwing dice. Some of the animals tended under these circumstances to "go to pieces"—to have a "nervous breakdown." Some of the animals, especially apes and humans, eventually formed a routine habit of exploring the doors in a set order and so avoided breakdown. Anrep's experimental neurasthenia in dogs was established in much the same way. By confronting hungry dogs with two doors, one marked by a circle and leading to food, and the other marked by an ellipse and leading to punishment, he found that the dogs quickly learned to choose the door with the circle and to disregard the ellipse. But when the ellipse was made so nearly circular that the dogs could no longer discriminate between the figures and the cue was now ambiguous, the routine habit was broken up and the essentials of a nervous breakdown were present. Even the ability to respond correctly to the original choice disappeared.

It is probable that the essential cause of every nervous breakdown in human beings is a failure to establish a routine habit response to a recurring situation. What is the process by which these necessary stereotyped habits are established? Under what circumstances do recurring disturbances tend to be answered with a routine and stereotyped reaction?

We can account for the strong tendency to repeat action patterns as they have previously occurred in terms of conditioning. When a series of movements has once taken place it tends to be fixed without the repetition of all the series of stimuli responsible for it in the first place. The reason for this is that movement-produced stimuli have become conditioners of the succession of movements. The serial response is now somewhat independent of its original causes. Once started it may maintain itself, particularly if excitement has made movement and movement-produced stimuli more intense or energetic and more extended.

We can observe in all behavior this tendency to "set" in integrated patterns. Not only the pattern of our signature but our walk, our laughter, our styles of play and work, our conversation, our very trains of thought betray this fixation. We repeat verbatim remarks we have made before. We cling for years to mannerisms and actions that serve no purpose and only occasionally are noticed by us.

Why should habit series not be stereotyped with one rehearsal? The answer is that an astonishing number of them are. Many a speaker preserves for years some button-twirling movement, some unintelligible gesture, some grimace that was an accidental feature of his first public appearance, or some set form of words that "signs" his address without his knowledge. The first performance of many tasks sets their style and manner for later performances.

If the later situation could be made a complete repetition of the earlier and if there were no intervening learning, serial responses would be duplicated on the second occasion. But these conditions can not be met. There is always behavior in the interval and some of the cues for movement have been attached to other movements. The situation is always somewhat different. The room and its contents may be substantially the same and the external events duplicated, but the individual is not caught in exactly the same posture or movement pattern.

We shall therefore never find perfect repetition of a movement, in spite of the conditioning of one movement on the stimuli produced by the last. Through this conditioning on movement-produced stimuli, behavior is adjusted to the more significant features of the environment and exertion tends to be minimized. The first acquisition of a new dance step consists in tentative movements which are directed by eye or the instructor's voice. On repetition, one movement becomes the substitute cue for the next and the series is partially independent of eye and voice. Learning to read music is learning to play phrases in response to the sight of the notes. Practice makes us independent of the notes because eventually the movement-produced stimuli of one phrase become the substitute stimuli for playing the next.

In the stereotyping of habit the first steps include movements that are merely chance responses to irrelevant stimuli of the first rehearsal. First attempts at reading include hand movements, foot movements, irrelevant lip and tongue movements. These tend to drop out with practice. The reason for their disappearance is that they were responses to irrelevant and adventitious stimuli which are only once or only occasionally present in the rehearsals. If, in his first lesson in reading, a small boy is holding a pencil, twisting his foot about the chair leg, grimacing, the second lesson may repeat these acts because they have been conditioned on the remainder of the situation. They will not always be eliminated. Only if successive lessons include stimuli to other conflicting irrelevancies will the first be lost. There is ample opportunity for this, however, because responses to irrelevant stimuli do not regularly occur in each lesson and one failure or one inhibition does away with them. The essential or relevant stimuli for reading always include the sight of the printed words. Responses to chance accompaniments disappear because they are displaced by responses to other irrelevancies. For the beginner learning the alphabet, "C" may stand for "cat" and insistently suggest "cat." After a year has passed "C" stands for very little without its special contexts, because it has stood for so much in general. It can not call up "cat" and "canary" at the same time because these are sounds made by incompatible movements. They can not even be thought at the same time because thought, even if it does not always depend on movement and movement-produced stimuli, certainly is derived from movement. We can not think what we have not once done.

Freiberg, Dallenbach, and Thorndike (1929) assembled evidence that the simple repetition of series of events in action or thought does not in and of itself lead to the omission of any terms of the series. The dropping out occurs, we may suggest, only when the terms are irrelevant in the sense that they depend on stimuli which are not essential to the action series, when they are not recurrent, and when they are replaced by stimuli to incompatible movement.

If, for example, we are engaged in any one of those repeated action series that lead to stereotyped habit, such as entering our home, the first occasion involves many movements dependent on adventitious stimuli. The postman is leaving and we stop to exchange a word with him; the dog greets us at the street and we respond to him. These are variable elements in the situation and responses to them are generally eliminated from our final habit series. These adventitious acts tend to be repeated, and are sometimes a part of the stereotyped habit, but they are eliminated if successive home-comings offer other stimuli that break them up, or if some of the external stimuli on which they depended are lacking. On the second home-coming the serial tendency to stop where we chatted with the postman gives way to our response to the sight of the entrance. We are not on this occasion looking at the postman. All that is left is the trace of the previous action which is a reminder of our meeting. We may think of the postman.

This reduction of habit to essentials makes many habits local responses no longer involving the whole body. When we are practiced we can drive and talk, or play the piano and smoke, or skate and greet a friend at the same time. At first this is impossible because driving, playing, skating all include a mass of action that is not essential to the performance but is present because it is part of the total associated complex bound together by conditioning. In time, many irrelevant movements are dropped out from the complex and the activity is limited to the muscles and the movements required for the performance. This process is, of course, never complete. Perfect grace, which means the use of only the essential muscles and this use only to the point necessary for the action, is only approximated, never reached. A graceful skater relaxes the muscles not engaged in skating.

We are concerned here with the fixation of habit rather than with the development of skills, which will be the topic of a special chapter. Fixation of response, which constitutes habit, may stand in the way of skill as well as assist skill. But one feature of this fixation which contributes to skill is so characteristic of habit formation that it must be considered here.

Practice of a stereotyped action generally results in speeding up the action. This may take place even when it interferes with success. This speeding up of habit is not an invariable feature of habit formation, but only a very common one. Under what circumstances does repetition increase speed?

Habit series do not always speed up. Timing of a serial response depends on the movement-produced stimuli and the rate of movement depends on the number of fibers in contraction in the muscles used. The phase of the movement determines the pattern of stimuli from the movement. Hence, in action that has become fairly stereotyped speed does not increase. But in action that still includes much that is "irrelevant" to the recurring stimulus pattern and hence much that is subject to adventitious change, the elimination of irrelevant movement may result in speeding up the serial response.

Besides this source of increased speed there is another. Many stimuli which have been acting for some time become conditioners of a later movement which is, as a result, elicited at the earlier appearance of the stimuli. Our behavior in general tends to anticipate the external event through conditioning of this sort. The chick first rejected the bitter caterpillar on tasting it. But while the movements of rejection were in progress the caterpillar was visible. On the next occasion the rejection takes place before the acceptance, and the result is avoidance. On the first occasion we may walk to the water cooler, take a cup, draw the water, then drink. On later occasions the sight of the cup may start the raising of our hand before we have stepped close. The other hand is ready for the tap before we have reached it. In the end the whole series has become one flowing action in which the originally separate acts are overlapped instead of distinct. Through such anticipation we learn to recover our balance before we are upset in a canoe. At first the upset is responsible for the attempt at recovery. The attempt at regaining balance takes place earlier and earlier until it occurs in time to prevent the catastrophe. It may even occur too soon and lead to over-balancing in the opposite direction. The beginner who has had a half hour's experience is apt to sit in the canoe with two opposed sets of muscles tense. The canoe is now in more stable equilibrium than the passenger, whose unstable balance is mental (by which we may mean due to learning). Fatigue may result in negative adaptation of this tension and leave the passenger with the slight and timely reactions that we call skill.

Dodge (1933) did not believe that this tendency to anticipate the event can be the result of simple conditioning, but I am convinced that from the simplest maintenance of equilibrium to the most complicated instance of foresight it can be reasonably maintained that conditioning is the fundamental process by which these results are achieved. In the last analysis foresight consists in reacting to signs of what is to come. The signs of rain are the substitute stimuli for a conditioned thought of an umbrella that earlier depended on the shower but now is stirred by the clouds, the weather bulletin, or the rheumatic pain. Search for an umbrella may appear a very far cry from a conditioned salivary flow, but the maintaining stimulus that gives direction to that search may be as simple a response as a subvocal murmuring of the word or a sustained readiness to grasp the object.

Speeding up a habit may be accomplished in a third way. When the habit is not adequate to its situation, when the machine operator is too slow for the machine, when the driver is not quick enough with his brake, the resulting confusion and its attendant conflict in response occasion excitement, general increase in muscular tonus, and so more energetic action. More energetic action means more rapid movement and, in so far as the activity is dependent on movement-produced cues, more rapid performance.

This speeding up through excitement may, however, introduce its own confusion if the speeding up is not uniform in the muscular system; it may often cause the disintegration of a habit.

Unless irrelevant parts of a habit are eliminated (and it must be remembered that they are not always eliminated), unless overlapping stimuli set forward certain movements in the series, or unless interference produces excitement with a resultant quickening of movement, habits will not normally be accelerated by practice. In fact we may correctly speak of the *habitual speed* of an action since excitement, which is the only internal cause of acceleration among those described, is itself dependent on conditioning in that the conflicting action and interference responsible for excitement can be conditioned. The rate at which a movement is performed quickly becomes a habit unless it is altered in one of the ways just described.

CHAPTER XI

Breaking Habits

IN THE last chapter it was asserted that in repeated encounters with a disturbing event organisms tended to establish toward the event a stereotyped response that represents minimum exertion. This occurs through conditioning. Events that do not disturb serve only to facilitate the actions in progress and hence do not form new habits. Under what circumstances do such stereotyped habits disappear?

What has been said of inhibitory conditioning probably furnishes the answer. Established habits disappear only when new habits displace them.

The mark of an established habit is smooth action and highly predictable action. The habit is sure and well integrated. Each movement of it is a conditioner of other movements, which accounts for its comparative independence of external variation in the situation. As we grow older our styles and our mannerisms grow more in evidence and increasingly certain. The stereotyping may preserve waste movement and excess movement, but it tends to eliminate interference among movements and movements that result in disturbing stimuli. Where daily routine is fixed and dependable a stereotyped routine of response insures minimum outlay of energy. Life is simplified. When we are young and in good health our ready recovery from fatigue and our physiological resources for excitement make this simplified routine unnecessary. Old age and ill health make mental health depend on the establishment of routine habits.

Pieron in *The Brain and Thought* described instances in which such simple, coördinated, well-established habits as making the sign of the cross were lost as habits although the movement could be performed without its former effortless grace. Brain injury was responsible for the loss. His conclusion that the habit had a specific "center" in the brain is not warranted because the wrecking of such a habit could be accomplished by the destruction of only a few of the brain pathways used in the cross-conditioning that makes up the habit. Some laboratory workers like Lashley have concluded from the fact that certain complicated sets of habits can survive the removal of any section of the brain, the complex system of habits being impaired in proportion to the amount of brain tissue removed, that brain pathways established through conditioning are not involved in such behavior. This conclusion is quite unnecessary because any habit is the habit of the whole animal, with all its sense organs and most of its muscles active. It is highly improbable that any one brain area is exclusively in use. Many parts of the nervous system are probably involved in even a simple action, and the destruction of a section of the brain interrupts some paths but not others. The detailed movements of the habit will probably always be found changed by the operation.

Because the simplest habit includes conditioning of movement-produced stimuli as well as of exteroceptive stimuli to eyes and ears there are probably no brain centers that are exclusively used in any habits that include general activity. When only a few local groups of muscles are involved, as in speech, the situation may be different, and the loss of speech habits may depend on the destruction of limited areas in the brain.

This mistaken notion that a habit has its brain center has been responsible for many wrong opinions about habit formation and habit elimination. The simplest habit is a very complicated event and at first involves the whole organism. Only after much repetition is it localized in a limited number of muscles.

In this connection it is interesting to note two observations on which there is general agreement among psychologists. The first is that we are conscious of a feature of our situation when that feature is dominating the response of the whole organism. The second observation is that as a habit becomes stereotyped it tends to disappear from consciousness. We no longer notice it, and are unable to recall whether or not we have performed the act. It can now perform itself without attention.

How is it that these "automatic" habits can ever be broken? They are obviously hard to break. Under what circumstances can they be broken?

We have admitted that repetition is generally effective in establishing a habit, but not that repetition is fundamental. An act is learned in the single occurrence. The need for repetition comes from the need for executing the act in a *variety* of circumstances. When most of the substitute cues are within the reactor's body, so that their occurrence as a total pattern is highly probable, habit may be established in one excited rehearsal. Tics are such habits, and their origin in emotional reinforcement has been pointed out by the Freudians. The effectiveness of repetition lies in the enlistment of new conditioners and in negative adaptation toward more and more potential distractions. Repetition is effective but not necessary in breaking habits and in making habits.

The simplest rule for breaking a habit is to *find the cues that initiate the action and to practice another response to these cues.* No matter how well integrated a habit or how well it is established by practice, if the initial movements of the habit can be thus "sidetracked" the habit can be avoided. It will not cease to be part of the behavior repertoire of the individual because it will remain integrated. *Sidetracking* a habit in this fashion is to be distinguished from a thorough *breaking up* of the habit, which requires the unconditioning of the cues within the habit complex that serve to integrate and to stereotype the habit.

Avoiding or sidetracking a habit is easier than breaking up a habit. The chief difficulty in the way of avoiding a bad habit is that the responsible cues are often hard to find, and that in many bad habit systems they are extremely numerous. Each rehearsal is responsible for a possible addition of one or more new cues which tend to set off the undesired action. Drinking and smoking after years of practice are action systems which can be started by thousands of reminders, and which become imperative because the absence of the object of the habit, the drink or the smoke, results in a block to action and so in restlessness and tension. The desire, which includes tension in the muscles used in drinking or smoking, disrupts other action. The writer who "wants a smoke" is disturbed in his writing and the disturbed state will continue until the aroused action tendency is allowed to go through. The original wakening of the desire may be caused by any of the chance accompaniments of previous smoking —the smell of smoke, the sight of another person smoking, or of a cigar, the act of sitting back in the office chair, sitting down to a desk, finishing a meal, leaving the theater, and a thousand other stimulus patterns. Most smokers, while busily engaged in activities not associated with smoking, can go for long periods with no craving. Others find that the craving is strictly associated with such things as the end of a meal, if it has been their practice to smoke at that time. I once had a caller to whom I was explaining that the apple I had just finished was a splendid device for avoiding a smoke. The caller pointed out that I was smoking at that moment. The habit of lighting a cigarette was so attached to the finish of eating that smoking had been started automatically.

When the cues for a bad habit are as varied and as numerous as they are in the case of smoking, it is clear that a general unconditioning of all cues is a long and arduous process. A more successful method of dealing with such a habit is to "sidetrack" by attaching other responses to the initial movements of the habit itself. A good resolution is an attempt at this method, an attempt at the substitution of emphatic rejection with verbal reinforcement for the beginning of the act. Practice the beginning of the act with rejection instead of acceptance.

The smoker who has succeeded in avoiding or sidetracking the habit has not forgotten the art. The skill with which he can fill and smoke his pipe may survive many years of no smoking. The habit has not been forgotten, has not been broken up. This could only be accomplished by practicing the habit under circumstances that destroy its integration. This is more likely to happen to valued skills than to bad habits. The marksman whose practice has been semiprivate may find that the beginning of a good score in a tournament, as soon as he notices it, proves a distraction and a source of stage fright and confusion. Premature rehearsal of his triumph interferes with his aim. The confusion of his habits may outlast the tournament and set him back in his later practice.

The effect of punishment in the breaking up of habits is often miscalculated. Punishment is often not severe enough or not sufficiently distracting to break up the habit and results only in reinforcing the habit by making its performance exciting. Under excitement fixation is more rapid and certain. Much of the "naughty" behavior of children is thus encouraged by mild punishment and by moderate parental opposition. The interest in the activity is heightened by its excitement, since interest is only more energetic pursuit of the activity. Drawing on the walls, saying "I won't," spilling food, uttering forbidden words, all take on the fascination that big-game hunting has for the adult, and for exactly the same reason. There has been just enough opposition and excitement to fix the interest and compel the act.

Severe punishment is an obvious means of breaking up or of sidetracking a habit. Which of these takes place depends, of course, on the timing of the punishment. Punishment in the course of the habitual action may disrupt it. Punishment at the beginning may leave the habit intact but result in its deflection. Punishment after the act may have no effect on the habit whatever. What effect retribution does have depends on verbal cues which are associated with both act and punishment. In many cases the cues for the action and the beginning of the action do not call up the words or other attendants of the punishment, and the punishment remains quite ineffectual.

Since punishment gets its effect at the time through stimulating crying and struggling and thereby breaking up the unwanted habit, it is clear that any other means of breaking up the action pattern may be just as effective. Any interference that captures attention and introduces a new activity will be successful. Picking up a small child and tossing him or swinging him by the heels is just as effective in overcoming a balky fit as is a sound spanking, and, of course, has a great advantage in that it does not leave the parent a cue for frightened aversion. The distraction must be so thorough that the muscle set of the obnoxious behavior which is the cause of its persistence is thoroughly changed.

Dunlap, in his *Habits, Their Making and Unmaking*, proposed a very interesting and new technique for avoiding or deflecting bad habits, and reported the successful use of this method on a wide variety of actions, from errors in typing, facial tics, and stammering to aberrant sex habits. His method he called the method of *negative practice*. Contrary to all common sense he had the subject repeat the undesired action over and over. But this repetition must be supervised very skillfully in order to have the desired effect of doing away with the habit. Negative practice must be conducted in full awareness that the habit is to be done away with. In the case of a facial grimace or tic he required that it be repeatedly produced by the subject and produced *before* it would normally occur. In the case of a persistent error in typing the error is practiced over and over, the subject being aware that it is an error. The result is that the typist can resume work and the error does not appear.

These results have a very paradoxical look. They seem a direct contradiction of the older laws of frequency and of practice. We repeat an act in order to establish it as a habit. Are we also to repeat it in order to do away with it? Dunlap offered very little explanation for this paradoxical effect beyond calling it a new law of learning. Any explanation of learning, he believed, should be strictly avoided (Dunlap, 1932, page 314).

This is an astonishing statement for a psychologist to make and it must be attributed to some very bizarre notion of what constitutes an explanation. A statement of the circumstances under which negative practice is effective and the circumstances under which it is not constitutes an explanation of negative practice. Dunlap suggested that the determining conditions are "thoughts, desires and ideals." Even if Dunlap has access to his patient's thoughts, desires, and ideals, in actual work with the patient he must use speech and gesture and action to accomplish his training. *Only the observable conditions under which learning occurs are of any use for a theory or for an understanding of learning*, and when these are described, the theory is already complete. One objection to Dunlap's own theory is that it uses unobservable conditions or conditions very vaguely described. We may therefore offer our own explanation, with the clear understanding that Dunlap, who is much more familiar with the application of his negative practice, would probably disagree with it. With Dunlap's opinion (1928) that the response has no effect on the future probability that the same stimulus pattern will produce the same response, or that the occurrence of a response actually decreases the probability of its repetition we must simply disagree. We may suggest that the phenomena of negative practice are illustrations of associative learning, rather than exceptions to the rule of association.

In the case of all these bad habits amenable to negative practice the reason they are beyond control is that the subject is unaware of the cues which serve to start them. He can not tell what it is that begins the wrong series of movements resulting in writing "hte" instead of "the," or what the preliminaries of the uncontrollable facial grimace are. These unknown cues begin the action and, once begun, it is so well integrated through cross-conditioning that it is certain to go on. To use Aristotle's comparison, the response is like a ball which has been thrown and is no longer under the thrower's control. Dunlap's negative practice makes the cues obvious, or establishes other known cues for the very beginning of the activity, before it has attained momentum. To these cues can then be attached other behavior. The importance of starting the obnoxious action with full attention would indicate that the success of the method lies in reconditioning the very first cues on which the habit depends. The subject can now "take it or leave it"; he has made it a voluntary act instead of an involuntary act, which only means that the course of the act will be subject to verbal deflection, or to deflection from the social situation. Our voluntary acts are acts that we can perform on request, or on our own request.

In dealing with children it is often more important to be able to ward off the formation of bad habits than to be able to correct them when formed. Nursery-school and habit-clinic writers are now pointing out that a great deal that children do is aimed at getting attention, and that one of the most effective ways to keep the occasional misdemeanor from becoming a regular habit is to pay no attention to it. This is distinctly a purposive explanation, an explanation in dramatic terms. It is a perfectly proper explanation as far as it goes, but we can go further in stating the circumstances under which undesirable forms of attention getting will be fixed as habits, and this more adequate explanation will be in terms of learning. A great deal of children's behavior from birth on is dependent on the attention of adults. Hunger, cold, pinpricks, discomforts in general, continue to produce restlessness and crying which will last until an adult has given her attention. The infant cries until the adults about are disturbed and care for him. Fatigue may negatively adapt all the unsuccessful efforts and leave the discomfort a cue for the successful method of attention getting.

Attention-getting behavior is thus acquired early and continues to be acquired in normal families. The child forms new needs for attention since his play habits may involve other persons. Play activities being initiated by the sight of others can not proceed until the other person gives his attention and takes his part. The result will be excitement and the ready fixation of habits which are effective in demanding attention. The bulk of the teasing, annoying, irritating behavior of children is fixed in this way, and random action that results in the startled attention of adults is very apt to be repeated. The complete disregard of a "naughty" performance on its first appearance is an effective way to avoid making it a habit. If the attention given it is in the form of scolding or mild remonstrance or argument, just enough emotional reinforcement may be furnished to fix a habit. A "rise" out of the child's parents makes many an otherwise dull afternoon thrilling and interesting. His parents themselves, if they are not aged, like a little excitement and risk or they could not have attained the status of parenthood.

The normal process of a psychoanalytic cure of a neurotic symptom has been described as practice of the cues for the paralysis, tic, hysteric "fit," or what not, with the general situation so controlled as to deflect the response. The psychoanalysts place emphasis on another phenomenon—the tendency for the neurotic habit to disappear when the circumstances of its first conditioning are recovered in full consciousness. A recall of the forgotten occasion on which terror or syncope was associated with bright artificial lights frees the patient from the habit of responding thus whenever he is in a brightly lighted room. This is reminiscent of Dunlap's description of the effects of negative practice, since one of the conditions for success in negative practice is full awareness of the action. The old fable of the centipede that could no longer walk when asked the order in which its legs moved describes a very common human experience.

When attention is given to an act that has been performed without attention, the very act of attention is frequently a disruption of the habit. Attention to one of our own movements renders that movement different because it now lacks some of its cues. In writing we ordinarily look at the words as they are formed, and there is no doubt that this determines in part the sequence of movements. If, in ordinary writing, we attend not to the written words as they are formed, but to the finger movements (which will be found difficult), the writing changes its character and becomes disorganized. There are conflicts and confusion. This is probably analogous to what happens in a psychoanalytic cure. The bad habit has depended on cues which were being responded to without attention. The recall of the distressing experience brings these cues to notice and so alters the response. This is not intended to mean entire agreement with the psychoanalytic doctrine that a hysterical fear is always done away with by being brought into consciousness. There are many cases in which embarrassment survives a full awareness of its origin.

Attention includes general movements of orientation, looking, listening, and so on, and includes also the inhibition of conflicting response. The stimuli attended to are by the movements of attention caused to dominate behavior, and even a minor change in action resulting from this may undo the habit.

CHAPTER XII

Reward and Punishment

ONE of the most ancient and one of the best established of beliefs concerning learning is the belief that learning is determined by its effects. Common sense puts this in terms of pleasure and pain. Action leading to pleasure tends to be fixed as habit, while action leading to pain tends to be "stamped out."

There can be no real quarrel with this popular theory. Children have been spanked or caressed on this theory for an undoubtedly long time. The theory is well established.

But the popular theory has several defects for scientific purposes. In the first place, when it is applied to animals we become a little puzzled as to how to tell pleasure and pain. And unless we can define them so that they can be unambiguously recognized they are of no use to a theory of learning; for a theory of learning must state the observable circumstances under which learning occurs and under which it fails to occur. Habits are formed by snails and earthworms, but no one has ever tried to describe what a pleased snail or a pained earthworm looks like. Pleasure and pain in dogs would seem a little more readily described.

We need then to substitute for pleasure and pain as the conditions of learning some less ambiguous condition, some condition that can be easily recognized by an observer, because we can not always ask the learner which he feels, and can not depend very much on his answer when he gives it.

This less vague and less ambiguous description of the conditions of learning Thorndike has suggested. He would substitute satisfaction and annoyance for pleasure and pain. These are the conditions that determine the fixing and unfixing of habits. He defined satisfaction and annoyance in strictly behavioristic terms so that they can be readily recognized by any observer. "By a satisfying state of affairs," Thorndike said (1932, page 176), "is meant roughly one which the animal does nothing to avoid, often doing such things as attain and preserve it. By an annoying state of affairs is meant roughly one which the animal avoids or changes." His principle, which he called the law of effect, is as follows (1932, page 176):

When a modifiable connection between a situation and a response is made and is accompanied or followed by a satisfying state of affairs, that connection's strength is increased. When made and accompanied or followed by an annoying state of affairs, its strength is decreased. The strengthening effect of satisfyingness (or the weakening effect of annoyingness) upon a bond varies with the closeness of the connection between it and the bond. This closeness or intimacy of association of the satisfying (or annoying) state of affairs with the bond in question may be the result of nearness in time or of attentiveness to the situation, response, and satisfying event in question.

This statement of the law Thorndike somewhat amended, in line with an admirable disposition to be guided by the facts rather than by his theory, a disposition which he often demonstrated. He no longer believed that the action of annoyers is the opposite of the action of satisfiers in all respects. The strengthening effect of satisfaction is more universal, more inevitable, and more direct than the weakening effect of annoyance. An animal that gets food by pulling a loop learns to pull the loop.

But if an animal in the same situation pulls a loop and either (a) gets a shock in its paw at contact with the loop, or (b) gets a blow on the back, or (c) gets a sudden pain in the bowels, the weakening of the connections is likely to vary. In (a) there will probably be much weakening by way of strengthening the connection between the situation and the response of drawing back from the loop. In (b) there will probably be weakening, but less, because the reaction will probably be jumping away from the place, which is not so inconsistent with pulling at the loop. If the animal in (c) reacts by screaming without letting go of the loop, there may be no weakening at all (1932, page 276).

In other words Thorndike's latest view was that punishment may or may not lead to unlearning *depending on what it causes the animal to do*. The important thing to be noticed is that his amended explanation is precisely in terms of the conditioning which he rejected as an explanation. The sight of the loop will later cause the animal that hurriedly withdrew its paw on being shocked to withdraw its paw on the next occasion. The animal that gets a blow on the back will on the next occasion tend to jump away. The animal with the gripe in its bowels will tend to do whatever it did in response to the gripe. That this is an appeal to pure conditioning is concealed by putting the emphasis on the loop pulling and speaking of this as weakened or strengthened. We can be, as Thorndike acknowledged, much more precise than to predict the failure of loop pulling. We can predict the recurrence of the specific behavior indulged in.

How it could escape Thorndike's notice that the effects of satisfaction are likewise readily and much more precisely described in terms of conditioning is hard to understand. Satisfaction is defined as a state of affairs the animal does nothing to avoid, or often acts to maintain. This is to say that a situation in which a maintained response is made tends on later occasions to evoke that response. "Doing nothing to avoid" a state of affairs does not mean doing nothing whatever; it means maintaining orientation, maintaining attention, and on the second occasion the general facts of conditioning would lead us to expect a repetition of the behavior.

In those cases in which the satisfaction is a satisfaction of some source of unrest, maintained hunger spasms or a continuous painful stimulation, it is quite reasonable to suppose that the precurrent behavior is associated with the hunger, but that this association is continuously destroyed by new associations. There is one act, however, to which hunger may remain a faithful conditioner. That is the act of eating; and the faithfulness of hunger to this association derives from the fact that hunger dies when eating occurs. As Stevenson Smith and I pointed out in our *General Psychology*, elements of the consummatory response tend to be present throughout a series of actions driven by a maintaining stimulus. Hull's paper (1932) on his goal-gradient hypothesis described the role that such traces of the consummatory reaction may play in guiding learning and in holding the animal to its purpose.

Thorndike explained the appearance of retroactive effect, the reinforcement by a satisfying outcome of an association that lies in the past, by suggesting a physiological event in the brain. Of this possible event he said (1932, page 314) that "the evidence that it is some condition favoring conduction across certain synapses is still strong. The physiological equivalent of a connection does not thus vanish utterly in the twinkling of an eye. Whatever it is, it is there a second after it occurred in a manner or degree quite different from that of a connection of an hour ago."

This cerebral hangover is a highly speculative and quite unnecessary assumption. The physiological attendant of a connection which "does not vanish utterly in the twinkling of an eye" may well be the maintained muscular contractions of the response. We know that these tensions in systems of muscles may be maintained for long periods. And while they are still maintained they are reasonably assumed to be subject to conditioning. The action that produces "satisfaction" is not over "in the twinkling of an eye," and by Thorndike's own definition of satisfaction it is an act that is maintained, or at least not broken up by the vigorous interference of punishment. Peterson in 1922 wrote: "Nerve impulses flash through the organism in but a fraction of a second. But there is considerable evidence to show that the effects do not so immediately fade away. Probably the responses of muscles and glands set up other nerve impulses, which . . . bring about further responses." And "these streams of impulses, therefore, will exist contemporaneously with subsequent stimuli and exert important directive influences on the nerve impulses these stimuli set up."

"The influence upon learning," Thorndike said (1932, page 312), "of both satisfiers and annoyers depends upon what they cause the animal to be or do." This is exactly what I am suggesting, namely, that the future response to a situation can be best predicted in terms of what an animal has done in that situation in the past. Stimuli acting during a response tend on later occasions to evoke that response.

I do not hold that all satisfiers tend to fix the associative connection that has just preceded them. When a satisfying situation involves breaking up the action in progress it will destroy connections as readily as punishment. In teaching a dog to sit up, tossing his rewarding morsel to a distant part of the room will prove a very ineffective method. There is no doubt of the satisfying character of the meat. The dog certainly "does nothing to avoid, often doing such things as attain and preserve," not, of course, the meat, but the eating of it. But the effect of the reward will be that the dog instead of sitting up stands ready for another dash across the room.

Just as satisfiers do not always "stamp in" a connection, so annoyers do not, as Thorndike himself perceived, always "stamp out." What we can predict is that the influence of the stimuli acting at the time of either satisfaction or annoyance will be to reëstablish whatever behavior was in evidence at the time.

"A satisfier," Thorndike said (1932, page 312), "which is attached to a modifiable connection always, or almost always, causes the animal to be or to do something which strengthens the connection to which the satisfier is attached; but we do not know what this something is. It may be to maintain relatively undisturbed the physiological basis of the connection; it may be to retain it longer than would be otherwise the case; it may be to confine it by some metabolic effect; it may be to alter it in some more mysterious way." I suggest that the mystery may be reduced by supposing conditioning to have taken place. This is, of course, to invoke another mystery, but one somewhat less mysterious because more familiar. The something that the satisfier causes the animal to do on the second occasion is the repetition of its behavior on the first occasion—always allowing for possible new elements that may interfere. The dog's lesson in sitting up may always be interrupted by the cat. If it is objected that this explanation seems to demand a retroactive effect on connections we can only say that backward association, in the sense that the cue may follow the original stimulus, is well established. This retroactive effect need not be actually anything more than simultaneous association. The substitute stimulus is probably always coincident with the response.

To this last quotation Thorndike added a footnote: "The satisfying after-effect obviously often causes the animal then and there to continue or to repeat the connection." So long as the substitute cue for action remains, this would seem a very natural consequence. One taste leads to another because the stimuli are still present unless the animal turns away from the food, which would be by definition the work of an annoyer. As in the case of the chick and the cinnabar caterpillar, rejection, the result of the bitter taste, may be conditioned on the sight of the caterpillar and replace the original impulse to peck. This is not a "retroactive effect," though it has that appearance. It is simultaneous conditioning. I venture to predict that learning would be much more uncertain if the caterpillar were of such a size that it was swallowed at one peck and not visible while rejection was going on.

We may go on to inquire how any stimulus becomes an annoyer in the first place, a question which Thorndike did not consider. He defined an annoyer as a state of affairs which the animal avoids or changes. But this ability to avoid is just what it is necessary to explain. Hammering the thumb or bumping one's head on a beam is not an annoyer according to this definition unless we assume that the learning has already occurred, for the victim can not avoid it after it has happened. If he avoids it at all it must be in time, and this implies that the learning which we hoped to explain has already taken place. We may, for the sake of argument, consent not to be annoyed by such events and to deal only with annoyances which satisfy the definition, that is, with continuous stimuli which we can do something about while they are still upon us, such as intense heat, a bumpy road, thirst, hunger, flies, radio programs, or, if we are laboratory animals, charged grids, immersion in water, confinement.

In his later publications on learning Thorndike was influenced by the Gestalt movement and described a number of conditions of perception which favor the establishment of an association. These include such perceptual characteristics of the response as "belongingness" (1932). This is illustrated by a type of experiment in which subjects practiced a list of sentences. The list was rehearsed straight through, but Thorndike found that the words in one sentence were more effective as cues for the next word in that sentence than the last word was as a cue for the first word in the next sentence. Thorndike concluded that belongingness was more important for the establishment of an association than contiguity. The relatively greater ease with which meaningful material can be memorized when compared with the memorizing of nonsense syllables is well known. The Gestalt psychologists have emphasized the importance of such perceptual organization and paid scant attention to association as such or to such problems as what gets associated with what. The writings of Köhler and Koffka, except for one passing reference by the latter, never raise the question of how one specific response came to be made rather than another. Tolman makes little or no reference to such a problem.

Katona in his *Organizing and Memorizing* describes experiments designed to show that in the higher reaches of behavior learning consists not in the association of specific responses but in the conceptual grasp of solutions. For instance if two men each practice a series of numbers such as 3, 4, 6, 10, 18, 34, 66, 130, the one who perceives that each term is two less than twice the preceding term not only need practice no further but has learned the continuation of the series to an indefinite length.

An associationist would not deny this except to object to the use of the term "learn" for the ability to continue the series; but he would point out that it was previous responses of multiplication and addition that were being called on and that the new learning involved associating a formula with the situation. The ability to follow the directions of a formula had been previously acquired through associations established in the grade-school training in arithmetic. In other words, the associationist does not deny that intricate perceptions enter into learning. He asserts that these perceptions are themselves acquired in conformity with association, not as violations of the principle.

Now we do not know, unless we have observed it on some previous occasion, what either animal or man will do in any of the annoying situations described above. Holt (1931) has well argued that the early and primitive response to such stimuli is approach. If the fingers are flexed the finger tips touch the palm. The touch on the palm then comes to be a conditioner of the finger movement. Holt suggests that the grasping reflex is thus learned before birth. In general the stimuli caused by movements come to be the conditioners of the movements which cause them. Holt has also described how intense stimuli may, through conditioning, become stimuli for withdrawal and avoidance. Annoyers are essentially intense stimuli. Their original effect, before we have learned to avoid them, is in some cases approach, but in all cases excitement. Intense stimulation brings about general tonus of skeletal muscles and reinforces action. We do not know what a man or an animal suffering an intense stimulus will do, but we do know that he will not be relaxed and that there will be variety and energy in his actions. He will be active, and being active his activity will be varied, because activity changes the stimuli which act upon him. Eyes and ears as well as muscles and tendons will be subjected to rapid change in stimulation. If these intense stimuli responsible for his excitement are maintained (we have elsewhere referred to them as maintaining stimuli) as they are in those situations which would satisfy Thorndike's definition, they have opportunity to become the conditioners of many and varied actions, but each successive action alienates them from its predecessor.

There is one act, however, of which these maintaining stimuli may remain faithful conditioners. This is the act which removes them. The maintaining stimuli are no longer present with the succeeding acts and so may remain conditioners of the movement which took them from the victim, or took the victim from them. If annoyance means avoidance, we had to learn to be annoyed at annoyers. At first they were only disturbers.

Dunlap (1932, page 30) treated reward and punishment in part in terms of feeling, rather than of satisfaction and annoyance. "That feeling in itself, without thought, is of any importance is improbable," he said, "except in so far as feeling may be an organic condition which is generally favorable or unfavorable to learning. From present information, we may infer that perhaps mild feeling is favorable and intense feeling possibly unfavorable, but we have no indication that any specific type of feeling is any different in its effect from any other, except the feeling which is involved in desire."

To this it may be suggested that the effect of intense feeling is not unfavorable to learning in general but very favorable.

But what is learned will be what is done—and what is done in intense feeling is usually something different from what was being done. Sitting on tacks does not discourage learning. It encourages one in learning to do something else than sit. It is not the feeling caused by punishment, but the specific action caused by punishment that determines what will be learned. In training a dog to jump through a hoop, the effectiveness of punishment depends on where it is applied, front or rear. It is what the punishment makes the dog *do* that counts, or what it makes a man do, not what it makes him feel. The mistaken notion that it is the feeling that determines learning derives from the fact that often we do not care what is done as a result of punishment, just as long as what is done breaks up or inhibits the unwanted habit.

My own view of the way in which unpleasant or unsatisfactory consequences of action affect learning may be further illustrated by a minor incident in the routine of a certain psychologist. He rented an apartment for the summer with a garage which had a large swinging door. From the top of the door hung a heavy chain. When he opened the door hurriedly the first morning the chain swung about slowly and struck a blow on the side of his head, a distinctly painful and "unsatisfactory" event. But this continued to happen each morning for some two weeks. Why the long delay in learning to stand aside?

The answer, I believe, is that the act of opening the door was performed while looking at the exterior of the door. The chain struck after the door had opened and the scene changed. Dodging was not conditioned on the sight of the door because sight of the door had not accompanied flinching from the blow. The flinching movement which occurred as the rear of the car came into view was too late. Only after the bruised ear became a chronic reminder and the incident had been talked about and finally told to a visitor on the way to the garage, did caution show itself in time.

The whole incident is to be explained not in terms of pain or annoyance, but in terms of the action and its cue. It is not the annoyance but what the annoyed person does that determines what will be learned. Annoyance, in so far as it means increased muscle tonus and more complete and vigorous action, is favorable to learning to do whatever is done in response to whatever cues are present. The mistaken belief that annoyance discourages learning comes from placing all the attention on one line of action. Annoyance often accompanies the sudden disruption of an activity and leads to unlearning that activity, but at the expense of learning something else.

As the outcome of this discussion punishment and reward are not summarily to be ejected from the place they hold in public favor. No doubt whatever has been thrown on their general effectiveness. Children may still be spanked or caressed. But we shall have a much better insight into the uses of punishment and reward if we analyze their effects in terms of association and realize that punishment is effective only through its associations. Punishment achieves its effects not by taking away strength from the physiological basis of the connection (Thorndike, 1932, page 313), but by forcing the animal or the child to do something different and thus establishing inhibitory conditioning of unwanted habit. Punishment is effective *only in the presence of cues for the bad habit*. The law of effect would not have made us aware of this.

Furthermore, when the effect of punishment is only emotional excitement, punishment facilitates the stereotyping of the undesired habit. Punishment and reward are essentially moral terms, not psychological terms. They are defined not in terms of their effects on the recipient, but in terms of the purposes of the individual who administers them. Theory stated in their terms is bound to be ambiguous.

The argument over the law of effect has been carried into the higher and less easily manipulated reaches of human behavior.

Gordon Allport (1946) has suggested that men do not endlessly repeat their successes as the law of effect would lead us to expect, but, having once succeeded, the specific problem and the motive vanish. Against the law of effect Allport proposes such tendencies as problem solving, satisfaction of the ego, and interest in novelty.

To this Rice has replied with a defense of the law in which he points out that problems exist by definition only when a repeated response is not available for a repeated goal. He suggests that a general interest in problem solving could be subject to the law of effect.

One of the theses of this book is that, as Allport has suggested, the law of effect is a secondary principle of learning; but the actual position taken here is very different from Allport's. Allport believes that the ego (which he treats as a principle but without any statement or rule) and such interests as an interest in novelty or in problem solving are alternative to or take precedence over the law of effect. The thesis of this book is that the law of effect is reducible to and conforms with the principle of association by contiguity. Allport assumes that association would lead to endless repetitions of successes.

The answer is that normally we do repeat behavior that leads to success when the occasion is repeated. The notion that a rule of association by contiguity would lead to endless repetition of behavior cycles is so widespread among psychologists that an illustration of its falsity is in order. Allport uses as an illustration the fact that students who get an A in a course (reward!) do not immediately reregister for the course. A simpler instance and one that is equivalent is afforded by the customer at the cigar counter who, having purchased a cigar, fails to continue indefinitely to purchase a cigar. We should bear in mind that there are men who, having just finished a smoke, do actually repeat. Why does not the man who has successfully entered the theater return and buy another ticket and reënter? Why does not a man who has solved a problem immediately embark on its resolving with the same device? We hope that, if the same problem recurs, the same solution will be repeated. Education depends very largely on that trait. But the conditions of life do not allow repetition. The solved problem does not exist as a problem.

Estes (1944) undertook the investigation of the effects of punishment by Skinner's methods. Skinner suggested that punishment causes a temporary depression in the rate of response and that this is followed by a compensating increase so that the total number of unreinforced responses necessary for extinction is the same as if no punishment had been given. Estes concluded that when a response is once strengthened by periodic reinforcement it can not be eliminated solely through punishment. The response may cease during punishment but recover to a reflex reserve equal to what the reserve would have been without punishment.

Estes found that "merely being shocked in the experimental situation has the same effect upon the animal's behavior in respect to the lever as being punished for making the response" (1944, page 25). This has a considerable bearing on the law of effect because punishment is affecting a response which had not been elicited or "emitted." Estes interprets his results in favor of association (of cautionary response to shock) in the general situation of being placed in the experimental box, not as a direct effect of punishment on the reflex strength of the response in question even when punishment followed the response.

CHAPTER XIII

Skill

AN OCCASIONAL habit can be described as skillful, but habit and skill refer to two features of behavior that are very different indeed. In trying to define skill we must include a new dimension in the description of behavior. Habit can theoretically be described in terms of muscular contraction or of glandular secretion. To define skill we must make reference to something quite outside the organism and something not contained in the stimulus situation.

In other words the stimulus-response terms which we have been using up to this point now become inadequate for what we wish to describe. A habit is a habit, whether it is good or bad, successful or unsuccessful; but in one sense of the word good, no skill is a skill unless it is good. Progress in skill is progress toward goodness of a kind. Skill, in short, can be defined only in terms of success, of achievement, of a goal. *Skill consists in the ability to bring about some end result with maximum certainty and minimum outlay of energy, or time, or of time and energy.* Skills are made up of habits, but habits stand in the way of skill as well as being the stuff of which skills are composed. Progress in skill is the formation of "good" habits and the elimination of "bad" habits.

The typical laboratory study of skill defines some achievement, such as hitting a target, getting cards sorted into the proper piles, typing a given number of words, reaching the end point of a maze. The point of the experiment is the attainment of such an end result. The movements by which it is attained are not recorded. So far in this book we have been concerned with the prediction of movement.

Between 1920 and 1940 probably more studies were devoted to one form of skill, the learning of a maze, than to any other. The maze used with rats consists of a system of runways, some of them "blind alleys," others part of the route to the maze terminus at which point is to be found (whether the psychologist speaks in terms of the Thorndikean law of effect or not) a reward, usually food. If food is to be the reward, the rat is usually hungry when placed in the maze. A record is kept of the time required to reach the food box, and sometimes of the "errors" or wrong turns. But as a rule no notice is taken of the animal's movements; only the result of the series of movements is noted.

Under such circumstances the rat on repeated trials normally reduces its time and the number of its "errors" and when these are represented graphically we have what is called a learning curve.

The rat must be hungry or it will spend its time (we are tempted to say, pleasantly) exploring the maze or scratching itself, or even briefly napping. Hunger is required to set the goal. Many psychologists conceive of the goal as a determiner of the learning. We can not do this because we have resolved to remain scientists and to undertake to find the *antecedent* conditions that determine learning; and until it has been experienced the goal is not such an antecedent condition. When it has once been reached this previous experience does, it is very true, become one of the antecedent conditions. But this is not what psychologists like Wheeler mean when they speak of learning as goal-determined.

In our *General Psychology in Terms of Behavior* written many years ago, Stevenson Smith and I described this type of goal behavior in the following words:

Many responses are of such a nature that they bring to an end the stimuli that caused them. Often, when a response is prevented, emotional reinforcement ensues, so that, when the stimulus is persistent or recurrent, negative adaptation toward it does not occur. This emotional reinforcement makes probable the occurrence of the response as soon as a change in the situation allows it. Such a stimulus may act throughout a long period, during which it interferes with responses to many other stimuli. Persistent or recurring stimuli whose responses are blocked with a resulting emotional reinforcement will be called *maintaining stimuli*. Maintaining stimuli are ultimately removed by the responses they themselves provoke. The final response that removes these maintaining stimuli, by altering either the external situation or the internal state of the animal, is called a *consummatory response*. The series of responses leading up to this final response are called *precurrent responses*.

To this general view of the nature of drive or motivation, which is substantially that proposed by Sherrington in 1911, I would still subscribe. An elaboration of it by Rexroad (1933) is so enlightening and clear that it deserves some review. Rexroad was considering the nature of goals and goal objects and the part they take in the determination of behavior. He suggested that goal objects may be divided into two types, "those *from* which the behavior is getting and those *to* which the behavior is getting." The first may be treated as simple stimuli. An animal on a charged grid, a barefoot boy on a hot pavement, a man sitting on a tack have as their goals mere escape from the intense stimulation that causes general tension and restlessness as well as specific movement. These stimuli continue to act as what Stevenson Smith and I called maintaining stimuli until some movement carries the subject away from the source of stimulation, or the source of stimulation away from the subject. Goal objects *toward* which the behavior is getting depend on maintaining stimuli that do not come from the goal object. "Food," Rexroad pointed out, "is not effective for causing eating unless the animal is hungry, water is not effective for causing drinking unless the animal is thirsty. . . ."

Goal objects toward which behavior is getting thus differ from simple stimuli in that the behavior toward them is "driven" by stimuli which are usually internal. The animal may as justly be described as fleeing from the acute spasms of hunger as seeking its goal, food. Rexroad continued, "A second difference arises from the fact that the direct response (the one made when the goal-object is immediately present) removes the internal condition upon which the goal object is dependent for its effectiveness. Eating removes hunger, drinking removes thirst. . . ." Goal behavior of both sorts is subject to ready conditioning because of the tension and excitement produced by the maintaining stimuli.

Goal behavior is the outstanding characteristic of living things. Haldane (1922) and Cannon (1932) described life in terms of the maintenance of certain essential conditions of life. We can, after we have observed it, predict that body temperature, the carbon-dioxide-oxygen balance in the blood stream, and numerous other states will be maintained, though we may not know as yet how they are maintained. This holds true also of goal behavior. We can as the result of experience with rats or men assert that certain goals tend to be reached under certain conditions. We can predict that a man will eat even when we can not predict how he will go about getting food. A number of psychologists like McDougall and Tolman and Humphrey hold that this striving for goals is the fundamental mode of human behavior and the behavior of animals. This is not to be denied. An organism is primarily a striving object. But even though we admit that goal striving is fundamental in human and animal nature, it is the conditions under which goals are reached, and the conditions under which they are established through learning that are the fundamental problem of the psychologist. If we attempt to understand goal behavior we are at once driven to consider the nature of learning, the mechanics of learning, because in all the more complex strivings of men and of animals it is through learning that goals are attained and through learning that desires, wishes, goals, and purposes are formed.

There are many psychologists who hold that the nature of the pursuit of goals, aims, purposes is misrepresented by the preceding account. For such psychologists a goal is in some sense the *determiner of the action*, not just the outcome of the action. Now there is a sense in which goals determine action, but it is the contention of this book that such determination of action by a goal proceeds always through the previous association of the goal with action. The goal as a future event does not influence the action. It is evident that we must consider the nature of goals and their manner of determining action very carefully.

In the first place, how are we to know in advance what is the goal of any series of acts, animal or human? How are we to know, for instance, that the food at the end of the maze is the goal of the rat? Or that a performance in record time is the goal of the typist? I must confess at this point a certain awe of the psychologists who, like Tolman (1932, page 10), say that "behavior . . . always seems to have the character of getting-to or getting-from a specific goal-object, or goal-situation." So much of my own behavior lacks this admirable quality, so often must I, when asked what I am about, seek desperately for a rationalization, that I am inclined to suspect even the higher animals of at least the occasional aimlessness which Wheeler, Tolman, and possibly Humphrey would deny them. And when I do select a goal in advance it is so seldom that the outcome resembles it. Not that there is ever a failure to get to and from places and things, since ubiety, or the property of position, remains even in death; but the things and places are so often not goals in the sense that they were selected in advance.

For a simple outcome of a series of acts to be a goal it is not enough that it be an outcome. Every event ends in something or other. Every action or series of actions has an outcome.

How can we know that food or, as Tolman has pointed out, a particular kind of food was the rat's goal when it was placed in the maze? What we do know in advance is, first, that the animal is a rat; second, that the rat has been without food for twenty-four hours; and this, coupled with the knowledge that this is a rat, will enable us to predict that the animal will keep in restless motion until fed or exhausted. We know by analogy that the rat's stomach is indulging in periodic spasms, and that the high points of activity tend to coincide with these spasms (cf. Richter, 1922).

We can with fair safety predict that the rat will reach the food eventually. We can also predict that on future repetitions of the performance the time required and the number of blind alleys entered will be gradually and somewhat irregularly reduced.

We also know more than this, thanks to the work of Tolman and others. When Tolman says that at the height of hunger the exploratoriness is specifically directed toward food, we must, however, be cautious. We know that food will stop the restlessness, but it is not true that activity will be directed toward food until food has been encountered on some occasion. If we have forgotten to place the food at the end of the maze on the present occasion this will have no effect on the rat's behavior.

Among the things we know from the experiments of Tolman and his associates are that the nature of the reward will affect the rate of improvement; that a delay in giving the reward leads to less improvement than prompt reward (Hamilton, 1929); that a change in reward will disturb the rate of improvement (Elliott, 1928); that the degree of hunger affects the rate of improvement (Tolman and Honzik, 1930); that learning a maze by wading through it in water will not materially affect the rat's ability to get through without errors when the rat has to swim (Macfarlane, 1930); that of routes differing in spatial or temporal length the shorter will eventually be taken (Gengerelli, 1930); that errors in the general direction of the food are less readily made than errors away from food (Tolman and Honzik, 1930).

All this knowledge about the course of improvement in the

performances of rats in a maze is the result of observing rat be-havior in a maze. It is derived from experiments of a new type, differing from those referred to in previous chapters in that these new experiments do not record or attempt to predict the action of the animal but only the results of the action. The resulting generalizations are consequently also of a new type, and they do not, of course, contradict the generalizations of former chap-ters but they do represent extensions of our knowledge of be-havior and of learning.

Tolman's theory in which he systematizes these results is, in a much abbreviated and probably considerably mutilated form, about as follows: The white rat has, by virtue of its membership in its species, certain goal tendencies. These include food, mat-ing, escape from confinement, avoidance of certain types of noxious situations, nursing the young on the part of the female, and other such behavior outcomes. These are end results which we can expect of the rat, knowing it is a rat. This is, of course, such a list as would have been called a few years ago a list of instincts.

Also we can be reasonably sure of more than this. We can be sure that these goal tendencies will manifest what Tolman calls "docility." By this he means that repeated occurrences of a par-ticular goal behavior will result in an increase in the certainty of goal reaching in the recurrent situation, and that there will be a reduction in the time required and in the energy required for the accomplishment of the result. In this one word, "do-cility," he lumps and dismisses all the phenomena which we have been considering under the name of conditioning or as-sociative learning. The manner of this learning, he suggests, may be conditioning; however, it is not the manner but the re-sults of the learning in which he is interested.

So far Tolman's theory is the familiar instinct theory which has received a great deal of undeserved scorn in recent years. Animals do have their ways, and a description of these ways offers useful information. Tolman's theory does not stop with this. It goes on to make use of the history of the individual animal and to predict what the animal will do in terms of the situation in which it is placed and the experience it has had with that situation.

I have suggested that such information can only be utilized in some form of association theory. The form of association theory which Tolman has adopted does not use the association of stimulus with response, but the association of cues, which he first called "sign gestalts" and later called "field expectancies," with a mental event. The early parts of the maze (Tolman, 1933) act not as cues for action, but as signs that the goal is to come, cues for the rat to expect the goal. By "expect" in this sense Tolman does not mean action or preparation, but a mental awareness of some kind. His "sign-gestalt" formula leaves quite untouched the problem of what a rat will do with a sign, or of how signs are translated into action. "These sign-gestalt expectations," he says (1933, page 249), "I assumed would be to the effect that the earlier parts of the discrimination apparatus would have become a sign or a set of signs to the rats that the encountering of the food-compartments was to be achieved by running through this discrimination apparatus." Signs, in Tolman's theory, occasion in the rat *realization,* or *cognition,* or *judgment,* or *hypotheses,* or *abstraction,* but *they do not occasion action.* In his concern with what goes on in the rat's mind, Tolman has neglected to predict what the rat will do. So far as the theory is concerned the rat is left buried in thought; if it gets to the food box at the end that is its concern, not the concern of the theory.

This objection to the sign-gestalt theory does not at all apply to experimental work done by Tolman and his associates. That hungry rats do get to food boxes, that practice reduces the number of blind alleys entered and shortens the time required, that errors in the direction of food are more common than errors away from food, that certain problems are much more difficult of solution by the rat than others, are generalizations based on observation and are real additions to knowledge, particularly knowledge of the ways of a white rat in a maze.

Whether or not these laws are reducible to conditioning (which Tolman and the Gestalt psychologists would deny) has been the subject of a number of papers by Hull (1929, 1930, 1931, 1932). Hull defends the theory that the apparent "drawing power" of the goal is based on the conditioning of cues for successful movement. There is some evidence (Borovski, 1927) that errors are eliminated near the goal before they are eliminated at the beginning of the maze. The presence of hunger contractions with eating renders hunger contractions a possible cue for eating movements. Inhibitory conditioning does not occur because eating removes the maintaining stimuli, which consequently do not become negatively adapted.

Such useless movements as entering a blind alley tend to be eliminated not because that is a general law of learning, but because blind alleys are left as well as entered, and always left after they are entered. The sight of them suggests leaving and not entering. Other irrelevant movements, like scratching, exploring, depend on chance stimuli which are not repeated at that point of the run on successive occasions and these adventitious movements are apt to be replaced by other movements on that account.

Not only do general movements of eating tend to be aroused by hunger contractions, but the specific movements demanded by the peculiar nature of the food are possibly in evidence. Hence when the rat runs the maze it is ready for whatever reward has been received in the past, sunflower seed or bran mash. This readiness is an actual muscular readiness, and is the actuality behind the "sign gestalt" and the "means-end-readinesses" talked about by Tolman.

The "goal tendency" or the purpose of a man or a rat is often made clear by his behavior. When hunger spasms drive the animal to action there is one action accompanied by the hunger spasms that is not succeeded by any other, and so is not subject to inhibitory conditioning. That is the act of eating. Eating removes hunger. Consequently hunger as a stimulus may remain faithful to those parts of eating behavior that are not incompatible with walking, turning, and so on. The hungry animal may often be seen to lick its chops, swallow, and exhibit other features of the consummatory response.

When in the course of a number of trials the reward is changed, confusion is introduced. Readiness for bran mash is now confused with readiness for sunflower seed and the two are as incompatible as readiness for a high and for a low pitch on the part of a baseball catcher. The rat, encountering the changed reward, is disappointed, which is only to say that the movements with which the rat approaches the food are not movements adjusted to the eating of this particular food and there is some resultant confusion.

Thus Tolman has been very sagacious in pointing out that the rat does not learn the maze, but learns the way to sunflower seed or the way to water. And when the reward is changed, confusion results. Furthermore, when a rat has learned the maze route to bran mash when hungry and is placed in the maze well fed but thirsty, it has a new problem. Thirst is not the cue on which the maze running has been based. The rat must learn the maze over again for water. Its first practice with food as a reward is not a total loss because there are some action sequences whose serial form is ready to reëstablish, but the primary maintaining stimulus that integrates the behavior and makes it *purposeful* is altered.

All this discussion of rats and mazes may strike the reader who is primarily interested in human learning as a digression having very little to do with understanding the acquisition of skill. It is not a digression, because the central and necessary element in every skill is its purposefulness, its achievement; and rats, especially as a result of Tolman's work, have contributed to an understanding of the manner in which this purposefulness enters into behavior. Every purpose has as its essential feature some maintaining stimulus complex. In the rat this lay in its hunger spasms and in the muscular readiness for the familiar food. If this muscular readiness were broken up the rat might remain restless from hunger but it would "forget" what specific food it was after, and "forget" where to find that food. By "forgetting" we mean here only that it would fail to keep on the path to the food.

Maze learning in rats and men, and similar tasks, represent a very special and limited form of skill in which a highly stereotyped solution is possible. Elliott (1934) has shown that under the drive of more urgent hunger the rat's path toward food tends to be more fixed and stereotyped. It is less open to distraction and inhibition from other habit tendencies. There is another class of skills which do not allow this solution in a single stereotyped series of movements. Skillful tennis, fencing, chess, games and sports in general, are very different affairs. In these skills no fixed order of action is possible. No two games are alike in the order of the responses necessary. Skill here consists not in acquiring one serial habit but in acquiring thousands of habits fitted to differences in the situation. In tennis the player must learn a thousand different ways of returning the ball according to its speed, according to the direction given it by his opponent. He learns to take his cue from the movements of the other player, and not to wait to see what the ball will be like. Remote conditionings must be acquired.

One difficulty in acquiring such skills is that the stimuli resulting from inadequate habits, the consequences of poor performance, do not appear in time to break up the bad habit. If it could be arranged that the stance and swing that result in "slicing" a drive in golf would in their course produce a sharp pain, slicing would quickly disappear. It does not disappear readily because the result of slicing is, in the first place, not immediate discomfort, which would break up the bad habit, but only a belated perception of a ball taking the wrong course. In so far as this belated perception leads to rehearsal with changes, improvement is possible. If an instructor is present, his speech may accomplish the "break up" and serve instead of a pain.

Dunlap, in a discussion of improvement in skill in throwing a dart at a target (1932, page 34), pointed out that in practice in which 90 percent of the darts are thrown wild, "in the total learning, the darts thrown wrong probably have been as effective as an equal number of those thrown 'successfully,' provided the thought factor has been adequate." This is, of course, a very vague statement and the adequacy of a thought factor would be hard to observe or to control. Dunlap's account does not go far enough. Improvement resulting from wild throws depends first on what has been referred to by experimenters as "knowledge of results." But the knowledge of results can not be left as mere knowledge or it will be useless to theory. What it undoubtedly consists of is the perception that the throw was to the right, too high, or too low, not merely the knowledge that it was wild. And we may venture to believe that only in cases in which this perception of "too far to the right" includes a *change of stance* or a partial rehearsal of a correction will Dunlap's "thought factor" be adequate. This correction of posture or movement, this rehearsal with a difference breaks up the wrong habit and makes improvement possible. It is often noticeable on the golf course.

The golfer watching his putt keeps his posture. The "thought" that his putt was a failure will not bring improvement. Better performance will result only if the sight of the ball rolling too far to the right leads to rehearsal of a corrected swing. He may overcorrect, but he has at least broken up the pattern of action that failed to reach his goal.

Before he has developed skill he addresses his ball tense with a fear of hitting too hard, and at the same time tense with a fear of hitting too gently. These "fears" are nothing more than conditioned corrections resulting from previous errors. Only long practice will reduce the conflict of opposed muscle groups and deliver the ball with the minimum exertion that we call grace or skill.

This reduction of the energy required is not a universal law of behavior, as Humphrey would have us believe, but it is fortunately a very common result of practice. And the part taken by the goal is not in the form of an attraction or influence. The player has learned the object of the play. When he is set for a certain outcome or goal, failure breaks up the habit and brings a readjustment.

Learning the typewriter is learning to make certain movements at certain cues. As practice begins, the would-be typist pronounces the letters to himself and makes a somewhat tentative movement at the key. This movement is at first apt to be an extensive one. It may include a nod with each stroke. When the letter appearing on the paper is not the one muttered there is a repeated effort, with changed movement. This is a combination of previous habit and slight trial and error. The quick readjustment tends to break up the wrong habit and eventually the letters will be struck as muttered; movements that depended on adventitious stimuli will be eliminated because these chance stimuli do not occur twice the same, and there is a resultant speeding up.

With further practice combinations of letters often repeated are integrated into continuous movements and will be "set off" by the sight of the combination as a whole. Later, whole words that have often been written become in the typing of them single acts. The final development is for the seen copy to begin the adjustment for writing another word while the writing of its predecessor is still in progress. At each stage new errors are introduced and broken up. One of the commonest errors in the typing of a semiskilled typist is to anticipate a word and begin it before completing the word or syllable preceding it. The wrong letter introduced into the copy is in many cases one that should properly occur shortly after where it is inserted.

There have been many thousands of studies of the acquisition of special skills. For many years these were inspired by the hope of discovering the "curve of learning." When put in graphic form with the number of errors or rate of performance as the ordinate and the number of the practice period or the elapsed time as the abscissa, these curves encouraged the belief that there was some standard or ideal form of the curve of learning from which particular instances departed because of the special conditions governing the particular experiment. There was general agreement that improvement was more rapid at the beginning of practice; that as practice continued the rate of improvement diminished until a final limit was reached, a limit supposedly set by the physiological nature of the learner. This regular improvement was often interrupted by plateaus or periods of practice during which there was no improvement. Speculation concerning the nature of these plateaus suggested that they were periods when improvement was concealed in the form of increasing integration, or that they represented the physiological limit of performance with the methods in use and that the resumption of improvement was due to some radical change in method. Failure of incentive might also be responsible.

All this discussion of the "curve of learning" parallels the investigation of the forgetting curve, which was also assumed to underlie the various forms of curves developed in experiments with different material.

There is, of course, no ideal or standard curve of learning or curve of forgetting. All depends on the nature of the activity learned or forgotten, on the amounts of previous practice of component activities, on the habits the individual may have previously formed and which may impede or facilitate a particular skill, on what is done during the intervals between practice which may attach other responses to cues used in the activity, and finally, since success is success however attained, on the fact that progress is badly infected with chance.

There is, in other words, no general curve of learning. There are learning curves for special skills, like typing, telegraphing, skating, shooting, when these are practiced under standard conditions. A factory making jute bags may keep careful records of the daily output of beginners from the first day's work on. The number of bags sewn per day increases more rapidly at first. About the third week there is for most workers a plateau at which improvement is lacking or very slow. This is followed by a second rise. Under these fairly uniform conditions we do find that the learning curves tend to have a strong family resemblance. It is possible to estimate within reasonable limits what 75 percent of beginners will be turning out at the end of six weeks. The piecework incentive is not uniform in its appeal to all, but the variation is not extreme. It is possible also to assign the cause for the plateau, because the end of it, in the cases where it does end, coincides with the sudden acquisition of the ability to turn the corner of the bag to sew the second edge without stopping the machine.

Learning curves are thus specific and not general, and the interest in them has considerably lessened on that account.

Another discussion that has filled many pages concerns the question: Under what circumstances does practice in one activity affect favorably or unfavorably performance in other activities? This question was raised in several forms. For instance, can the ability to remember names be improved by practicing a specific list of names? Does exercise of the memory improve the memory in general? Or does it merely strengthen the items practiced? In strong revolt against the old conception that lay at the base of phrenology, the notion that because memory is a name for a class of actions it must be a faculty and perhaps even have a local residence in the brain, many psychologists undertook to deny very vigorously that practice of one set of actions classed as memories would affect favorably or unfavorably another set of memories. Psychologists divided into two camps, with the skeptics in the majority. The debate extended far beyond the laboratory because it involved a theory of education, the theory that certain educational disciplines like Greek or logic might be lacking in direct usefulness but that they trained the mind in general, or certain faculties of the mind such as judgment, discrimination, reasoning power, and the like.

The dispute went on and in the meantime many laboratory studies were undertaken to answer the question: Can practice in one skill have effects that will transfer to others skills? Although the results of the experiments proved very disillusioning to the upholders of the theory of formal disciplines, they were not at all unambiguous.

Practice in skill A may affect skill B favorably, skill C unfavorably, and have no effect on skill D.

At this point Thorndike proposed a solution. Practice in skill A affects skill B favorably because they have identical elements. Studying mathematics has a favorable effect on the ability to get good grades in philosophy because certain habits contribute to both abilities. A habit of refusing invitations to go to the theater acquired while working at mathematics would favor good work in philosophy. The habits necessary for sitting still with a book for protracted sessions would be common to both ventures.

The general outcome of the discussion was that psychologists were willing to go so far as to advise students to practice as nearly as possible what they wished to be able to perform. Students are no longer advised to learn to think by studying mathematics and logic and then use the acquired thinking ability in other courses.

This remains fairly sound advice, but it does not settle the question of transfer. Thorndike's principle of identical elements did not do much to settle it either, since there is no method for counting identical elements or for judging their relative importance. We are forced to be content with a position like that taken on the curve of learning. Special studies only will determine whether practice in mathematics affects favorably or unfavorably performance in philosophy, whether practice in golf improves or interferes with performance in baseball, whether typing aids or hinders piano playing. There is no formula by which these questions can be answered in advance of experiment on the specific issue. There is no general answer to the problem of transfer of training. The writer is tempted to add that there is no general problem of transfer. The problem is always a specific one. There can be no doubt whatever that the person who has had a course of training in the classics or in engineering is different from what he would have been without that training, but the nature of the difference can be told only by special investigation of the effects of the training on specific activities.

Several other generalizations like Thorndike's rule concerning transfer have been attempted. Experiment brought out the fact that in a number of forms of skill or of memorization the rate of improvement was markedly affected by the distribution of practice periods. Practice in typing for one hour a day developed a given number of words per minute with a smaller investment in time than did a practice period of two hours a day. Even with rats one trial a day in the maze produces more improvement per trial than do two trials a day. Memorizing a poem or a list of nonsense syllables requires less total time when one short period once or twice a day is used than when practice is condensed into longer sessions.

In general these results have stood the test of experiment on varied materials. The generalization is that of two arrangements

of practice periods the one that uses longer intervals up to perhaps two days has the advantage.

In the case of typing. there is obviously a point in the length
of a session at which fatigue introduces confusion and the breaking up of habits, so that beyond that point continued practice is
worse than useless. What habits are being formed are apt to be
bad and there may be a negative value in protracted sessions.
Where this point is depends on motivation, of course. We suspect
that added practice has negative value only from the point at
which fatigue or loss of interest begins to introduce errors. Such
errors may be established as habits and be hard to eradicate.
There is no doubt that the student who continues study beyond
the time when he is able to appreciate what he is reading becomes habituated to sitting scanning the lines of his book and
daydreaming. Listening to a boresome lecture or sermon makes
it more difficult to listen to future lectures, whether good or bad.
Having the radio turned on continuously makes it more difficult
to listen to music. Goodenough and Brian (1929) have summarized the results of experiments on the length of practice
period in the conclusion that ". . . the greatest efficiency may
perhaps be gained by appropriate interruption of practice at
times when the setting up of undesirable habits seems to be re-
tarding practice."

Other than this there is no law of the distribution of practice.
The effects of different periods will vary with the nature of the
material and the emotional reinforcement of the activity. Ruch
mentions (1928) among the conditions affecting the results of
massed and distributed practice in learning, the number and age
of the subjects, the nature of the material, the length of the
period chosen, the interval between periods, and the criteria by
which the amount of learning is measured.

Much the same comment can be applied to the relative merits
of "whole" and "part" learning. Is it more efficient to practice

such material as a poem by reading it through from beginning to end or by memorizing it one stanza at a time? Is a piano composition more efficiently memorized when practiced as a whole or in parts?

The first results tended to favor "learning by wholes" and much was made of this in advice concerning many types of learning. This seemed the plausible result because when material is memorized part by part, after the parts have been memorized it is necessary to learn the order of the parts—the cues for each part. But here again conflicting results began to appear and the only generalization that can be made is that much depends on the material and the circumstances of practice. In learning piano pieces, for instance, R. W. Brown found (1928) that the "whole" method was most efficient except for the most difficult music. The evidence in general is that where the material is of such great length that fatigue may affect a single repetition, there is no advantage in the "whole" method. So again, before we can offer practical advice, we must find by experiment the better method for the material we have in mind. There is, of course, no doubt whatever of the wastefulness of a very common practice in memorizing, namely, the rehearsal from the beginning to the end of a first section, then from the beginning of the first to the end of the second section, etc. This "overlearns" the first section and leaves the last in a precarious state.

CHAPTER XIV

Trial and Error in Learning

MY OWN views of how behavior through experience is adjusted to recurring events have been set forth at some length in the chapter on skill. It would be quite unfair to the reader who has not read a considerable amount of modern psychological writing to give the impression that these views are universally held among psychologists.

The principal objections to analysis of learning in terms of conditioning have come from Köhler, Koffka, R. M. Ogden, and Wheeler, to mention a few of the more outspoken defenders of the point of view called Gestalt psychology. An adequate account of the differences between the Gestalt psychologists and the views to which they object would require a book in itself. The chief issues can be condensed into much less space.

Unfortunately, much of the discussion concerns issues having little or nothing to do with science, which is limited to the concise description of the world as found and the use of its concise descriptions or laws for the prediction and hence the possible control of nature. The laws of science describe the *observable* conditions under which certain classes of events take place.

Another unfortunate aspect of the controversy is the frequent use of the device popularly known as the "straw man." A great deal of writing has been directed against views held by a mythical misguided person but not held by any actual psychologist.

Since Wheeler is the most ardent partisan, we shall take him as the representative of the Gestalt views. We quote (1929, page 316):

> It is evident that learning does not proceed by trial and error with accidental successes fixed by pleasure and errors eliminated by annoyance [by this Thorndike is probably indicated]. Likewise it is certain that learning does not commence with random movements which are subsequently eliminated by mechanical agencies [this would probably be Wheeler's characterization of the present account]. "Trial and error" refers to an imposition of a goal upon the learner to which he is not responding. . . . He [the learner] fails to repeat the unsuccessful movements because he has perceived a *different* goal; another remote end has been established. . . . The *successful movement is repeated for the same reason that it was made in the first place,* namely, when the stimulus pattern in which the goal figured presented relationships on the learner's level of insight, that is, fitted his level of maturation, since learning is a species of growth process, a given level of maturation is not only maintained, under optimum conditions, but continues to rise with respect to a given task until the limits set by the learner's organic structure are reached.

It should be remarked in the first place that no actual writers use the phrase "random movements" in the sense in which Wheeler implies. All psychologists assume that any movements made by an animal are determined by the stimuli acting, the animal's history, and its present state. Movements are random only when viewed in relation to some goal or outcome.

Nor is it clear what Wheeler means by "accidental successes." The word "accidental" does not refer to the event as such but to our ability to predict the event. The accidental is that which is not provided for in our rule. If these successes are not accidental, they must be indicated in advance by the circumstances. But a formula that will tell which of all activities are going to be successful and which are going to fail is unthinkable. This betrays a very serious weakness in the Gestalt psychologists' formula—success is determined by insight. Success occurs, Wheeler says, "when the stimulus pattern in which the goal figured presented relationships on the learner's level of insight, that is, fitted his level of maturation."

How either the observer or the learner can make use of this "principle" for discriminating good moves from bad ones is quite beyond the writer's own level of insight. Some of the learner's movements turn out to be good; some turn out to be bad. In advance of experience no possible general formula can tell which will be which. Only after the event can good moves be told from bad. But after the event is rather late for prediction. So far as the insight formula is concerned, success remains accidental.

Let us examine one of Wheeler's applications (1929, page 252):

. . . when you train your fox terrier to sit up and beg, you reward him with a tidbit . . . in order to provide the dog with a definite goal with respect to which it will execute the desired act. Dog fashion, it will then understand what you want of it for responding to food-goals falls well within the repertoire of dog insight! Dog insight is relatively feeble and slow of development, especially under artificial conditions. Consequently considerable time will elapse before it will make the movements just as you want them. Meanwhile it is making numerous other movements, all at about the same time, jumping, barking, and running around; which of these is to function as the "tool" for the securing of the food is the difficult problem you have imposed on it. As the dog keeps trying, the insight into the problem grows. . . .

This invites a great deal of comment. In the first place, this running about and barking, etc., is precisely what writers on learning have meant by trial and error. And just why the success of sitting up when that does occur should not be called accidental from the dog's point of view is very obscure.

In the second place, "growing insight" seems a very vague notion. Our whole investigation of learning is aimed at discovering *under what circumstances an act will be learned as a response to a given situation.* The only circumstances hinted at in this account are the exhibition of food and the doghood of the dog. A growth of insight is promised, but this does not promise just what the dog will learn to do—bite your leg and make you drop the food, look bored and so discourage lessons in silly tricks, or whatever else a bright dog might have in its repertoire.

In the third place, as a set of directions for teaching the act this is very imperfect. Consider similar advice given to a school-teacher. To make pupils learn to spell a list of words the teacher is to establish a goal, such as escape from the schoolroom, and then wait for insight to grow, which is promised if the pupils are at the proper level of insight. The most important feature of the proper directions for the dog's training has been omitted. The trainer should be advised to hold the food and possibly manipulate the dog in such a way that the dog will sit up. As he accomplishes this he should give his signal. The act can be rewarded by giving the dog the food.

The food is offered according to Wheeler "to provide the dog with a definite goal." There can be no objection to this provided we understand the nature of a goal and recognize that the sight of the food (because of past associations) gets immediate attention from a hungry dog, starts its saliva and movements of eating (because of past associations), inhibits responses to potential distracting stimuli around the room, and, because the withholding of food blocks the normal immediate eating, makes the dog alert and tense and so favors the establishment of habits.

Contrast Wheeler's prescription for training a dog to sit up with the directions in books on the training of dogs. The practical trainer regularly emphasizes (1) the means for compelling the specific action desired, either force or persuasion, and (2) the necessity for giving the command as the act is executed. We quote Whitford's *Training the Bird Dog* (1928). "Force," he says, "is so applied that the desired thing to be done is the most natural thing for him to do, and once the habit of doing the desired thing is fairly well fixed, the force is no longer necessary.

. . . We use a check line in such a way, in teaching the dog to stop to order, that the order to stop, the check, and the enforced stop all happen at the same time" (page 30).

The "integration" of the dog's behavior on which the Gestalt psychologist places so much emphasis is quite evident. But, instead of being an unanalyzable mystery, an irreducible first principle of behavior, this integration is a matter of degree and is controlled by circumstances. The primary cause of the integration of the behavior of animals is the fact that they are "all of one piece." The animal can not, like Stephen Leacock's knight, go dashing madly off in all directions because it is tied together by ligaments. There are other conditions of integration which have already been mentioned. In the case of the lesson in sitting up, the sight of the food effects a distinct new integration of the dog's behavior by capturing its attention and by arousing in it energetic tendencies (actual movement or muscle tonus) to eat, which dominate its behavior.

Of explanation in terms of association Wheeler says (1929, page 266), *"But it is inconceivable that two sets of principles, based upon logically opposite and incompatible assumptions, should be applicable to . . . behavior.* So much for a general comment on the laws of association." The opposite principles referred to are insight and association. It is reassuring to find him later on remarking (1929, page 271) that "recall is a response induced by certain of the stimuli that conditioned the original experience," and that "certain words function as stimuli for a great variety of others through proprioceptive channels. That is, thinking of words involves incipient movements of the speech muscles, and these movements furnish stimulation because the muscles are supplied with sense organs."

The truth is that the Gestalt psychologist must speak in terms of association or conditioning when he is explaining the occurrence of any *specific* behavior *because no other hypothesis has been so much as put forward.* The purposive behaviorists like

Tolman and McDougall and the Gestalt psychologists like Köhler and Wheeler have suggested a theory of the circumstances under which certain end results tend to be accomplished without reference to the means by which they are accomplished. Association theory is a theory of the circumstances under which certain movements or certain responses will occur. The two sets of principles are, Wheeler notwithstanding, entirely compatible. They do not apply to the same fields of prediction. It is quite true that a hungry dog tends to find food *somehow*. It is also true that if we wish to know how a particular dog will go about finding food our best information comes from his past behavior under similar circumstances. And this is to use an explanation in terms of association. Hull (1934) has an excellent description of the way in which an animal may acquire a varied repertoire of ways for reaching a goal when disturbed by such a stimulus as hunger. The path chosen on any particular occasion obviously depends on previous learning, and also on present obstacles.

Both sets of explanations are quite legitimate and give useful information. The insight level of a child is the subject of a great deal of research. The average ten-year-old can be depended on to solve problems of a higher degree of difficulty than the average six-year-old and the details of this are important. But a scientific account of learning is devoted to finding the circumstances under which new responses occur and new insights develop. And the Gestalt psychologists have given the problem of learning almost no attention. Wheeler in his Gestalt vein dismisses it with the remark that insight somehow grows or matures. Tolman is content with calling behavior docile or teachable and letting it go at that. Wheeler does not always confine himself to his Gestalt viewpoint, and has in his text a considerable account of learning, but this is presented largely in terms of association as we have seen.

In my opinion, insight, if it were defined in terms of new successful response to a new situation, would be unpredictable.

Science can not deal with unique events. Only in recurring events can we discriminate between mere antecedents and necessary and sufficient antecedents. In so far then as insight means the ability to meet a new and unique situation with an adequate response it must remain in the category of luck. The work of the inventor, of the creative artist will never be entirely accounted for by scientific explanation. We can say, as a result of observation of repeated cases, that in a given set of circumstances this action or that will follow (in a certain percentage of the instances) or even that success will somehow be attained in a given percentage of the cases, but we can not say that in a certain unique situation we may expect anything in particular. If we could predict the thinker's conclusions we would have made the thinker superfluous.

There remain a few incidental features of the Gestalt doctrine which deserve attention. To his general statement of his theory of learning (1929, page 271) Wheeler adds a footnote: "The theory supposes, with Köhler, that there is always a particular organization of stresses within the nervous system which in part conditions the 'recall'" (pages 272 ff. and 311 ff.). A great deal has been made of this theory of the brain as a dynamic electrical field in which any change in detail alters the whole pattern. The theory is of course, quite safe from experimental verification or disproof by any technique thus far developed, and as an attempt to state the circumstances under which action or learning occurs it is quite useless because it calls on unobservable determiners.

Another concrete example will make clearer the differences between Wheeler and myself. According to that author (1929, page 252), when a trainer whips a bird dog that has crushed a pheasant "the punishment is applied to furnish a goal for the animal's behavior; it creates a special stimulus-pattern on the dog's level of insight. The goal is a situation to be avoided; carrying a bird gently comes to be the means by which the goal is avoided." In my opinion this gives very inadequate information to the trainer. What can be done to keep the dog from crushing the bird? One old device is to insert pins in the bird. Crushing the bird brings about stimuli which tend to open the dog's jaws. Success is a compromise between letting go and crushing. And the compromise becomes a habit. This can be accomplished without any awareness on the dog's part that carrying a bird gently is "the means by which the goal is avoided." The very fact that few of us can at all describe the way in which we perform skilled acts or have any notion of what our skill consists of shows that insight is not the primary event. The greater part of human skills are developed without any awareness of the slight readjustments that correct our faults. We make responses to stimuli whose presence or absence we are unable to report at the time or later. The golfer often volunteers an explanation of his improvement, but it is only the credulous who take him literally. To assert as Wheeler does that all improvement is "at the level of conscious behavior" (1929, page 240) the writer believes rather absurd.

One further item. As an indictment of the theory that learning depends on conditioning, Köhler and Koffka both use a very familiar and well-acknowledged fact that response, especially perceptual response and recognition, may be established to a visual pattern and then be found later to be elicitable by the same pattern in another size. The force of their argument is clear when it is realized that a child who has learned to name the letter H in his book can name it later on when it is written large on the blackboard. His acquaintances whose names are learned at one distance are recognized when they are farther away. And this means that as visual patterns on the retina they are stimulating *a different group of sense organs*, one not involved in the original experience. Here we have a case in which stimuli which *were not acting* at the time of a response appear to be acting as cues for that response. My view of this objection to the notion of the conditioned response was expressed in an article in the *Psychological Review* (1930) as follows:

That we do respond to patterns as such is not open to question. And this would seem to involve the complete breakdown of any theory of conditioning such as is being presented, for at varying distances the actual receptors and afferent paths activated by a visual pattern must be quite distinct. The fact, indeed, cannot be questioned, though it should be noted that it is not a general or uniform occurrence. The child who has learned to read the raised letters on his blocks will not ordinarily recognize the letters when he sits on them. The effectiveness of patterns applies only within very limited fields.

Is it not entirely possible that the method by which we come to recognize a face at different distances as that of one and the same person is essentially the same method by which we come to recognize the rear aspect of this same person as his own back? In this case of recognition there is no question of similar patterns, for the back of his head resembles his face less than his face resembles the faces of others. If we maintain an attitude, or repeat a response to an object while that object is the occasion of shifting stimulation and of new stimulus patterns the maintained response may be conditioned on the new stimuli. Our response to a person at different distances is the same, with differences appropriate to the distance. Why may we not attribute this sameness and this difference to the sameness and the differences originally present in the stimuli furnished by our original behavior in his presence?

If we accept conditioning as an explanation for responding appropriately to a person on hearing his footstep, which offers a stimulation pattern quite different from the visual pattern to which we previously responded, why should we consider it mysterious that the appropriate response could be called out by the stimulation of a quite different group of visual receptors? The fact that they have the same pattern is irrelevant.

The Gestalt psychologists assert not only that we respond in similar ways to similar patterns, which we undoubtedly do, but also that we do this *without any opportunity for conditioning,* which the writer does not at all believe. In the case of the hen which performed its trick using the eye which had been blindfolded during learning it is entirely possible that the cues for the proper movement were not primarily visual, but were furnished by movements connected with vision before the experiment was begun. Animals and man both have movements of skeletal muscles congenitally associated with vision. These movements may be in part identical for stimulation of either retina. If the act is conditioned on these movements, it might be elicited from either eye, without regard to which eye entered into practice.

Koffka (1924, page 160) points out another difficulty in the acceptance of conditioned-response explanations. This was also pointed out by Stout. A cat which has once freed itself by pulling a string with its foot may on another occasion use its teeth for the same result. Here the cat has learned to do something, but what it has learned to do is not to move its foot but to pull the string by one means or another. The response does not employ the same muscles that were employed in practice and this can therefore hardly be called a conditioned response.

In the first case stimuli assertedly *not* present with the response now elicit it. In the second case a response *not* associated previously with the stimuli is elicited.

This is not an isolated case but a common mode of behavior. We do learn to attain certain results as well as to make certain movements, and one method may be substituted for another. But this fact does not make it less probable that our action depends on conditioning. The essential of the situation may have been that the cat had learned to fix its attention (i.e., a muscular orientation pattern) on the string, and on different occasions in the past the cat has taken with its claws or teeth the objects it has looked at. The conditioned response was not the foot movement (though the cat undoubtedly repeats its method as a rule) but the attention. This was considered in the chapter on reward and punishment.

One further objection to associationism made by the Gestalt psychologists and we shall leave the subject. Köhler devotes much argument to the point that animals respond in general not to the stimuli—light, sound, touch, etc.—which play such a part in the explanations of conditioning, but to relations between stimuli. Trained to choose the darker of two shades of gray, A the lighter and B the darker, and then confronted with B and C, C being darker than B, the animal will choose C.

This of course would not require experiment for its demonstration because none of our visual responses are to absolute values of the stimulus. As twilight comes on we recognize our friends, although the absolute illumination of all parts of their faces is much lower. But Köhler believes that this is somehow fatal to the notion of association as dependent on stimuli—fatal to what he calls "machine theory." His implication is that the body considered as a mechanism could never respond to relations between stimuli but only to stimuli.

Now all stimuli are relations. This is the accepted use of the word. In order to act as stimuli, physical forces must be changing. Response to a constant force very soon ceases. If we stare at a brightly colored spot with constant illumination we cease to see the color. A touch on the skin that is kept constant ceases to act as a stimulus. The stimulus is in reality a change in a physical force or a chemical state.

Moreover, even so simple a structure as a beam balance responds to the relation between the weights on the two pans, not to their absolute value. The right-hand pan will be depressed if it has a heavier weight than the left. That neural activity in any one tract is dependent on the relative difference between two stimuli, and that this difference should constitute what we have called a stimulus pattern is quite acceptable and does not seem to me to be any objection to the concept of association. All objects on the surface of the earth are continuously responding to the relation between gravitation and centrifugal force. We do not need, on this account, to credit them with any awe-inspiring ability to abstract or to integrate.

CHAPTER XV

Learning With and Without Intention

MANY studies on learning have been devised to bring out the difference between learning with intention and learning without intention. Nonsense-syllable lists may be repeated almost indefinitely without being memorized if there is no intention to learn. A ritual may be repeated for years, but will not always be memorized unless the subject "made up his mind" to learn it. It would be absurd, of course, to claim that there is no unintentional learning. All of us have annoying habits that we had not intended to acquire. But the "intention to learn" undoubtedly seriously affects the ability to memorize and the acquisition of skill. Bryan and Harter (1899) found that telegraphers of long experience whose rate of sending and receiving had been stationary for years took a new spurt and reached new high levels when interest was shown in their rates of performance.

If "intention" can thus affect the rate of learning or determine whether or not learning will take place, it becomes necessary to inquire into the nature of intentions in general. We may be able to find out what there is about an intention that makes it so important in learning.

Many psychologists with strong antipathies for the very earthy and glamourless language of behavior have asserted that human intentions can be known directly only to their possessors, that they can not be stated in terms of action, that they are purely mental affairs. If all this were so, we could make no progress whatever toward the use of "intention" in understanding learning. Fortunately it is not so. The psychologist can define what he means by intention in such terms that he is independent of the subject's inner and strictly private knowledge of his intentions and can judge at least some intentions by external observation. The courts have always been inclined toward objective interpretations of intentions. Intentions testified to only by their possessors on the basis of strictly private information are not evidence in the courtroom. The court judges the intention of the accused from the record of his overt acts.

In our *General Psychology* (1921) Stevenson Smith and I offered an objective definition of intention that made the essentials of an intention (1) the presence of some maintaining stimulus complex, (2) the blocking of direct response which would remove the maintaining stimulus, (3) the presence of precurrent responses which "commit" us to action, and (4) the presence of a readiness for the consequences of the act, anticipatory behavior of preparedness. Our acts can be judged unintentional when we are not set for their consequences. We intended to do what we did if we are found prepared for it, just as in court the presence of a gun and a mask on the accused is taken to show an intention to use the gun unlawfully, or the presence of a railroad ticket and a packed bag shows an intention to make a journey when other behavior is appropriate.

It will be noticed that this account of the nature of an intention makes it something very like what Tolman's rat, making its way through the maze, has in its preparedness for eating sunflower seed. The dog at the kitchen door licking his chops is intent on eating.

What is there about the nature of intentions thus described that would affect learning? Such intentions serve the same guiding purpose that is served by the traces of eating in the dog or rat. By them the behavior is integrated. Past action associated with these cues is called up. The general conduct is subordinated to the intention. Intent on eating, the home-going dog disregards those stray items of notice that would delay him if he were not hungry. He is kept to the point by his intention.

Can this be applied to human beings? If we are willing to go beyond what has yet been demonstrated in the laboratory to what is on general grounds very plausible, yes. It is more than possible, it is highly probable that the difference between reading a prose passage with the intention of learning it and reading it without that intention is an actual difference in the nature of practice. One reader is practicing recitation as he reads; the other reader is not. One learner has his attention on what he is doing. The other has not. Lack of attention to an activity is a failure to get certain types of stimuli from that activity.

A phenomenon called automatic writing is usually given some space in books on abnormal psychology; in it the subject, with writing materials in hand, is engaged in speech but at the same time encouraged to write. Occasionally he does write while carrying on a conversation with the experimenter, or, in cases when the phenomenon appears without encouragement from an experimenter, with attention not on the writing. Afterward—and this is the reason for calling the writing automatic—the subject has no memory of what was written. Some psychologists describe this in terms of a division of the personality, which is perhaps a legitimate description but not the only one applicable. We may prefer to believe that the movements of writing have led from one movement to the next, through associations established in the past. But why is the writing not remembered, as we ordinarily remember what we write? Probably because it was not read, not followed with speech as it was written. We remember what we write in normal circumstances because we see it and read it as we write. The automatic writing, which we have not seen or pronounced, could be recalled only by the arm movements by which it was written.

The essence of an intention is a body of maintaining stimuli which may or may not include sources of unrest like thirst or hunger but always includes action tendencies conditioned during a past experience—a readiness to speak, a readiness to go, a readiness to read, and in each case a readiness not only for the act but also for the previously rehearsed consequences of the act. These readinesses are not complete acts; they consist of tensions of the muscles that will take part in the complete act. When you are told that the electrodes you hold in your hand are about to be charged by current from an induction coil, the muscles which would jerk the hands away develop some tension. A sharp noise or a tap on the shoulder will often set off the act of withdrawing the hands, though there has been no shock. Often it is possible to keep the hands in place only by tensing the opposed muscles and grasping the electrodes.

The defense of a man charged in a Washington court with shooting his neighbor was an admission that he set out to kill the neighbor. Armed with a rifle he took ambush behind some shrubs from which he could see the door of the neighbor's cabin. As he waited with his rifle pointed at the door he began to reflect on what he was doing and eventually decided, so he told the court, not to go through with it. The neighbor suddenly appeared at the door and the rifle was discharged. The killer had no memory of pulling the trigger. His attention was not on the trigger or the door until the sudden appearance of his neighbor released the prepared action. The court took a very skeptical view of this account, but it was essentially consistent with what we know about voluntary action and intentions. We can not argue the legal aspects of the case, but psychologically the man had, and at the same time had not, the intention to kill his friend. His original intention had undoubtedly broken down except for one important particular, the readiness to pull the trigger.

The maintaining stimuli and the readiness of certain responses to these stimuli do not constitute a full intention unless they *are dominating the animal's behavior* or, what is the same thing, *are being given attention.*

The bearing that this discussion has on the role of intention in acquiring a skill may now be evident. A skill is a system of habits organized to further some specific end result. It is defined by this result and is measured by the relative amount of energy or time taken to attain the result, or by the proportion of success to failure.

Practice at any skill thus assumes an intention to accomplish something—to clear the bar at six feet in the high jump, to make the pencil drawing resemble the landscape, to plow the three acres by nightfall. Being built around an intention, every skill has a core of maintaining stimuli. These may change from one moment to the next. The tennis player must have a rapid succession of intentions dictated by the action of his opponent. Through this runs an underlying intention to win, to gain the cup, to make the gallery take notice. All these intentions betray themselves in anticipatory movements. The player's glance darts toward the point where the ball is to be placed. This eye movement not only betrays his intention but is usually necessary for the carrying out of the intention. It is the cue for the stroke. A great deal of practice would be required to look one way and deliver the ball elsewhere and even here there must be a fixed connection between glance and movement. This ability may be cultivated in order to deceive an opponent and its cultivation means learning some other eye movement as a cue for the stroke.

Every person who has taken part in physical contests knows the important part played by the intention to win. This intention is by no means a mental affair in the sense that it is not of the body; it lies in the way the game is played. Sportsmen refer to it as a psychological factor, and this is an entirely correct use of the word because it is a matter of learning, habit, and association. The intention to win means a set, a preparedness for taking points, a state in which the action indicated—and by "indicated"

we mean associated with the preliminary cues by past training—
is ready to go.

Skill at tennis means the accumulation of thousands of habit
responses attached to the proper cues, the advance signs of the
developing situation. It includes sustained attention to the results which constitute the goals or objects of the game. Because
attention is on these and because they are parts of the intention,
or the events for which the player is set, any failure tends to
disrupt habit and make improvement possible.

Continuous failure leads to the anticipation of failure and to
what is sometimes called a defeatist psychology. The anticipation of failure follows regular failure because the action dictated
by failure is eventually elicited by more and more remote cues
in the manner described in the chapter on time factors in conditioning, and the player may eventually enter the game prepared
to lose.

Skills are formed rapidly in contests because a living and
thinking opponent is capable of offering continuous surprise.
Struggle with an opponent is different from learning a maze or
memorizing a poem on this one account. And surprise has as its
main result the introduction of confusion and interference in
action with a consequent building up of states of tense excitement. It is this lack of stereotyping that characterizes play and
accounts for the excitement which gives play its drive.

So-called intellectual skills are not different from physical
skills in the manner in which they are established. Playing chess
and playing tennis are learned in fundamentally the same way.
Both are contests and hence expose the player to the unexpected.
When one player is so skilled that his opponent can no longer
surprise him, the game loses its interest. Both games require
long practice because they offer a tremendous variety of situations to which responses must be prompt. Thinking is at a dis-
count in both games because thinking indicates lack of familiarity
with the situation—the absence of a prompt habitual reply to

each move of the opponent. Thinking marks those situations which ambiguously condition incompatible movements and hence lead to a period of blocked action. During this blocking, tension increases and equilibrium becomes less stable. Luria's book, *The Nature of Human Conflict*, describes this state. Small children confronted with a choice, that is, with stimuli to incompatible movements, immediately go into confused action. The small hand touches one piece of cake which is then obscured, leaving another which entices and is touched. An adult, however, pauses, and the action is prepared and organized before it is executed. The conflict has led to a state of mutual inhibition in which added cues may occur. Luria believes these to be primarily linguistic. These movement-produced cues reinforce one action or the other and the conflict is resolved. This is very like Thurstone's view (1924) that thinking is checked action and always develops out of overt action.

To return to the nature of chess, we may remark that the skilled chess player does very little thinking. Long experience has presented so many combinations on the chessboard, and the confusion of failure has so successfully broken up bad associations and left the good, that a glance at the board gives the cue for proper action. This explains why the skilled player can take on ten or twenty opponents at once and stroll from one table to another, give a quick glance, recognize the situation, and make a good move. The more thinking his opponents have to do the less is their chance of winning.

It may be remarked incidentally that chess and tennis are alike in another respect, but that here tennis has the disadvantage. Neither skill deteriorates seriously over a lapse of time in which there is no practice. Tennis loses more by such periods because some of the moves of the game are parts of other sports or of the daily routine of an active man. Skill at chess will withstand long periods of no practice because the situations of chess are not approached in daily routine and so habits are not disrupted; cues are not alienated from their proper responses by being conditioned to other behavior.

Both games have a major purpose governing play—defeat of an opponent. The opponent and his moves are the maintaining stimuli which dominate attention. Both games have minor and shifting purposes—returning a drive, placing the ball in a hard spot, taking an opponent's piece, maneuvering into a good position. These minor purposes are the player's transient intentions. Popular speech is strictly psychological when it describes the player as being intent on these minor goals. He is intent in that he has begun action associated with them. He is "tense" with them. In an important chess match this tension often results in muscular tremor. This tension of the muscles appropriate to the action tends to maintain itself through circular reflexes until the action is inhibited by a change in the situation, and in addition to maintaining itself it tends to dominate behavior and to integrate it.

Both tennis and chess are affected by what is called "confidence" or by its lack. Confidence is nothing more than preparedness for victory. Preparedness for defeat makes winning impossible because it means acting too soon as if defeated.

All football coaches and many boxing trainers take great care not to put their charges up against opponents that are too formidable. A series of football defeats or a few experiences with a rough opponent put the contestant on the defensive, which means only that he is now using caution before the occasion for it. The opponent's moves have become substitute stimuli for protective movements first called out by actual punishment.

CHAPTER XVI

Perception and Thought

IF WE were to speak by the book we could not refer to hearing the streetcar, seeing that the day is cold, smelling flowers, feeling the house shake. The proper object of hearing is noise; of seeing, light; of smelling, odors; of feeling, the shaking not of the house but of ourselves. We see not the man, but the light reflected from one side of his body surface. We speak of hearing someone in the next room. What we hear in the strict sense is a noise which may or may not have been made by a person.

The simplest instance of perception is an elementary conditioned response. C. Lloyd Morgan (1930) uses the caterpillar and the chick as his stock illustration. The chick seeing the caterpillar pecks it and the bitter taste of the caterpillar stimulates the chick to vigorous ejection from its bill. But the light from the caterpillar is still stimulating the chick's eyes while the movements of rejection are going on and the sight of the caterpillar becomes a substitute stimulus for rejection. On the next occasion the chick has what Morgan calls a foretaste. It reacts as if it had tasted the caterpillar before it pecks, and this reaction inhibits pecking. The bitter taste has been anticipated. Vision now serves instead of taste to produce the results of taste. This is perception in its most elementary form, a response to a situation which is in part determined by past learning, a response which includes certain features because these features were present on some former occasion together with some of the present stimuli.

This is to describe every perception as an instance of conditioning. We perceive the contents of the cup before us as coffee because this same stimulus pattern in the past has accompanied the taste of coffee, the odor of coffee, the warmth of coffee, and the mere sight of the cup now gives us a foretaste, a "foresmell," a "fore-warmth" as the result of conditioning. The sight of the cup or the smell has become a substitute stimulus for former responses to the various stimuli that coffee may offer.

To this description of perception in terms of conditioning many very telling objections can be made. In the first place it is pointed out that the conditioned response is not just a replica of the previous response. The chick's movements of rejection at the sight of the caterpillar are not identical with the movements of rejection that occurred after pecking as the direct result of the actual taste. We quarrel with a friend and on the next meeting we do not reproduce our quarrel, we avoid his glance or turn aside or speak with polite restraint. We fall on the icy pavement and on later occasions, instead of falling, we walk cautiously when we see the smooth surface of the ice.

This objection to treating perception as a simple conditioned response is a valid one. Perception is conditioning but not simple. The perception differs from the original experience, but it remains true that in the perceptual response can be found movements which were present on the former occasion. Our careful progress on the icy walk includes tensions of the muscles used when we fell. Our hands and arms are ready to fly out to break the fall. The caution is a compromise between walking and the protective movements that would inhibit walking if they were carried out. The chick's avoidance of the caterpillar on sight includes some actual movements of active rejection, and it is the presence of these movements that has broken up the tendency to peck. Our coldness toward the friend with whom we quarreled is the result of the inhibition of our usual cordial greeting by quite diverse responses learned while we were quarreling. But it represents the resultant of conditioned quarreling and what is left of former cordial habits.

We may therefore still hold that perception is the result of conditioning, even though we grant that the perceptual behavior does not resemble any former behavior in its total appearance. The behavior of the present moment is affected by the total situation acting on the sense organs. As a totality it is unique because total situations are unique. Our only hope of predicting behavior lies in selecting in it elements that are not unique, that have occurred before.

To make our prediction, our data must be observable antecedents. They include past observations of the species, past observations of the individual, and present observations of the stimuli acting and the state of the animal. The behavior to be looked for from any stimulus is the behavior that occurred when this stimulus pattern was last presented. If we know nothing of the past of the individual before us we are limited to "instinct" in our prediction. We expect from him what other members of his species do in these circumstances. If what they do differs according to their individual histories, we can not know which of these different responses he will make until we know his history. And if we know his history, our prediction, in so far as it is based on any one feature of the situation, will be that he will respond to this as he last responded. This is merely another way of stating the principle of conditioning.

A problem faces us immediately. What if different features of the situation may lead to different predicted behavior? To this there can be only one answer. Only if we have had experience with a similar conflict of these same features can we venture any prediction. If we have had such experience we may be able to say in advance that one feature of the response will be dominant or that the result will be mutual inhibition and excitement, or a compromise in which both responses have lost their distinctive features in combining.

Now of course every response is such a compromise, and it is only a question whether the altered nature of the conditioned response will leave it recognizable. There can be no general rule for this beyond the very vague one that the chances of a recognizable repetition depend on the number of conditioners present. There is strong evidence that two cues are better than one, three better than two, and so on.

Our prediction in terms of conditioning will therefore be somewhat halting and tentative. We can make no accurate count of the conditioners. Many of them, especially those that stimulate proprioceptive sense organs, would be difficult to observe. Our predictions will have a large error save in cases like Pavlov's where the total situation is under maximum control. But with all this difficulty what small knowledge we can have about behavior in advance lies in our expecting a stimulus pattern to be reacted to as it was last reacted to.

A generation ago it was current practice to distinguish two sources of a perception, the present stimulus pattern and a past experience. The contribution of the past experience was called apperception. It was sometimes supposed to be a contribution of the central nervous system to the total result. The experience left "traces" in the brain. This distinction served very well for a very cursory description. Twenty persons hear the word "Italy." One pictures to himself an avenue bordered with poplars; a second, maps of various sorts; another, the Coliseum or a can of olive oil. The stimulus is much the same for all. The differences are "apperceptive" and originate in the various pasts of the hearers, vaguely believed to be somehow or other "stored" in the brain.

The more modern view is an improvement. The perceptual response, even in the form of a visual image, is a response to the present stimuli that are acting. But the present stimuli include a great deal more than the sound of the word "Italy." They include as well the stimulus patterns of the responses to that word, or the responses prevailing when the word is uttered. The responses to the word depend on past conditioning (apperception based on past experience) but are occasioned by present stimuli. Perception is thus based on past learning and is occasioned by present stimuli.

The most important factor in perception is undoubtedly the influence *of what the organism is doing,* an influence exerted through proprioceptive sense organs in muscles, tendons, and joints. This is the most important determiner of perception but it is at the same time very elusive from the observer's point of view and in many cases has to remain hypothetical. It is what Marcel Proust used in explaining the sequence of memories as he lay in bed in the morning. A change of posture, a movement, a shift carried with it a changed memory setting and another detail of his past.

The most important service of the Gestalt psychologists has been rendered in the field of perception. They have made rather light of prediction in terms of association or conditioning, though they use it. They point out a general tendency in behavior that seems more or less independent of the history of the individual and his associative learning. This is the tendency for perception to be integrated, to "click" into place. For instance, we are seated at a desk. Someone enters the room and utters something which we can not "make out." Not until we notice the fountain pen in his hand do we suddenly realize that he has asked us, "May I have some ink?" When our glance falls on the pen there is a sudden completion of the perception of his meaning. Up to that point we are puzzled. This has very aptly been called the "Aha! phenomenon," and is a characteristic of many perceptions.

We have the same experience at the telephone. Puzzled at

the meaningless jumble of sound when we take up the receiver, we suddenly recognize the voice, and the meaningless jumble becomes an invitation to dinner.

Several years ago a student offered me a newspaper clipping which reported a conversation in a restaurant between a prospective diner and the waiter. It ran as follows:

F-U-N-E-X?
S-V-F-X.
N-E-M?
S-V-F-M.
L-F-M-N-X.

The reader is of course somewhat baffled. If, however, he reads this aloud and happens to be familiar with the dialect which Milt Gross has so successfully captured in print, the conversation suddenly becomes meaningful. Our perception of it is conditioned on the sounds but not on the sight of the letters. With most persons the minimal "forming" of the letters as they are seen is inadequate; it is necessary to speak them aloud.

Two students are standing at the foot of the stairway of a college building. One is heard to utter the sound, "Squp." This does not "click" until we see that the students with one accord turn and ascend the stairs.

Most of the illustrations used by Koffka and Köhler are somewhat simpler than this. If a group of letters is exposed for a very brief time in an exposure apparatus, the subject tends to report that he has seen a word. Different subjects may report different words, but there is a marked tendency toward perception of the fragment as a complete word. If a large segment of a circle is exposed the subjects tend to report seeing a complete circle. We overlook proof errors in printing very readily.

What accounts for this tendency to complete the perceptual response? In the writer's opinion it is essentially the phenomenon which Hollingworth has selected as the fundamental explanatory notion in learning—redintegration. Part of a former stimulus situation tends to evoke the complete response of the earlier occasion.

The reason that the response tends to be "redintegrated" (and this is the writer's difference with Hollingworth, who would explain conditioning in terms of redintegration and not vice versa) is that the elements of the former response are con-

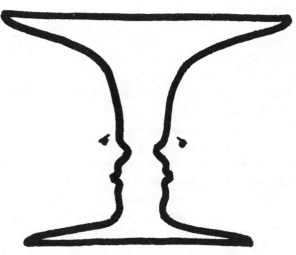

Ambiguous figure. One perceptual response or the other tends to be integrated. The figure is seen either as a wineglass or as two faces.

ditioners of each other, so that the response tends to be reëstablished at all.

The Gestalt psychologists have also pointed out that when a subject is confronted with a pattern there is a distinct tendency for part of the stimulus field to "stand out" from the rest as a figure, for which the remainder constitutes a background. This is for them a general law of perception, like the tendency to completion. For this general characteristic of perception an explanation in terms of conditioning and redintegration is also possible. Out of the patterns competing for attention one response or another tends to be redintegrated; that is, with an initial advantage once established, the elements of the response reinforce each other and so competing responses are elbowed out.

In such ambiguous figures as the classical staircase, the outlined cube, or the wineglass we have stimulus patterns which have been associated with two different perceptual responses, a stair seen from above or from below, a cube with the near face below and left or above and right, a wineglass or two human profiles. *One response or the other* tends to be integrated because any part of one response conditions the others and the union excludes the rival response.

These generalizations of the Gestalt psychologists and the experimental work on which they are based have materially extended our knowledge of perception. Their unwillingness to explore the effects of the past experience of the individual in order to understand his present behavior is not so commendable. They are content with pointing out the general tendency to integration of perception and with demonstrating certain integrations which are almost universally made, and they neglect the added understanding possible from learning. The role of past learning in accounting for common forms of perception has been set forth by Washburn (1926). Lines 1 and 2 are not mere lines, the Gestalt psychologist points out. They appear to enclose a space. But the addition of lines 3 and 4 alters all this. Now the enclosed spaces are between 3 and 1, and 2 and 4, not between 1 and 2. Washburn would explain this by past learning. Our commonest experiences with these patterns are in terms of boards, strips of paper, rulers, etc. In the right-hand figure we are set to make two distinct movements to pick up the strips; in the left-hand figure, one movement for one strip. The difference between lines 1 and 2 in the two patterns is that the addition of 3 and 4 changes our response, is associated with quite different action in our past.

We find ourselves thus in close agreement with the Gestalt

laws of perception; we disagree only in that we would search for the origins of specific differences in the perceptions of different individuals in their individual histories of conditioning.

The "click" or the "aha" which the Gestalt psychologists have so much emphasized is subject to delay. We shall not be too far from common speech in using the term "judgment" for the cases in which the response is organized after a delay. The delay in a judgment, the failure of response to integrate and

Lines *1* and *2* tend to be seen as enclosing a space. When lines *3* and *4* are added, the space between *1* and *2* is seen as part of the general background and the figure becomes two enclosed spaces.

"click" occurs when the situation is ambiguous, when different features of it have been associated with conflicting and incompatible response. Luria's account of the delay period has been mentioned. It is characteristic of the higher animals. Indecision is less common among barnyard fowls and mice than it is among men and apes. It appears during childhood and develops gradually. In their capacity for it adults show extreme variation. It is not a trait that attaches to all the behavior of any individual except under certain conditions. A man may prove a man of action in dealing with his business affairs but be "sicklied o'er with the pale cast of thought" in his relations with his family. His decisions may be prompt when he is working with the tools of his trade but protracted and distressing when he is dining with more sophisticated friends.

Judgment is the outcome of conflicting perceptions, perceptual responses which are incompatible, which interfere each with the integration of the other.

What happens in the moment of delay that precedes the resolution of the choice? What behavior fills the interval? Luria states (1933) that children, like most animals, go into action immediately and do not exhibit this period of hesitation. Köhler has described the moment of quiet observation in his apes, followed by an adequate action. He calls this insight. What precedes insight? From the writings of Köhler and Wheeler we get the impression that insight is just a "gift." You have it or you haven't it. There is very little to do about its absence but sit and wait for it to grow or mature, according to Wheeler.

It is quite obvious that insight depends on experience. Not only the immediate perceptions but the delayed judgment of an experienced physician is apt to be more adequate than those of a man without training. To some extent insight can be taught. It can certainly be encouraged by establishing opportunity for experience.

When we are confronted with a choice, action is blocked by mutual interference. What happens then? Probably something of this sort. Tension develops, so that any action that does go through is apt to be more vigorous. But during the interval of block both conflicting systems are in partial contraction. Each tends to call up associated behavior. This may facilitate one of the rival systems and inhibit the other. Tension serves to make the balance unstable. The associated items are often verbal, and in their turn serve as cues for action which will facilitate or inhibit one or the other of the systems.

There is no clear line between thought and action. Whether the restriction of action, through learning, to minimal contraction of muscles can be carried to the point of neural activity without muscular contraction as Dunlap urges (1932, page 19) is still a matter of speculation. The possibility has certainly not been disproved. Studies of minimal tongue movements accompanying the thinking of a sentence have shown such movements present in only some of the subjects, not in all. I incline to the belief that some peripheral activity is necessary, some trace of muscular contraction which will furnish movement-produced stimuli for the continuance of the thought train.

My reasons for this belief are several. First, there is ample evidence of minimal action in a great deal of thinking. Perception, memory, and imagination all are commonly accompanied by appropriate movements so slight they are not ordinarily noticed by the thinker. Second, I am inclined to take seriously Jacobson's statement (1929) that his subjects found it impossible to "picture" objects without noticing tension in eye muscles, or to "think" a sentence without noticing tension in speech muscles. Third, the manner in which one "idea" can bring up another "idea" is quite understandable if the first idea represents an actual stimulus pattern that can act as a substitute stimulus for the following idea. How a train of thought could maintain itself otherwise is something of a mystery. Fourth, the speed of thought is not so great as it might be if thought sequences were dependent only on nerve conduction from one part of the brain to another. If the reader will think the series of numbers from one to fifty he will find that it requires an appreciable time, perhaps fifteen seconds. Why this delay? Even if no faint disturbances in the throat are noticed, it is quite possible that they exist and that the delay is explained by the fact that one number depends on the slight movement stimuli in the throat as its cue, movement stimuli furnished by thinking the number before it. The fifth consideration is that action appears to be the precursor of thought. Verbal thinking in small children seems clearly to be prefaced by a stage in which speech is whispered or merely "mouthed." Being convinced that the serial action of habitual behavior is dependent on movement-produced cues for its completion, I incline to believe that thought series are maintained in the same way. A sixth argument is the ready convertibility of thought and action. What James wrote about "Ideomotor action" (*Principles,* vol. 2, page 522) in which "movement follows *unhesitatingly and immediately* the notion of it in the mind" becomes much more intelligible if we find that the notion of action is a motor beginning of action. The question whether all thinking is to be identified with action remains open, however. The arguments cited are not compelling and involve some speculation.

If we accept this account of thinking, the distinctions between perception and memory and fantasy are made distinctions of degree. In all three the thought sequence is determined by substitute cues. In perception some of the important determining cues are what is seen or heard, events external to the body. In memory and fantasy the thought is determined not by conspicuous external cues but chiefly by cues from the body itself. The memory of a scene is *behavior as if in the presence of the scene* —not entirely "as if," since we do not usually dive into our memory picture of the lake or perform all the movements of eating when we recall the supper. We do, of course, often make a noticeable abortive beginning of the dive, or swallow frequently while recalling the supper.

Perception, memory, and fantasy, all three depend on present cues. The memory is a perception of our revived behavior. The perception of a word before us is a memory of other occasions when the printed word became a cue for its response. The distinction between a memory and a fantasy is that the memory is perceived as a revival and the fantasy is not. All three are products of learning and, if our view of learning is correct, of conditioning or association.

The account of thinking offered by the associationists had no adequate treatment of one of the central features of thinking—its purposiveness. For thinking is normally directed to and is to be understood in terms of a goal.

Thinking is, as the Freudians must be credited with reminding us, generally wishful, guided by desire, driven by a motive. What we see and hear is affected by our wishes; what we imagine, still more so. And our memories of the past are selectively evoked and generally distorted by our loves and fears and wants.

How shall we describe this wishful character of thinking and action? The psychoanalysts have undertaken the task by naming (but unfortunately not describing) sex as the general goal of all behavior, with minor goals or definite wish objects formed out of this general urge through associative learning as the result of experience. The Gestalt psychologists have described certain characteristics of perception, such as the tendencies toward completion and integration, and the general tendency to get whatever is wanted, or insight, together with a doctrine of tension and relief (Lewin) and a general tendency toward minimal exertion (Wheeler). Tolman would list certain goals which tend to be attained, together with a general "docility" in behavior which leads to the goal with minimum effort.

No one of these generalizations is wrong. Not all of them have the universal validity that their authors would attribute to them, it is true. Much behavior is aimless. But the chief objection to most of these methods is that they are indefinite. They can be neither verified nor refuted by observation. Without additional explanation in terms of stimuli and associated response there is nothing to indicate what form the completion or closure will take, what path toward minimal action will be followed, why insight once integrated should be suggested on another occasion, whether the libido will express itself in highway robbery or in rivalry at pinochle. With association left out, the principal source of prediction of human and animal behavior is lost. The most certain and dependable information concerning what a man will do in any situation is information concerning what he did in that situation on its last occurrence.

As in action, so in thinking, goal seeking can be so described in terms of associative learning that our understanding of it is more complete and our anticipation of it more accurate.

Thinking often has a goal. What is the nature of goal-directed thinking? It would probably be much more correct to say that thinking generally has a topic. In so far as perception, memory, or fantasy is directed toward a goal this is because (as Rexroad has pointed out) stimuli are disturbing the organism. Perception is affected by wishes because the maintaining stimuli of the wish are part of the stimulus situation. The real goal is always relief from these maintaining stimuli. When we are hungry our ears are tuned for the dinner bell because the bell is associated with hunger; our fantasies deal with food; our memories concern meals we have enjoyed in the past. Under the spur of hunger memories of indifferent meals become savory. They become savory because the slight disgust or nausea that is normally part of the memory is thoroughly inhibited by hunger. If instead of being hungry we are embarked on a rough sea or have eaten too heartily, perception of the food about us changes, our memories and fantasies deal with former occasions on which we have been replete with food, or disgusted, or nauseated. When the lumberjack has finished his hearty meal he often attempts to stop the appetite of the remaining diners with his stories.

Thinking has topics rather than goals. And the topic is set by the insistent maintaining stimuli through associations established in the past. Appetites and desires are specific only through learning. In the infant without experience hunger is a general restlessness indistinguishable for an observer from the excitement and restlessness that follow a pinprick, or falling, or being firmly held still, or having the edge of a card drawn along the sole of the foot a number of times. Hunger in an adult is directed into the lines of past action when hungry. It is not a vague restlessness but a specific interest in a particular dish at a favorite restaurant or, if not that, a conflict between tendencies to set out for two or more places where hunger has been allayed.

It is true that once such a specific desire is aroused, there may be great variety in the means by which it is satisfied; but all these means, in so far as they do not depend on trial and error, which means on associated behavior modified by the situations encountered, are initiated through association, that is, as conditioned responses to the cues from the stomach. And thinking as well as action depends on conditioning in the same manner. Thinking occurs where action is blocked, but it is nonetheless a conditioned response to the acting situation, including the situation within as well as the situation without. Thought is as much ruled by habit as is behavior.

A specific goal, a desire, is a line of action that is started but can not be completed. It persists as long as the fundamental disturbance persists; or if it lacks a persistent maintaining stimulus like hunger spasms, it may, once started, maintain itself as a posture is maintained. Desires of this latter sort can be erased by conflicting action; they are forgotten because they are broken up by other behavior. If it is a mere appetite aroused by the day's routine, we may forget our desire to eat by reading a book or carrying on a conversation. We are sure to lose it if the house is discovered to be on fire or we fall downstairs. *Nor is this loss any change that has occurred in the goal. It is a change in stimulation.* We have lost the desire and the goal has ceased to be a goal because the maintaining stimuli have been withdrawn. The psychologist who placed his trust in the goal as the indicator of action to come is left in a very embarrassing position.

CHAPTER XVII

Pluralistic Theories of Learning

TOLMAN

A RABBIT hunt is easily possible without a rabbit, but it is not possible to have a rabbit hunt unless someone in the party has at least a general notion of what a rabbit is. Men do not set out upon X hunts. What weapons would be used? What would they look for? Where would they search?

When Skinner asks whether learning theory is necessary and answers this with a "No," it is hard to agree. Without some preconceived notions of the nature of learning Skinner would not undertake to investigate learning or to write a book about it. Not even psychologists set out upon X hunts with unknown objectives.

If we examine current learning theories, however, it becomes obvious that the authors are not all in pursuit of the same game. If we wish to understand the various theories of learning mentioned in this book, it will be profitable to ask ourselves how the author we are studying defined learning and what questions about it he set out to answer. It is by this method that we shall understand the radically different approaches to learning theory to be found in recent psychological literature.

If learning theories are examined from this point of view, the apparent confusion is much reduced. Their authors have set out to answer very different questions.

One theoretical position which has won considerable support in recent years is E. C. Tolman's. The question Tolman asks is:

What can men and animals learn to achieve? This question looks simple, but its simplicity is very misleading. By directing his interest to achievement rather than movement Tolman is committed to the language of purpose rather than the language of means. Achievements are changes in the world and not, at least as a usual thing, changes in the organism. They may require muscular contraction but they can not possibly be described in terms of muscular contraction.

The title of Tolman's book, *Purposive Behavior in Animals and Man,* commits his theory to purposive categories. The theory is stated in terms of straight association, the association of stimulus situations not with movements—and therein lies the distinctive character of Tolman's associationism—and not as in the Gestalt theory with goal achievement, but instead of these, with concepts, perceptions, and "expectancies." It is with these essentially mental events that Tolman is concerned. The question he sets out to answer is not: How do animals and men alter their response to situations? Instead it is: What sorts of things can animals and men learn to do? One might ask the salesman for a computing machine company: What are the capacities of the machine? What tasks will it perform? These are legitimate and important questions. The answers are far more significant to prospective users than the answer to the question: How does the machine work? Only the manufacturer and the maintenance man are interested in that question.

The theory presented in this book is directed at the question: How does learning take place? The same question in slightly different form is: Under what circumstances does learning occur? The fact that human beings are begotten and not manufactured and the fact that up to a certain point they are capable of looking after themselves are facts which give point to Tolman's treatment of learning. There would seem no need for blueprints or maintenance manuals. But, after all, psychologists are engaged in tinkering with human behavior. For them it is important to know how learning occurs because they propose to interfere with it and control it. This requires something more than knowing what it can accomplish.

The fact that Tolman is dealing with another question means that his theory is not in the strict sense a rival of the theories of Hull, Skinner, Spence, or Dollard and Miller, or of the theory in this book. Tolman's theory is a general classification of human or animal capacities for performance. In this it resembles the salesman's views of the nature of his calculator. It lists six kinds of learning, which turn out to be six kinds of things men can do.

It is true that Tolman introduces into his theory, without emphasis, and almost as an incidental remark, a statement that associations are formed and that they are established by the mere fact of contiguity of stimulus pattern and perception or cognition. In this respect he agrees with the viewpoint of this book rather than with the "reinforcement" psychologists like Hull. But this passing recognition of the role of association does not alter the fact that Tolman's emphasis is on the kinds of results that learning may have and not on the process itself.

It will be noted in the following pages that Tolman is particularly concerned over the nature and complexity of the response that is associated. In fact his interest might be described as an interest in the nature of perception and concept formation rather than in learning. The error of this description lies in the fact that perception and cognition are involved in learning and that the theories devoted to explaining how learning occurs have not faced the problems raised by perception and cognition. This is true of Hull's theory, Dollard and Miller's, Spencer's, and Skinner's; and unless certain suggestions made later in this book prove acceptable, it is true of the stimulus-response account given here.

Tolman (1949) distinguishes six kinds of learning: (1) cathexes, (2) equivalence beliefs, (3) field expectancies, (4) field-cognition modes, (5) drive discriminations, (6) motor patterns.

By cathexes he means "the acquisition of a connection between a basic drive like hunger and a specific type of goal object," like milk or meat. Or the connection may be between a negative drive like fright and a specific object of fear.

By equivalence beliefs he means "a connection between a positively cathected type of goal" such as food for which a taste has been acquired, and a "type of sub-goal"; or the corresponding negative cases, a negatively "cathected" type of disturbance object and a subdisturbance object.

A certain amount of ambiguity seems persistently to reside in these categories and I myself am not certain what may be regarded as cathexes and what as equivalence beliefs. Is food a goal, or is the "cathected" goal the ingestion of food or its presence in the stomach or, perhaps, the results of its metabolism in the tissues of the body? Food in the mouth does not alleviate hunger. Whatever Tolman conceives to be the "cathected" goal, it is clear that an "equivalence belief" means something closely associated which serves the organism as a goal in the sense of directing behavior toward or away from itself.

Tolman's third category of learning, field expectancies, was formerly called "sign-gestalt expectation." This covers an important feature of behavior. By the term Tolman means that on successive experiences in a particular environment an organism acquires sets (or field expectancies) which make it possible to take appropriate short cuts or roundabout routes. This phenomenon is involved in what Tolman and Honzik many years ago called "latent learning." An animal left in a maze for a period without any reward becomes familiar with the locale; when, later, it is made hungry and allowed to discover food, its mastery of the path from starting box to food box is far more rapid than the progress shown by an animal new to the maze.

Tolman cites an experiment by Gleitman, who trained rats on a T maze with food in each of the two end boxes. The boxes were radically different and after the first training the rats and the end boxes were taken to another room. The animals were placed in each box a number of times; they received a shock in one box but not in the other. They were immediately returned to the T maze, where 22 out of 25 rats avoided the path which led to the end box in which they had been shocked. This is a demonstration of what Tolman has called a field expectancy.

Tolman's fourth kind of learning he calls field-cognition modes. By this he means that field expectancy depends not just on memory but also on perception and inference.

Field-cognition modes can carry over to other experiments and be utilized by the animals in other situations. Tolman uses an alternative term, field lore, for field-cogntion modes. This category appears to cover the forms of space and time perception which the philosopher Kant called modes of intuition and believed to be innate forms which all our perceptions inevitably took; the three-dimensional nature of space perception is an instance.

As to memory Tolman suggests that "the one innately given principle seems to be that, if a certain sequence of events has occurred on one occasion, this same sequence of events is likely to occur on subsequent occasions" (1949, page 152). This principle, he says, is "innately strong."

Inferential lore Tolman believes also has its innate basis in the "simple rules of space, time, force, and quantity. . . ." Verbal training, however, adds much to these simple forms of perception. "As to the conditions and laws for the acquisition, de-acquisition and forgetting of such perceptual, memorial and inferential modes . . . I believe we have as yet practically no information" (1949, page 153).

Tolman's fifth category of learning he calls drive discriminations. Hull and Leeper are cited as offering evidence that the ability to distinguish between different drives must be learned sometimes by rats and often by men.

The sixth category of learning, motor patterns, Tolman

identifies with what in this book have been called "movements" as distinct from "acts." "And in default of other experimental theories about the learning of motor patterns," he says, "I am willing to take a chance and to agree with Guthrie that the conditions under which a motor pattern gets acquired may well be those in which the given movement gets the animal away from the stimuli which were present when the movement was initiated." However, he believes that rats and cats do learn stereotyped motor patterns, *but only when these specific patterns get them to food.*

Learning cathexes probably requires reinforcement, Tolman thinks. Reinforcement plus traumatic experience explains the acquisition of equivalence beliefs. Field expectancies are acquired according to Gestalt principles rather than through association. The acquisition and loss of field-cognition modes and the learning of drive discriminations Tolman believes are not explained. Motor patterns are possibly acquired by simple conditioning or association by contiguity.

"Other theorists," Tolman says in the introduction to his paper (1949, page 144), "will certainly not support what I am going to say. Not only will each of them feel that his theory is basic for all kinds of learning, but also each of these others will be sure to object to the general conceptual framework within which my distinctions alone make sense."

The conceptual framework of Tolman's theories offers a striking contrast to the framework of Skinner's system and to the framework which supports the theories of this book and the theories of Norman Maier which are included in this chapter. Skinner approached the problem of learning with his mind made up to reduce it to a point at which it could be treated objectively and mathematically—to a point at which the methods of natural science could be applied. In his original studies, Skinner's facts are as objective as anyone could desire. He records elapsed time and the motions of a bar (beyond the critical point at which it operates the recording device). These are facts which notably satisfy the definition that a fact is an event so described that any observer may accept the description. No observer would challenge Skinner's items of record. The rat's behavior in the box is not recorded. With this extreme limitation of his area of interest Skinner succeeds in getting lawful regularities which prove to be of great possible significance.

Tolman, instead of cutting down his observations to the movement of a lever beyond a critical point and the record of elapsed time, lets his attention and interest range over the full area of living behavior, animal and human, simple and complex. He has been unwilling to specify and make precise the area and aspects which he will cover, though such delimitation is essential for the development of laws or even of principles and scientific models. Science gains its precision by such restrictions. Physics refuses to take into account a man's religion and politics; it looks on him as a creature to be described in terms ultimately of centimeters, grams, and seconds. His fondness for a particular food or a certain symphony, even his psychological traits which he shares with other men, such as his mode of learning, have no place in a physics textbook and can not be described in physical terms. Not all men would reject physics on this account. Physics is a description of the behavior of matter in space and time. Men are physical objects, and for certain purposes can be treated as physical objects. They are, of course, much more than physical objects. They have loyalties and loves. Every man's life has aspects which no science can ever touch.

Tolman is unwilling, for the purpose of an account of learning, to disregard some of these more complex aspects of man which can not be fully explained by such principles as association. We assume that the earth and the rocks in a valley are all gravitating objects; but it would be insane to believe that with only a knowledge of the law of gravitation we could predict the forms that future erosion will take in the valley.

Skinner attempted to set the limitations required for the demonstration of lawfulness in behavior by disregarding the actual movements of his rats (to the point of hiding them from view) and using as his unit of response the class of all movement patterns, potentially infinite in variety, which operate a bar mechanism in a box.

This book has undertaken a very different form of restriction for the purpose of understanding, namely, the restriction of the basic facts to stimuli to sense organs and to animal movements, with the limited admission of certain movement groups or classes defined by their end results. This is the highly controversial stimulus-response formula. Unlike Tolman's view, movements are not regarded as alternatives to the formation of likes and dislikes, to the perception of space and time, to the possession of the equivalent of a map, or to the sets which make short cuts and localization possible. Every horse owner knows that his animal has a strong tendency to maintain an orientation toward the stable where it is fed even when this place has been out of sight for some time. But orientation toward the stable is not something the horse uses *instead of* movement patterns. Orientation can be demonstrated only by movement patterns. Men can demonstrate virtual possession of a "map in the head" by speech. But in this book speech is regarded as a form of motion. It is much more. But it is also motion.

Therefore, when Tolman suggests that movement patterns are acquired by simple conditioning, this is all that this book contends. Acts are defined by consequences but executed by movements. Goal-directed activity is also stimulus-directed activity, not an alternative category of behavior. Presbyterians move about and on occasion declare their faith. Without movement we could not know them as Presbyterians. They could not be Presbyterians.

One more issue is disputed with Tolman. Cathexes are defined by him as attachments of types of positive goal objects to basic drives. Just what is associated here? Without denying for a moment that we form interests in specific foods, specific sweethearts, specific fears, between what are the associations established? This book takes the ground that these specific likes and dislikes *are names for certain modes of behavior* and involve movement.

If movement patterns are acquired by way of associative learning it is clear that Tolman's first five categories are intended by him to represent mental processes different from and alternative to the acquisition of movement through association.

In an unpublished Ph.D. thesis recently submitted at the University of Washington, Culbert describes his study of certain interesting temporary effects of recent experiments on visual perception, within the area of Tolman's "field-cognition modes." After looking at certain grid patterns in a very dim light (to minimize afterimages), the subjects judge whether certain lines are horizontal or slope up or down. After an interval of several minutes of looking at lines which slope up to the left, lines which are actually horizontal are seen as sloping up to the right. Perception has adjusted itself to the inclination and a new standard has been formed in terms of which succeeding perceptions are for a time distorted.

Tolman believes that these field-cognition modes are acquired in accordance with Gestalt principles and *not in accordance with associative learning*. It is argued here that associative learning is probably involved. The phenomenon with which Culbert dealt is obviously an associative effect in some sense and it is quite possible that it takes place strictly in accord with the principle of association by contiguity. Tolman is, of course, entirely correct in saying that such phenomena are in accord with Gestalt principles and are not explained by the principle of association. The principle of gravitation does not explain erosion, but erosion must be explained either partly in terms of gravitation or in terms consistent with gravitation. It does not constitute an exception to gravitation. What I suspect, in the case of the horizontal lines which are perceived as sloping after gazing at lines that slope the other way, is that the observer in question actively compensates for the perceived slope in his response—possibly by inclining his head. The later sight of horizontal lines revives this adjustment in accordance with the principle of association and the observer views the new lines, which are actually horizontal, with a bias which he acquired while responding to (compensating for) the first lines.

This is a familiar phenomenon. In Seattle a cable car used to run up a steep hill. When the track flattened out at the top of the hill, the houses seemed to be leaning at a ridiculous angle. This perception was in turn quickly adjusted to and the houses appeared normal.

We can argue that the five kinds of learning which with movement patterns make up Tolman's classification are not alternative to the learning of movement by association and do not exclude such associative learning, but that they are modes of thought and perception which are difficult to "explain" in associative terms or which Tolman believes are adequately explained in the terms which make up his own body of principles, like his principle of the cognitive map (1948). ". . . The central office itself is far more like a map control room than it is like an old-fashioned telephone exchange. The stimuli, which are allowed in, are not connected by just simple one-to-one switches to the outgoing responses. Rather, the incoming impulses are usually worked over and elaborated in the central control room into a tentative, cognitive-like map of the environment. And it is this tentative map . . . which finally determines what responses, if any, the animal will finally release" (page 192).

The map-owner-like behavior of rats is interesting but difficult of explanation. Tolman's scientific model is the map control room *but with the navigation officer and his enlisted help left out.* The charts do not control the movements of the ship; hence this particular scientific model is seriously lacking in predicting the rat's movements.

A machine which actually charted the movements of a plane or a vessel could be constructed. Such a machine could possibly be made to direct the retracing of the course, but this would involve a mechanism that approximated association by contiguity.

Perhaps one of Tolman's arguments will successfully illustrate the differences between his theoretical position and the one taken in this book. He cites an unpublished Ph.D. thesis by Hudson in an account of an interesting experiment. Hudson set out to discover whether rats would learn an avoidance reaction in one trial. At one end of the rat's living cage there was a small striped visual pattern on which a food cup was mounted. The rat approached and as it touched the cup it was given a shock. Weeks afterward, on being replaced in the cage, the rat showed strong avoidance of the pattern. But if the pattern disappeared at the instant of shock the association was not established in many cases. Or if at the shock the lights went out for a second and the pattern and food cup dropped out of sight, a "large percentage" of the animals showed no avoidance.

Tolman interprets this as meaning that the rat, after the shock, is actively engaged in the "building up of his cognitive map," and is not "merely passively" receiving and reacting to all the stimuli present.

The difference between the present account and Tolman's account is not that one holds the rat's behavior to be passive and the other holds that it is purposeful and active. The present account maintains that active, intelligent, alert rats, engaged in building up their cognitive maps or performing any other bits of bright behavior, are doing so through the association of situation patterns with response. It is here argued not that animal behavior is not purposive but that purposive behavior is accomplished through associative learning. Purpose describes the end result; association describes a general principle to which all behavior modification conforms. The attainment of purpose is not inevitable.

Tolman's six varieties of learning may well prove to be no more exceptions to the rule of association than eating an ice cream soda is an exception to the law of gravitation. Gravitation simply does not cover the case completely. We must know something about the dynamics of vacuums and the nature of gases and liquids, the motivation and tastes of the high-school drug-store customers, and the history of the ice cream soda before we can be said to understand this particular instance of consumption.

The meandering form of a river in a wide valley obviously requires more than the law of gravitation to explain it. The inertia of the flowing water of the river which cuts into the alluvial soil of the outer bank on every turn is a principle distinct from gravitation. Similarly when hunger is "attached to" a particular food as a goal object or when a man falls in love with a particular girl, which Tolman calls a cathexis, the possibility is not excluded that various motor and glandular behavior is involved in the association. Such cathexes are noted for carrying with them the idiosyncrasies of the behavior of their first associations. Allport's concept of "functional autonomy," which describes the tendency of habits to persist in spite of obstacles, to be modified in such a way as to be retained, and Gardner Murphy's concept of canalization, which recognizes the tendency for basic drives to be expressed later in the motor forms which were the accidents of their first gratifications, both describe phenomena which take very readily to statement in terms of association. Freud's doctrine that infants are "polymorphous perverse" meant that the perversions of later life are accidents of early associations with sex responses and that any infant could develop any perversion if the perverse behavior were caused to take place in connection with the stimulation of erogenous zones. In terms of the association theory in this book, one addition would be required. The principle of association must be supplemented not by a rival or competing principle but by special considerations governing special situations which determine the outcome in accord with the principle of association but which require information in addition to it. For example, adventitious behavior associated with a basic drive tends not to remain associated unless it ends in the relief of the drive. The behavior which takes the organism out of the drive stimulation tends in the long run to be the behavior associated with the drive because all other behavior leaves the animal under the lash of the drive, and what it is doing is bound to be replaced eventually by other behavior. Perhaps this point, namely, that association is a general principle but never a complete explanation of a particular event, will bear further illustration. If a boy throws a stone at a companion, the boy's movements and the parabolic path of the stone all conform to the principle of gravitation, but none of us would be content with gravitation as the explanation of the event. Associative learning is as much and as thoroughly exemplified by the stone throwing as is gravitation, but an understanding of the act requires more than either or both of these general principles.

In other words, it is here suggested not that the behavior named in Tolman's first five categories—cathexes, equivalence beliefs, field expectancies, field-cognition modes, and drive discriminations—does not occur or is not important and interesting, but that it does not represent categories coördinate with motor patterns, that motor patterns are concerned in all five categories, and that basically it is to the association of stimulus situation with motor pattern response that all the modification of behavior which we call "learning" conforms. The present theory of learning is put forward not as a generalization from the observation of the behavior of rats, but as a "scientific model" representing how such a phenomenon as learning could occur. It is suggested that if there are angels and if angels learn, they may learn by associating situation patterns with response complexes. It would require some acquaintance with angels to assert that this is how they do learn; but in the meantime the theory attempts a conceptual structure of a method by which, if there were angels, angels might learn.

NORMAN MAIER'S THEORY OF FRUSTRATION

It may appear odd to include in a discussion of learning theories the ideas of Norman Maier when Maier's experimental field and area of interest have been not learning theory but animal behavior analogous to a nervous breakdown in human beings. The reason for discussing his point of view in some detail is that he has been led by the results of some original experiments in what he has called "frustration" to review the whole conceptual account of behavior and to outline a very thoughtful systematic account of behavior that includes, because he makes frustration an alternative and coördinate category of behavior, a brief account of the nature of learning.

Maier's *Frustration*, published in 1949, was based on work and ideas developed over a considerable span of years. The theory is included here because it offers an illustration of the ways in which theories develop—the natural history of theory— as well as representing what one active contemporary investigator has arrived at as an interpretation of the results of an extended research program.

Maier's research on certain forms of "frustrated" behavior in rats has won wide attention. His basic method used an experimental apparatus that consisted of a platform on which a rat could be placed, and an opposite wall separated from the platform by a space and including two doors so equipped that one of them could be opened if the rat jumped across the gap and struck it. Usually one door could thus be opened; the other was locked so that if the rat jumped against it the animal would fall. Behind the open door there was usually food.

The platform was also equipped with an air blast which could be used if the animal refused to jump. A similar apparatus was used by Lashley in studying learning in rats. Maier used the method to attack a new problem—the response to disturbing situations for which there is no solution. If the right-hand door is always openable and the left fixed, a rat learns in a few trials always to jump at the right-hand door. If the openable door is marked with one pattern and the fixed door marked with another, the rat learns to jump for the correct pattern even if it is sometimes on the right and sometimes on the left.

This is normal learning. Since Maier was not really interested in learning theory but, instead, was concerned with nervous breakdown, he adopted without argument the theory that rewarded acts are preserved and punished acts are discontinued. This is a very simple punishment and reward theory. He combines this with straight association and so has a dual theory. He believes that there are two kinds of learning.

But Maier's rats exhibited some odd behavior that did not come under this theory. When they were exposed to what he calls frustration, behavior patterns were in evidence which he could not account for in terms of punishment and reward. These new modes of behavior appeared when the animals were subjected to frustration.

Maier investigated the behavior of rats when neither position and neither pattern were consistently right, so that each position and each pattern were equally likely to reward or to punish the animal. This situation is what he calls frustration. He was interested in the rats' response to frustration which he believes can not be explained as learning.

The usual response is for the rat either to develop a tendency to jump to one side (a position stereotype) or to one pattern (a symbol stereotype), or to develop what Maier calls an abortive stereotype—a response that is not adapted to success in any instance. When the animals were subjected to a series of "no solution" trials this stereotyping of response tended strongly to develop. In such trials the animals developed a ". . . degree of stereotypy that perhaps exceeds in specificity the execution of responses developed or maintained under ordinary learning conditions where reward is given in connection with the response" (1949, page 30). Maier found that these stereotyped responses had certain characteristic differences from behavior learned with a simple reward when the reward was reserved for a "correct" response. One difference was that animals that have once developed a stereotype in response to an insoluble series of trials are less likely to learn to respond to a rewarded pattern than are animals that have already learned one rewarded response and are now exposed to another. The fixation they develop in an insoluble series is more persistent than the response they develop to a reward series. By a fixation Maier means a strong and persistent nonadjustive response.

The development of fixations tends to have a certain "all or none" character. Animals that were trained in a series in which one position was correct and were then confronted with a series in which one symbol pattern was correct tended either to abandon the position habit promptly or not to abandon it even after many trials. Seventy-four percent abandoned the position habit (now wrong) in less than 100 trials. The rest failed to abandon it in 200 trials.

Maier interprets this as meaning that frustration tends to freeze or to fixate a response even when that response brings consistent punishment. For this reason he holds that frustration represents a category of behavior alternative to and exclusive of learning. How he could be led to this conclusion even though he remarks that "the behavior fixated seems to be the stereotype they have practiced" (1949, page 35) is of interest as an illustration of the way in which the theory maker in any field is confronted with choices at many points in developing his theory but, once having made a choice, finds many other features of the theory now determined. Hull chose early in his task of theory building to make reward or reinforcement the basic category of explanation and to make association depend on it. This book presents a theory in which association by contiguity is assumed to be the basic rule and the response of animals to rewards and punishments is derived from that rule or explained in terms of it.

Maier's theory of learning excludes unadaptive fixations from learning by definition. The definition of learning used in this book makes fixation an illustration of learning.

Maier begins his account of learning (1949, page 6) by asserting that there are two types of learning which are basically different. One of these is associative. The other is selective. One is represented by Pavlovian conditioning in which mere association appears effective. The other is represented by learning in a maze or puzzle box where learning appears to be guided by its outcome.

There are, Maier says, four ways to alter behavior. One involves the "extension of a response (conditioning) so that it will be expressed in a variety of situations" (1949, page 4). A second method "is to change the consequences of an action." A third involves "a change in perception or stimulus interpretation" (1949, page 8).

A fourth type of behavior change occurs in connection with problem solving. Behavior is blocked because a difficulty has arisen in connection with progress toward a goal. Trial-and-error behavior solves some problems of this sort, but in other cases the person suddenly perceives the solution. . . . This type of behavior is goal oriented, and the behavior changes because a method of reaching the goal is discovered in the problem situation. In insightful problem solving the goal influences the nature of the insight and resulting behavior. In trial-and-error problem solving the goal has a different function because a solution is selected out of past experience. Thus it influences the behavior selected but does not play a part in creating the behavior (1949, page 9).

This was the original thesis of Köhler's *The Mentality of Apes*. In my own opinion due examination would show that insightful behavior does not differ from trial-and-error behavior in that trial-and-error behavior is based on associative learning and insightful behavior is not. Insights appear to be dependent on past experience just as truly as the simplest conditioning. On what else could insight be based even in angels? The Gestalt psychologists and Maier both assume that once an insight is formed it will be available on reminding cues. I believe that the occurrence of the first insight can be experimentally demonstrated to depend on previous learning—that Köhler's apes which showed such cleverness with sticks would not have shown it without much previous experience with sticks.

In his discussion of learning Maier makes another assumption which is not explicit. This is that learning is by definition adjustive because it is directed by reward and punishment. He makes this assumption in spite of his early recognition of learning by association. The persistent unadaptive responses which Maier finds in his rats after an insoluble series of trials can not, he thinks, be the effects of learning because learned responses would answer repeated failure by change.

Having assumed that "learned behavior is subject to change when it ceases to be adequate for obtaining a goal" (1949, page 18), Maier is compelled to conclude that *frustrated behavior* which shows resistence to change *is not learned*. The response developed with an insoluble problem is more persistent than the response developed with a reward series.

This reasoning leads Maier to postulate a mode of behavior change distinct from and incompatible with learning, namely, fixation, or the development of persistent stereotyped response not amenable to learning.

The details of these fixations observed by Maier are striking. An animal trained by reward always to jump to the right or left window and then subjected to new training in which the reward is shifted about and is accompanied by a visible symbol on the window may develop a fixation in the form of a strong resistance to jumping and an eventual abortive jump that does not carry it to either window. When a rat has established a position fixation on one side, the other window may be left open with the dish of food in plain sight and the animal will, after orienting toward the open window, turn and jump against the locked barrier (1949, page 43).

Maier finds that the introduction of frustration, as in a series of trials in which neither window is consistently right or consistently wrong, leads the rats to "settle on some form of behavior and to cease expressing the variable behavior usually expressed in a trial and error learning situation" (1949, page 78).

The strong resistance to change even under punishment is not the only difference between frustrated and learned behavior. Fixations are also more specific and stereotyped than learned responses (1949, page 80). In normal reward learning the animal may exhibit a variety of ways of depressing a lever. It may be here remarked that if the behavior of rats is like the behavior of the cats which are described in another chapter, or like the lever pressing shown by a rat in Neal Miller's film, *Motivation and Reward in Learning,* the variety of ways which Maier noticed in ordinary reward learning may prove to be made up of a limited repertoire of rather remarkably stereotyped responses.

Maier's original decision to accept a definition of learning that restricts the term to adaptive changes in behavior or to changes which can be directed by reward and punishment forced him to postulate a principle of frustration as distinct from his four modes of learning and to contrast learning and frustration as mutually exclusive. This in turn forced him to postulate another principle to account for the selection of the fixated response.

Some responses become fixated and others do not. What is the rule of selection? Maier concludes that the "facts point to a principle of *availability* as a factor in determining the particular response that is fixated" (1949, page 82).

Maier (page 93) adopts three principal categories of behavior change: (1) *stimulus-response reactions* "determined by neural connections only," (2) *motivated behavior* determined by the consequences to which such behavior leads, and (3) *frustration,* which is not guided by consequences though it appears to be readily amenable to change through "guidance" (page 79), which suggests that Maier believes it to be possibly determined by the elemental form of association which acts only through neural connections. His observation that the response that is fixated tends to be the response that happened to be in process when the fixation occurred, and his observation that fixation depends on the stimulus situation also point to the belief that he is really including fixation in a category of straight association by contiguity and that he is in the group of psychologists who admit the phenomenon of association by contiguity but look on it as a low and occasional order of behavior (as Locke did) mediated only by neural connections. He leaves unclear what may be added to neural connections in reward learning.

In spite of the fact that Maier refuses to classify the behavior of frustration as learning, he notes that the development of a fixation tends to relieve tensions. By an abortive jump the animal avoids further exposure to the air blast. This would class fixation in Hull's system as a response reinforced by tension reduction. In the theory outlined in this book the conditions of learning and retention are satisfied by the fact that the air blast disturbs the rat until it makes a jump, whether the jump is abortive or a "success." Jumping takes the animal out of the air blast and therefore remains its last response to a complex situation that includes the blast.

Frustration, according to Maier, has several alternative end effects. One of these is aggression, which relieves tensions and completes a behavior cycle, provided the source of frustration is no longer present. Another alternative is regression, which utilizes what Maier calls the principle of availability. The revived old response was "available." Another possible end result is resignation.

Of all these it may be said, in terms of the theory in this book, that they set up conditions for establishing response patterns which become the organism's response to frustration. Why these modes of behavior should not be called learning, even with Maier's sweeping assumption that all learning ends in adjustment, is difficult to see. They all take the animal out of a state which has included restless action and tension.

The principle of availability really serves only to call attention to the fact that which response occurs will depend on what stimuli are present and what their associative connections have been. No response is made that is not available in the sense of being included in the animal's repertoire, but this seems too obvious to need formulation as a principle. "In regarding regression as an end response to frustration," Maier says (1949, page 110), "and in utilizing availability as the principle that determines the form of expression . . . one seems to remain closer to the facts. At the same time the view explains why the regressive responses spontaneously disappear when frustration is relieved."

This theoretical solution does stay close to the facts. My own objection to it is not that it is at variance with the facts but that it is unnecessarily complicated. It appears to me far simpler to assume the principle of association by contiguity, which includes availability but makes it a general principle instead of a special attribute of frustration. It also explains why regressive responses spontaneously disappear when frustration is relieved. Their associative cue is gone.

It should be remarked in passing that the concept of regression which is usually illustrated by the case of a grown woman who behaves childlishly, is badly in need of overhaul. No 150-pound woman can act like a baby by means of the revival of old habits. Infantile behavior in a 160-pound adult would require the development of new skills. What many clinicians take for regressive behavior is sometimes the assumption of a new role rather than a revival of old habits. Sears (1943) has made a critical review of the objective studies of regression.

A theoretical position which confines itself strictly to the realm of observed movement but is at the same time reminiscent of Tolman's field expectancies was suggested by Brogden, Lipman, and Culler (1938), and by Culler (1938). They established the superiority of avoidable shock over unavoidable shock as a reinforcing agent in conditioning guinea pigs to run at a signal. When running in response to the signal was made to prevent shock, the signal became 100 percent effective in a period of training. When running was always "reinforced" with shock, the animals did not reach 50 percent response to the signal even when the training period was over twice as long.

The interpretation given this result by Brogden, Lipman, and Culler is to the effect that straight association by contiguity is relatively ineffective and that effective learning involves an incentive also.

Sheffield (1948) undertook to repeat this experiment, giving attention to certain features not recorded by the original experimenters. The apparatus consisted of an activity cage which rotated when the animals ran. The shock was administered by a charged grid that was the floor on which the animal stood. By making a polygraph record of the detailed movements of the wheel Sheffield discovered that the unavoidable shock did not invariably cause running but often caused the animal to crouch. The conditions of association by contiguity were therefore not properly represented by speaking of the running as the response to the unconditioned stimulus.

Furthermore, when performance on individual trials was examined and compared with the record of what the guinea pig had actually done last in response to shock, this was found to be an important determiner of what the following trial would show.

Sheffield also found that successive avoidances of shock led to extinction rather than to the strengthening of the running in response to a signal.

Culler's interpretation was to the effect that what is conditioned is not the response that actually occurred but a preparation for the stimuli of which the signal is a warning, even though this preparation may be a new response. This reminds us strongly of Tolman's field expectancies because Tolman's assumption is that when association has established an expectancy this mental state will result in appropriate behavior whether or not this behavior has been practiced.

In terms of association by contiguity we would expect only such preparation (Culler) or such adaptive or rational measures (Tolman) to be made as have actually been associated with the signal. Both Tolman and Culler predict that the stimulus situation will cause the animal to do something clever or near-clever. My own belief is that we learn our cleverness and are strictly limited to acting on the basis of past experience or present luck.

CHAPTER XVIII

Hull's Reinforcement Theory

THERE is no question that the most sustained and consistent attack on the problem of learning has been made by Clark Hull at the Yale Institute of Human Relations, and by his students, who include a large proportion of the most distinguished contributors to learning theory. Hull's first formulation of a learning theory was published in 1929. A recent article (1950) offers a condensed statement of his theory in its present form.

It was remarked earlier in this book that there are two very different approaches to scientific theory, the empirical and the deductive. The illustration used was the prediction of the falls of a die; this can be done either by throwing the die and tallying the number of times per hundred that each face turns up, or by arguing *a priori* from the physical properties of a cube of homogeneous material that each face has an equal chance of turning up. The second method is a much simpler example of the *a priori* use of a scientific model than the set of differential equations which are the basis for Einstein's theory of relativity, but both the cube and the set of equations represent *a priori* and deductive models.

Hull's theory, like Einstein's, has a mathematical statement, but the method of arriving at Hull's equations is far different from the Einstein method, Hull himself (1950) describes his method as beginning with the selection of two or three principles from an empirical study of learning. These are generalized as equations. An effort is then made to see whether these equations will fit data from other experiments and if they do they are retained as principles.

This is much like Skinner's professed method, except that Skinner does not use actual equations so much as certain general descriptive terms for his curves; his curves behave as if they were contained in an envelope though neither envelope nor curve is given a mathematical formulation.

Hull's method has the characteristic of the first or empirical source of theory—the difficulty of generalization. Empirical results never fit any generalization perfectly. Even in physics Boyle's law, which states that with other conditions held constant the product of the volume of a gas times its pressure is constant, is not illustrated by an actual experiment. It is impossible to hold other conditions absolutely constant; furthermore, every gas has its own peculiarities. The law is said to hold for an "ideal" gas since it holds for no real gas.

Hull's generalized equations are made up from the results of a very limited number of experiments and these experiments of a very special variety. As in the case of the dice, the empirical method based on actual throws of a die may involve characteristics which are peculiar to the die used in the experiment. Hull avoids this to some extent by putting his generalizations in a form such that some parameter of the curve remains to be determined by the data to which the curve is to be fitted. This tends to end in a demonstration that certain types of curves can be fitted to a variety of experimental results.

Hull presents his system as a series of postulates, theorems, and corollaries modeled after the Euclidean geometry. For a complete exposition of his theoretical position it is of course necessary to read his *The Principles of Behavior* (1943) and the supplement in the *Psychological Review* (1950). Here we can undertake only a brief statement of some of the outstanding points.

It may be remarked at the outset that as in the case of Skinner's theory we may seriously question the notion that the theories are derived from observed facts. In both cases the facts were selected by the theory in advance. The basic nature of learning—the theory that it is describable in terms of stimulus-response connections which are established by an association of a stimulus and a response, provided that the response is followed by reward or reinforcement in the form of drive reduction—was not discovered in some experimental results and then adopted by Hull. That conception of the basic nature of learning in terms of reward serves to pick out the facts which will be observed. The experiments that justify Hull's basic theory are experiments which were originally set up in terms of that theory.

Hull's 1950 version of his theory consists of eighteen postulates and twelve corollaries. Postulate I states that organisms at birth have certain stimulus-response connections that tend to reduce the needs which are expressed in drives. Postulate II states that a brief stimulus acting on a receptor occasions an afferent, self-propagating nerve impulse which rises to a maximum and then more slowly subsides. Postulate III (primary reinforcement) states that "whenever an effector activity . . . is closely associated with a stimulus afferent impulse or trace . . . and the conjunction is closely associated with the diminution in the receptor discharge characteristic of a need, there will result an increment to a tendency for that stimulus to evoke that response" (1950, page 175). From this principle Hull derives as corollaries what he calls "secondary motivation," in which a neutral stimulus associated with a drive becomes a conditioner of a secondary drive, and what he calls "secondary reinforcement," which names the tendency for a neutral stimulus to acquire "the power of acting as a reinforcing agent."

Postulate IV states the law of habit formation: "If reinforcements follow each other at evenly distributed intervals, everything else constant, the resulting habit will increase in strength as a positive growth function of the number of trials" according to the equation,

$$sHr = 1 - 10^{-aN}$$

where sHr is habit strength measured in terms of latency, vigor, certainty, or resistance to extinction. The failure of these measures to vary together makes a somewhat ambiguous concept of habit strength, unlike Skinner's rate of responding.

Postulate V deals with the rise and fall of drive under prolonged need and asserts that every drive generates a drive stimulus. Postulates VII and VIII concern the effect of different amounts of reward and delays of reward. Postulate IX defines *reaction potential* (sEr), which means the probability of the reaction under specific circumstances; it is determined by "(1) the drive operating during the learning process multiplied (2) by the dynamism of the signaling stimulus at response evocation . . . , (3) by the incentive reinforcement . . . , (4) by the gradient of delay in reinforcement . . . , and (5) by the habit strength."

Postulate X concerns inhibitory potential and states that any response produces an "increment of primary negative drive" which reduces the reaction potential of the response. This inhibitory potential is dissipated with time. It has been referred to by other writers as refractory phase. When a response is repeated at short intervals this inhibitory potential may be summated, and stimuli closely associated with the presence of appreciable inhibitory potential become conditioned inhibiters of the response.

Postulate XI deals with stimulus generalization. When a response has become conditioned to a stimulus S_1, so that the "habit strength" may be represented by $_{s1}H_R$, another stimulus (S_2) in the same mode (visual, tactual, and so on) acquires the power to evoke the response and the habit strength may be represented by the equation:

$$_{s2}\overline{H}_R = {}_{s1}H_R \times 10^{-ad}$$

in which d represents the number of just noticeable differences

by which S_1 differs from S_2. Pavlov's original demonstration of
this generalization consisted of using a touch on various parts
of the dog's body as the conditioned signal for salivary flow; he
reported that when S_1 represented the touch used in practice and
S_2 a touch at some distance, the amount of saliva secreted varied
as the distance between the points of application of S_1 and S_2.
There are many confirming experiments which show that stimuli
not practiced with a response can evoke the response if they resemble the practiced stimuli. Our chapter on generalization did
not make this a basic characteristic of learning and explained it
not in terms of the similarity between S_1 and S_2 but in terms of
identical components of the responses to S_1 and S_2. If, for instance, both S_1 and S_2 are sounds, both will be listened to and that
involves the dog's orienting his head and his ears. If two sounds
differ only in pitch, the movements of orientation or other responses to them will be practically identical; and since these
movements have obviously been associated with the response
just as much as the sounds themselves, the response may be
thought of not as a response to S_2 which has not been associated
with R but as a response to the orientation response which was
associated when R was evoked by S_1.

Postulate XIII concerns "behavioral oscillation" and is Hull's
method of dealing with the fact that the evocation of responses is
subject to an unpredictable component which he is not willing to
relate to the complexity of all actual situations and to factors
that are not subject to either control or recording. He holds that
the reaction potential oscillates from moment to moment. This
behavioral oscillation is the most speculative component of
Hull's theory. There are fluctuations of attention. If the responses involved in attention are subject to Hull's ninth postulate, this alone will provide ground for many failures of
response. Postulate XIII makes a dubious addition.

Postulate XVIII, concerning individual differences, states
that the constants in Hull's equations vary from species to

species, from individual to individual, and from state to state in in the same individual "quite apart from the factor of behavioral oscillation" (1950, page 180). By leaving these constants to be determined by the data under investigation it is possible to make the types of exponential curves used by Hull fit a wide variety of data. The original curves were derived from a very limited set of observations and it is not these specific curves, with the parameters of the original data, but only the genus to which they belong that makes up the quantitative elements in Hull's principles.

Some general comments on Hull's method are in order. It should be noted first that he has constructed the most explicit and clearest statement of theory yet offered. His publications and teaching have exposed his system to criticism, and in response to the difficulties raised by himself and others he has made the numerous extensions and corrections embodied in the postulates just summarized. It is my own opinion that two possible wrong assumptions have so entered into the choice of facts for the record that severe restrictions on the usefulness and generality of Hull's theories have resulted. One of these assumptions is that the formation and the strengthening or weakening of associations between stimulus and response depend upon reward or its absence—referred to by Hull as reinforcement and described as drive reduction. The association that is followed by drive reduction makes the associated stimulus an effective cue for the response. The complications and contradictions to which this assumption leads are numerous. It requires an elaborate theoretical account of how near the associated stimulus-response combination the reward must be in order to make the association effective, a theoretical account that is hard to reconcile with many facts.

Hull's answer is Postulate VIII

$$J = 10^{-jt}$$

n which the gradient of reinforcement is made a function of the time elapsed between conditioned stimulus and the reduction of the drive. In our observation of cats Horton and I saw nothing faintly resembling this. Serial responses which appeared to be concatenations of movement depending on the accidents of a first time in a new environment seemed to us to be preserved without reference to their nearness to any observable goal achievement or drive reduction. It is true that the final movements of escape tended to remain part of the pattern but they did not exhibit any time or space gradient. They remained—or so we interpreted their remaining—not because they were in any sense stronger that the earlier movements, but because there was no chance for conditioned inhibition to be unlearned in the absence of the necessary cues. Even with Hull's theory this would be true. No new association with a stimulus pattern can be formed without the presence of the pattern.

The assumption of a time gradient of reinforcement makes it necessary for Hull and the reward theorists to go to rather fantastic lengths to find the reward whenever an association occurs. If a rat is put in a Skinner box and the box arranged so that instead of the rat's being fed the light is turned out, learning occurs. It then becomes necessary to say that the light acts as a drive for the rat and that darkness is a reward. It also becomes necessary to interpret reward as relief from punishment instead of examining what punishment makes the animal do. In my opinion we gain more exact prediction of the effects of both reward and punishment if we interpret them as original stimuli and look for the conditioning of the responses caused by reward and punishment. Habits can obviously be broken up and "habit strength" reduced by reward as well as strengthened by reward, as was described in the chapter on reward and punishment.

A second assumption Hull has made in common with Skinner, namely, that learning is a continuous function of the number of reinforcements. It is my own belief now, as it was in 1935 when this book was first published, that in the long series of trials

which are used in developing this notion of learning as a continuous process psychologists have confused the strengthening of a
simple stimulus-response association with the improvement of a
skill which requires not the strengthening of *a* response but the
elimination of many responses, the alteration of others. The
basic phenomenon of associative learning occurs in one conjunction of situation and response. When a rat is exposed to 150 pairings of a signal and a response and the association appears to be
more certainly effective, the increased certainty of response
is explainable in terms of the conditioning of many variant patterns in the situation. A repeated signal is not always timed when
the animal is in a posture from which the response is possible.
The result is numerous failures of response. Hull explains such
failures in terms of "oscillation." I attribute the failures to un-
controlled factors and suggest that practice conditions more and
more variable elements in the situation.

It should be noted that Hull's concept of habit strength is not
directly comparable with Skinner's notion of response strength,
which is measured by the number of unreinforced responses required to extinguish and includes the state of drive. Hull's habit
strength is a hypothetical measure underlying such available and
observable measurables as the probability of response evocation.
An empirical measure of it is the number of times per hundred
that the stimulus is followed by the response in the general
situation that is taken for granted. A second measure indirectly
giving habit strength is the latency of reaction evocation, or the
time elapsed between stimulus and reaction. A third measure is
the number of unreinforced reactions necessary to produce extinction, and a fourth is the amplitude of reaction. This last,
in terms of the number of drops of saliva secreted, was Pavlov's
chief reliance.

Unfortunately these measures are not easy to use as indica-
tions of a single underlying habit strength because, as Humphreys has shown (1943), they are not highly correlated. The

reduction of these measures to a scale in which the unit is a *hab* can hardly be said to be an immediate prospect.

This proposed unit of habit strength raises some general questions concerning the aim and purpose of learning theory. If research verifies the contention of this book that movement patterns, once executed, tend strongly to be integrated and to occur "all or none," prediction which assumes a continuous scale of degrees of strength will not be applicable. Learning theory will be directed at predicting the occurrence or nonoccurrence of a specific response pattern much as a pregnancy test is directed at predicting the presence or absence of pregnancy, rather than the degree of pregnancy. Degrees of amplitude of response and degrees of latency are familiar laboratory phenomena. Both point toward a possible response strength conceivably like what Hull would measure in *habs*. The probability of response evocation is in a very different category indeed. This assumes not a scale of response strengths but a calculus of probabilities dealing with responses which do not vary in strength but either occur or do not occur. It is of very doubtful legitimacy to use zero as a measure of the strength of a response that does not occur and 1 as a measure of the strength of a response that does occur, and to find that the response strength is 0.31 when the response failed 69 times in 100 and appeared 31 times. The figure 0.31 is not a measure of strength but a measure of probability; it depends on our knowledge and ignorance rather than on the strength or weakness of a response. A response that occurred on trial 27 in a series of 100 trials but on no other trial was strong enough to occur on trial 27 and possibly not strong enough to occur on the other 99 occasions. Or it may have been potentially just as strong on the other 99 occasions and failed because there was no effective cue.

There is a serious objection to a treatment of learning which makes habit strength a continuous function of such a variable as the number of reinforcements or rewards which have followed an association. There is ground for believing that behavior tends

to be organized into all-or-nothing patterns. In the stream of behavior there is continuous determination of events by their
antecedents. What an organism will do is influenced by the
stimuli it encounters, but these stimuli are in turn the effects of
what the organism has just done. By a slight turn of the head the
whole visual field is shifted to a completely new set of objects
and events. By listening or not listening the organism's behavior determines what will be responded to and thereby determines what will be done. The initial movement—the very
beginning of a movement—serves to make certain alternative
actions impossible. Rival responses do not partly occur. The
rival response would have depended on initiating sense-organ
orientation and a chain of movement, would have produced
stimuli which, because the first response captured attention, are
now eliminated from any possible occurrence. The determination
whether or not a response will occur depends on the first step.
The first step may in turn be controlled by what the organism
is doing. On receiving the signal to which the observer is attending, the animal may be in a posture or a movement such
that the initial step is ruled out and the response in which the
observer is interested will not take place at all. It will not take
place slightly.

This tendency for behavior to be organized into all-or-nothing
patterns is not a law. It has plenty of exceptions. There are conflicts between actions. A warning shout at a man who is making
a run preparatory to jumping a small stream may disorganize
his behavior so that he does a sort of mixture of jumping and not
jumping and lands in the water. But all-or-nothing is a common
characteristic of animal and human behavior. If we say that the
strength of a pupil's tendency to answer "63" to the question
"What is nine times seven?" is 36 *habs*, what do we mean by
that? Actually the pupil in question will say either "63" or
some other phrase such as "I don't know" or "67." He will not
be found saying "63" twenty-seven times in one hundred or
whatever else 36 *habs* may indicate.

However, if by learning we mean not the tendency of a response to follow a given situation but, instead, the tendency of some end result like typing a page or running through a maze or solving a puzzle box to require less and less time with successive repetitions or to involve the elimination of errors or "useless" effort, then it is a mistake to talk in terms of units of habit strength in particular movement responses. The repetitions required in acquiring skill involve eliminating more responses than must be established. Skinner's early work with rats involved a combination of drive and skill. Probably every rat dropped its first movement response for a changed method during its confinement in the box. It is safe to hazard this guess because Skinner did not see or record what the movements were. If the rat ceases to press the bar with its right paw and substitutes its nose, shall we say that the habit strength of pressing-with-right-paw suddenly drops to zero after 18 "emittings"? Would it not be more profitable to look for the antecedents which led to the two different responses and to find whether R_2, the use of the nose, having been occasioned by special circumstances, now occurs in the situation which led to R_1 before those circumstances?

Skinner, facing this same problem, has pointed out that in a "chain" of responses only the initial response is open to type-R conditioning, that is, to being emitted. The movements following the first response are all cases of type-S or Pavlovian conditioning. In the same problem I should be inclined to look for possible stimuli for the very first movement, not to assume that a new mechanism for association is involved in producing the initial movement. One place to look for such stimuli is the drive.

Spence's Elaboration of Hull's Theory

At the time of its publication (1942) I believed that Spence's chapter on theories of learning in Moss' *Comparative Psychol-*

ogy was the best short account of learning theories in print. Before and since that time Spence has made a large number of contributions both in experiment and in the extension and defense of Hull's reinforcement theory of learning. His endorsement of Hull's basic concept of reinforcement was made after a careful and fair review of rival theories and of a large body of experimental results. One of the experiments which carried great weight with him was Loucks' ingenious method (1935) of investigating the conditionability of leg flexion in a dog when the flexion was produced by direct faradic shock to the motor area of the cortex. Here there was no unconditioned stimulus and presumably no sensory event. Conditioning did not take place. However, when food reward followed flexion, conditioning of flexion occurred. Spence interprets this as establishing the essential role of reward in the formation of an association.

The notion that reward is basic need not imply any backward-acting cause in learning. Hull proposed a temporal gradient of reinforcement such that reinforcement could be effective for a long period after the stimulus-response event it reinforced. He assumed that this S-R event leaves a diminishing trace which would be simultaneous with the reinforcement. Spence believes this device unnecessary and replaces it with the theory that secondary reinforcements can be assumed to be established in the behavior leading to reinforcement. Hull's doctrine holds that stimulus events which have consistently and often occurred together with drive reduction can themselves act as reinforcement of the S-R associations that immediately precede them. From my point of view this underscores the heavy burden which secondary reinforcement is required to carry in the theories of Hull, Spence, and Miller and Dollard. In order that the chaining of a long series of movements ending in food or escape or other reward be recognized as a product of associative learning, it is necessary to suppose that each movement produces stimuli which have acquired reward value and acts as a secondary reward for the movement just preceding. But since this secondary reward value can be gained only by association with a primary reward, it is not clear how the effect is passed backward along the chain of reactions. This problem will be mentioned again in the discussion of Miller and Dollard's theory.

Spence's name has been prominent in discussions of two opposed theoretical accounts of discrimination learning. Krechevsky (1938) and Lashley (1942) held that the animal exposed to a problem in discrimination, such as the selection of one pattern rather than another as a cue for response, responds to a series of features of the situation and eventually and suddenly comes to respond to the relevant cue. Spence believes that the relevant patterns are building up or losing excitatory strength and that when the difference is great enough to offset any existing preference (difference in excitatory strength in favor of) for such features as position, the animal will react properly to the relevant pattern. In terms of straight association as contrasted with reinforcement theory, the discrimination will be made after the animal has by practice been led to respond while attending to the relevant positive pattern, and also to refrain from the response while attending to the negative pattern. I suspect that close examination of the detailed behavior of the animal in the problem situation would confirm this. This position would not admit the critical nature of the test which Spence contends would decide between the noncontinuity theories of Lashley and Krechevsky and his own theory. Such a test consists in reversing the significance of the patterns after rats have been trained in a Lashley jumping apparatus. Spence holds that the noncontinuity theorists should grant that the previous training with one pattern as rewarded should not slow up the acquisition of a new habit, the result of substituting punishment for reward, and vice versa.

The theory that the rat suddenly changes hypotheses predicts that there will be little or no loss in acquiring the second habit. In terms of a theory of association by contiguity, the rat has acquired a family of responses amounting to a skill; and when punishment breaks up this skill, the second skill involved in jumping to the second card instead of the first requires that numerous stimulus patterns be reconditioned.

In general, Spence has been a defender of Hull's whole systematic account of the nature of learning and a designer of numerous experiments to test Hull's theory at points where it has been challenged.

DOLLARD AND MILLER'S THEORY

Two other students of Hull's have suggested modifications of his system in the direction of simplification and application, particularly in the direction of psychotherapy. Miller and Dollard recently published (1950) their *Personality and Psychotherapy.* It was in *Social Learning and Imitation* that their simplification and extension of Hull's system was first published. Dollard and Miller hold that there are four determiners of the behavior changes called learning. These are (1) drive, (2) cue, (3) response, and (4) reward. Action is dependent on the presence of drive, which consists of strong stimulation. The result of any very intense stimulation is pain and a strong tendency to action. Hunger, thirst, and sex are drives that are innate. Other drives, such as special fears or special appetites, can be acquired.

Drives insure that there will be response. Stimulus cues determine the form of response. When the response has been made, learning is possible. Learning consists of the strengthening of the tendency of cues to be followed by specific responses when they have been rewarded, and of the weakening of the tendency when not rewarded. Reward of primary drives consists in reducing the drive. Rewards are defined by their strengthening effect on S-R connections rather than by their reduction of drive since secondary rewards do not always result in drive reduction.

This position is somewhat modified in Miller's chapter, "Learnable Drives and Rewards." There he takes the position that learned drives depend on responses that produce strong stimuli. Fear is readily attached to new cues. Learned rewards are produced by responses that remove sources of strong stimulation. Primary drives and learned drives both depend on strong stimulation, and reinforcement or reward is of the same nature in both primary and learned rewards. In both cases the reinforcing effect is achieved through reduction of strong stimulation.

This formulation of Hull's theory in a more simplified form and without the mathematical expression is in most respects very similar to the theory presented in this book. In both descriptions action is essential to learning. In both, action is occasioned by stimuli, persistent and energetic action by persistent and strong stimuli.

In both theories learning consists of the attachment of a signal pattern to a response in the sense that in the future the signal will tend to be followed by the response. The difference between the two theories is that Miller holds that this attachment takes place only when the occurrence of the stimulus has been followed by the response and this by a reduction of drive, whereas my own perference is for the statement that the attachment always occurs when the S-R sequence occurs but that this in turn is likely to be broken up by new attachments of S to other responses unless the organism is removed from S by its actions or their consequences so that S-R can not be unlearned.

In actual practice it is very hard to distinguish these two series of events. Tension reduction is normally accomplished by removing the stimuli responsible for tension. Therefore tension reduction or drive reduction is in most cases tantamount to removal from the situation, and straight association and association by reward would be indistinguishable. If they are actually indistinguishable I prefer the simpler assumption, namely, that association is effective in its own right and does not require reward (although it usually involves it).

That the two theoretical positions are not as close as this, however, is clear from the following problem put to me by Miller in a letter:

Following up our discussion of your revision of *The Psychology of Learning*, I wish you would attempt to make a relatively rigorous derivation of the following behavior. A hungry rat running down a straight alley to an end box will leave the starting box faster and faster on successive trials and will continue running as long as he is hungry and finds food in the end box. Remove the food from the end box and the effect of trials on which the cues in the starting box are associated with starting and running is not (as I would think would follow from your theory) to condition running to a greater number of variable cues in the starting box and hence to continue to strengthen the habit. Instead, these trials produce extinction. Note that the rewarded sequence ends with the acts of stopping and eating which would seem to me to be as incompatible with running as are the acts of continued searching at the end of the non-rewarded sequence. Also note that the speed of starting decreases first and more than the speed of running in the section nearer the goal.

Since this illustration brings out so many theoretical issues and possibly so many theoretical weaknesses it deserves careful examination. In the first place it should be remarked that the experimental design stems from Hull's theory that the learning process is a continuous function of such variables as number of repetitions and that the strength of a stimulus-response tendency can be measured by vigor of response. The situation, in other words, is selected with such a theory in mind. We are all aware, if we have had experience with rats in a state of nature, that a rat that discovers the feed sack in the stable will be back the next night. The rat that appears on the birds' feeding table one morning will return. Tolman would say that this is behaving as if the rat had a cognitive map of the terrain and a goal expectancy which stirs ideas of food at the sight of the terrain it went over before the discovery of food. I heartily agree with Tolman that the rat shows signs of grasping the terrain and its meaning. The difference between Tolman on the one hand and Neal Miller and me on the other is that Tolman is content to point out and classify this bright behavior of the rat, whereas Miller and I are interested in describing *how* it is achieved. Tolman's suggestion that the rat acts as if it had a cognitive map can be accepted; but this is a statement of what learning brings about, not how it is brought about. This is true of all of Tolman's six categories of learning. They represent six kinds of learning outcomes or products, not six kinds of methods by which these are achieved.

We may assume that Miller would explain the rat's faster running on successive trials as increments of response strength occasioned by the cumulative effect of successive reinforcements. If we accept Hull's postulate that asserts a time gradient in reinforcing effect, the reinforcement theory has trouble with the fact stated in Miller's last sentence: "Also note that the speed of starting decreases first and more than the speed of running in the section nearer the goal." Here the start is further removed from the cumulative inhibition produced by nonreward and should be affected less.

But Miller's example brings out a type of weakness in my own theory. The theory is not primarily adapted to dealing with the special class of learning studies which may be described as studies of progressive change in response with indefinite repetitions of situation. These studies I regard as of slight importance for the understanding of learning, because in order to achieve curves they disregard the basic nature of learning. Miller's rat, if free to travel anywhere, would or would not return to the spot where it had discovered food and eaten. It probably would return, and after a visit on which no food was present it would probably continue to return occasionally. I suspect, from what I know of animals and men, that when the rat was next hungry a chance encounter with some portion of the path to food would start it retracing its course. But the problem which Miller's example sets remains. How can an encounter with these earlier cues be affected by the presence or absence of food on later occasions? If, as a theory of association by contiguity requires, the stimuli just preceding a response become the signals for that response, how can such things as an increase or decrease of speed be set back to the beginning of the series?

My own answer may prove too complex and too much contrived for the special case. Whereas Miller says that the acts of stopping and eating are as incompatible with running as are the acts of searching at the end of the unrewarded sequence, these acts are actually far more incompatible. Continued unrewarded search is very similar to running after food. Eating takes the rat clear out of this search, whereas nonreward leaves the rat in search and open to new learning. In this case the new learning involves acquiring a different attitude toward searching in this context. It may be pointed out that what Tolman describes as the establishment of a goal expectancy is certainly achieved and that the increased or decreased speed of Miller's rat is an instance of that achievement. But Tolman offers no explanation. Miller, with his principle of reward, offers what is to my mind a very dubious explanation in which a deferred ultimate reward is supposed to "stamp in" a long series of S-R associations from the beginning of a "run" to the goal. In watching cats escape from a puzzle box Horton and I observed long series of actions repeated over and over again, although they did not lead to reward. I believe, however, that at least a partial answer to Miller's problem is hinted at in these action series which are characteristic of animals in the puzzle-box situation. The simple run down an alley which Miller's example allows does not make conspicuous the fact that a serial pattern has been established in the animal. These serial patterns, I believe, can be subject as a whole to association. Skinner also has suggested that only the initial movement needs explanation since the following movements result from what he calls S conditioning, or association by contiguity. Hull has pointed out that, in a search for food, behavior is directed and integrated by partial goal responses. When a hungry rat has discovered food the series of movements leading up to the discovery was accompanied by partial goal responses—a set to eat, some of the behavior last associated with hunger. In many cases it is easy to tell a hungry from a well-fed animal almost at a glance.

The presence of these goal responses may carry with it such attendant symptoms as increased energy. The zeal with which the sight of food is met by a hungry animal serves to energize eating. In the absence of food it can energize action. This energy is subject to associative evocation as well as is action. A hungry animal that, set to eat, enters a goal box and finds no food is compelled to channel its excitement into activities other than eating. Such activities may include escape efforts. In a series of consecutive actions there are many features which run through the series. Hull has interpreted the facts in terms of neural traces left by stimulation. I tend to look for the aftereffects of action in peripheral events. Running involves general postural sets, special types of orientation, and many other features which extend through a series of movements. The difference between a rat that has entered a maze from a release box and a rat that has been picked up and placed in a maze lasts for some time. It furnishes cues which can lead to the setting forward of responses in the serial pattern, to anticipation. I believe this to be the behavioral side of Tolman's "expectancies." These can be exhibited as actual behavioral preparations for an event.

There are not only overlappings of response in the form of response features carried through a serial pattern, there are also stimulus patterns which extend over sections of the series. The beginning of Miller's runway is almost identical with the end portion and the running behavior is carried through. I would expect some features of the rat's anticipatory responses to be evoked by the stimuli involved in a near approach to the goal, and others to be evoked by features of the situation more remote from the goal. Readiness to eat, originally a part of eating, may be evoked by being picked up by the experimenter because the effect of being picked up may persist in behavior for some time after the event. The rat that is given a slight shock at the beginning of a run down an alley will run differently the rest of the way. Response to shock lasts for some time after the event. Response to shock is therefore available as a signal for anticipatory reaction.

Another way of stating all this involved reply to Miller's problem is that serial movements may become functional units and respond to associative cues when the actual association is with late elements in the series, if these late elements are present throughout the series or if they occurred earlier in it. As we approach a door the visual pattern of the door increases rapidly in size, but certain features remain much the same. Our response of taking out a key, originally made as we stood just before the door, may later be made at some distance from the door. All repeated actions tend to be modified by this tendency to become functional units tied together by the overlapping of parts that were originally separate.

In his contribution to a symposium on learning published in the *Psychological Review* (1951) Miller elaborates his argument that association should be interpreted as dependent on reinforcement. He interprets the position taken in this book as a definition of reinforcement as "events that radically change the stimulus situation" (p. 379), together with an assumption that such events reinforce the responses being made just previous to the change. He then suggests that if a rat is shocked on a charged grid and makes a response which enables it to escape the shock, this response will be learned, and to this I agree. But Miller goes on to suggest that if a rat that is lounging at ease on the grid is suddenly shocked, the shock will radically change the situation but will not reinforce lounging. It is scarcely necessary to try this on fifty rats to agree with Miller that, under the circumstances, lounging is likely to be made less probable as a response to being placed on the grid, not more probable.

"I would think," Miller continues, "that Guthrie would have to predict that turning on the shock whenever the animal scratched his ear would teach him this response, since it always would be the last response made to the situation of relaxed sprawling." This argument centers about the notion that shock effects a radical change of situation *before the response to shock occurs.* If the change waits on the animal's response to shock, the last response made while lounging is a violent reaction to the shock, not continued lounging; and this reaction may be expected to be associated with lounging, or with scratching, or with whatever the animal was doing when shocked. The point of the theory presented here is that new behavior elicited in a given situation becomes associated with that situation.

The addition of a stimulus like an electric shock does not remove an animal from the situation. It may result in behavior which does remove the animal; and that behavior remains faithful to the situation, because dissociation from a signal is impossible in the absence of the signal. This is true even in reinforcement theory. It is not directly the shock that removes the rat from its cues; it is the rat's responses to the shock. And it is this response to shock that becomes associated with the stimuli present when that response occurred. In a theory which holds that association is in itself effective, the results of reinforcement are explained in terms of association. Reinforcement may be brought about in a number of ways. Stimuli which help assure the response reinforce. Resulting situations which protect an association from being unlearned also reinforce.

Miller's extension and simplification of Hull's theory in terms of drive, cue, response, and reward, in which the eventual reward establishes the cue as an effective signal for response, gets into certain difficulties when it is extended into the field of learned drives and learned rewards. Miller takes the stand that drives can be learned and he offers generous proof. Learned fear can motivate an animal to discover methods of escape from confinement. Miller suggests that learned drives viewed as responses obey the same laws as do overt responses; and he also suggests that learned drives may be viewed as having the same drive and cue properties as strong external stimuli. If fears are learned as overt responses are learned, this requires, according to Miller's theory, that the cue-fear sequence be followed by drive reduction or reward. If learned drives have the same drive and cue properties as strong external stimuli, the conditions for learning, according to Hull's or Miller's theory, appear to be excluded because both these theories make drive reduction an essential determiner of the establishment of an associative cue.

It appears obvious to me that both men and animals learn responses that augment drive and tension. Children learn to do what causes excitement—to run and shout, to hammer and pound, to tease and annoy. Play is made up of such activities, all established by learning. Drive reduction does not explain why it is so difficult to keep small children from sounding an automobile horn. Here the thrill appears to be a reward. Only for the senescent does drive reduction have a certain plausibility as a universal requirement of learning and a guide of life.

In their *Personality and Psychotherapy* Dollard and Miller have set out to supply the basic learning theory necessary for clinical practice. They assume that neurotic behavior is learned and that it can also be unlearned. But to be able to direct its unlearning, the clinical psychologist should have more than case studies and his own experience to guide him. He should have a rationale or theory which can be made the basis for teaching and observation. Only by the light of a theory can facts be collected.

The theory selected by Dollard and Miller has one radical difference from Hull's reinforcement theory from which it is derived. That difference lies in the fact that the basic datum of Hull's theory is not a single reinforced association but a series of reinforced associations repeated under similar circumstances. Hull's postulates are stated as equations of curves, normally a certain type of exponential curve. These curves can not be made specific until certain features (parameters) are derived from the particular series of reinforced associations being considered. When a series of observed reinforced trials (or unreinforced, in the case of extinction) is provided, the constants which determine the specific curve can be calculated and the curve can be drawn. Until such a series is provided, the law of the event is not known. To illustrate: in order to determine the rate of strengthening a Pavlovian salivary reflex reinforced by feeding it will be necessary to make a series of trials in which under constant conditions a dog is given the signal and the response is followed by feeding (reinforcement) or by not feeding. The occurrence or nonoccurrence of the response, or the latent period, is recorded. This series is the basic datum in Hull's system. The series, once given, furnishes the constants which allow the curve to be plotted and the future course of a prolongation of the series to be known.

This obviously has little to do with the problems of a practicing psychologist. The experiences of patients do not come in controlled reinforced or unreinforced series. Both trouble and cure are more adequately understood in terms of episodes or present states.

Dollard and Miller have therefore made Hull's theory far more practical by making the single episode, the reinforced or unreinforced association, their basic datum.

They are left with four basic concepts: drive, cue, response, and reinforcement (or its absence). Some drives are innate and some are learned. Very strong stimuli of almost any sort can act as drives, make the organism restive, and lead to learning whenever activity produces drive reduction. The cues are the stimulus patterns that happen to have preceded a reinforced response, a response followed by drive reduction.

In their application of this to neurotic behavior Dollard and Miller are remarkably successful in giving a rational and plausible account of how neuroses are established and how they are cured through reassociation or extinction. Their theory is generally indistinguishable from that presented in this book because what they call reward or drive reduction is normally also a removal from the inciting stimulus situation responsible for the activity. Our theory holds that all associations are established by the mere fact of concomitance, and that some of these associations, like the final movements of escape from the puzzle box, are protected from being unlearned by virtue of the escape. To unlearn them would require reëntry into the puzzle box and the association of some different behavior with the cues found there. Dollard and Miller assume that the successful association is preserved and strengthened because of the tension reduction consequent on escape. The difference between the two theories is of great ultimate importance but of slight practical and immediate importance.

CHAPTER XIX

Skinner's System of Behavior

ONE of the most original developments in learning theory was described in Skinner's *The Behavior of Organisms* published in 1938. Skinner's theoretical system has led to a very considerable body of experiments, which is one of the tests of the merit of a theory.

Skinner begins with a use of the term "stimulus" which insures that his system will be radically different from any others yet proposed. "The environment," he says (1938, page 9), "enters into a description of behavior when it can be shown that a given *part* of behavior may be induced at will (or according to certain laws) by a modification in part of the forces affecting the organism. Such a part, or modification of a part, of the environment is traditionally called a *stimulus* and the correlated part of the behavior is a *response*. . . . For the observed relation between them I shall use the term *reflex*."

The study of psychology is the study of the quantitative properties of representative reflexes (1938, page 12). Responses have certain measurable features which Skinner calls laws. There is a critical *threshold* of stimulus intensity below which a response does not occur; there is a *latent period* between stimulus and response that differs between different reflexes and varies inversely with the intensity of the stimulus; responses have *magnitude*, which is a function of the intensity of the stimulus; responses may persist after the stimulus has ended, a period of *afterdischarge*; the prolongation of a stimulus or its repetition has within limits the same effect as increasing the intensity.

Skinner's definition of stimulus as a part or a modification of a part of the environment rules out from his system the use of an organism's own movements as determiners of coming action. It was in agreement with this use of the term stimulus that his earlier experiments were performed with the animal in a box which did not allow any observation or any recording of its movements or posture. The only record was the lapse of time and the incidence of movement of a lever by which the animal obtained food. This brings out a further difference between Skinner's system and the account presented in this book. For Skinner the response, defined as the part of the behavior correlated with a stimulus, is what has been here defined as an act rather than a movement. The response of bar pressing which Skinner makes the item of record can be achieved by an indefinite variety of movements, as a recent film made in the Yale laboratories by Neal Miller demonstrates. A bar can be depressed by either paw, by the snout, or by a remarkable variety of any one of these means.

The quantitative features of response—namely, threshold, latent period, magnitude, period of afterdischarge—which Skinner calls "static laws," are the basis for the measurements involved in observing certain *dynamic laws* of reflex strength. These are the law of the *refractory phase*, that reflex strength is at a low or zero value immediately after elicitation; the law of *reflex fatigue*, that reflex strength declines during repeated elicitation and is restored during inactivity; the law of *facilitation*, that the strength of a reflex may be increased by a second stimulus which would not itself produce the response; the law of *inhibition*, that strength may be decreased by presenting a second stimulus "which has no other relation to the effector involved."

Skinner's whole system turns upon the concept of *reflex strength* and its determiners. But the development of this concept must follow a basic division of behavior into two radically different kinds. Skinner points out that most adult behavior and much early "spontaneous" behavior have no clear relation to eliciting stimuli. It will be recalled that his definition of stimulus excludes proprioception and confines stimuli to changes in the environment. He therefore proposes to distinguish two kinds of behavior: elicited response as *respondent behavior*, and non-elicited or at least not observably elicited response, which he calls *operant behavior*.

An operant is an identifiable part of behavior of which it may be said, not that no stimulus can be found that will elicit it . . . but that no correlated stimulus can be detected upon occasions when it is observed to occur. It is studied as an event appearing spontaneously with a given frequency. It has no static laws comparable to those of a respondent since in the absence of a stimulus the concepts of threshold, latency, after-discharge, and the R/S ratio are meaningless. Instead appeal must be made to frequency of occurrence in order to establish the notion of strength (1938, page 21).

Some criticism of this twofold division of learned behavior into operant and respondent will be undertaken later in this chapter. This criticism will not be taken too seriously by Skinner himself because he does not think of the twofold classification as a theory but as a convenient way of dealing with the results of two very different kinds of experiment in which contemporary psychologists are engaged.

In accord with the division of behavior into respondent and operant, Skinner formulates two sets of laws of conditioning. The first of these applies to respondent behavior in which, as in Pavlov's experiments, there is a clear eliciting stimulus. This Skinner calls conditioning of Type S. The law of conditioning of Type S is: "The approximately simultaneous presentation of two stimuli, one of which (the 'reinforcing' stimulus) belongs to a reflex existing at the moment at some strength, may produce an increase in the strength of a third reflex composed of the response of the reinforcing reflex and the other stimulus" (1938 page 18). Skinner says that the observed data for this law "are merely changes in the strength of a reflex." This is perhaps a legitimate stand, although it involves the conception that all Pavlov's dogs—in fact, all dogs—have a salivary reflex to the sound of a flute and that this reflex is at zero strength in all dogs but the ones later conditioned to that sound.

Complementary to the law of conditioning of Type S is the law of extinction of Type S: "If the reflex strengthened through conditioning of Type S is elicited without presentation of the reinforcing stimulus, the strength decreases" (1938, pages 18–19).

Note that both these laws assume that reflex strength is a *continuous* function of the number of pairings and that Skinner's method, dictated by this theoretical position, does not involve any play-by-play examination of associative changes in behavior. The theory has dictated what facts will be observed.

Corresponding to the laws of conditioning and extinction of Type S (Pavlovian) are laws of conditioning and extinction of Type R, learning or operant learning, in which we refrain from or are unable to specify the original stimulus responsible for the reflex. The law of conditioning of Type R is: "If the occurrence of an operant is followed by presentation of a reinforcing stimulus, the strength is increased" (1938, page 21). The law of extinction of Type R is: "If the occurrence of an operant already strengthened through conditioning is not followed by the reinforcing stimulus, the strength is decreased" (1938, page 21). In both conditioning and extinction of Type R or operant responses the term strength refers to their frequency of occurrence. Skinner's practice assumes, though he does not say so, that this frequency of occurrence means frequency of occurrence in a very special set of environmental conditions. He deals chiefly with rats placed in an opaque box in which there is a lever so connected with a food dispenser that depressing the lever may or may not cause a pellet of food to drop into a food box where the animal can eat it. In his experiments, response strength means frequency of response in this particular box, or in the situation in which the response has been conditioned (rewarded).

Respondent and operant behavior may be closely interwoven. When an animal is faced with food, an operant response may be called out or not depending on whether or not the animal has been deprived of food or is satiated. But the operant response having been begun, the series of graspings and swallowings that follow are respondent behavior elicited by the early stages of eating. These early stages of eating may be regarded as stimuli because a bit of the environment is changing its locale. Skinner's definition of "stimulus" as a part of the environment or a change in a part of the environment does not allow him to recognize the motions of mastication or the initiation of swallowing as stimuli which in part determine the next movements, or—and this is a crucial difference between his and a number of other systems—to recognize that the posture of a crouching cat is an essential condition of the spring to follow or that action and posture are the most important data available for prediction of the immediate action to follow. In other words, Skinner's identification of stimulus with change in the environment, excluding changes in the organism itself, bars any possible interpretation of drives as stimuli. Deprivation of food, deprivation of water, illness, which all affect the strength of a group of reflexes, are called *operations* (1938, page 23) and are not interpreted in terms of stimuli such as might be incidental to fullness or emptiness of the stomach, even though fullness might act as a stimulus because it represents the intrusion of a part of the environment.

Skinner is, however, not consistent in this view of the nature of stimuli as confined to the environment; he recognizes a possible role of proprioceptive stimuli in the ordinary sense when he formulates what he calls the law of chaining: "The response of one reflex may constitute or produce the eliciting or discriminative stimulus of another" (1938, page 32). No use, so far as I know, is made of posture and movement as determiners of behavior. Skinner prefers to deal with such determiners or with possible interoceptive sources of hunger or nausea not as stimulus situations but in terms of the *operations* which bring them about. Feeding and deprivation are such operations, as are electric shock and restraint. These are controllable acts of the experimenter and Skinner is intent upon working with data that can be directly measured in the laboratory. The possible interoceptive stimuli directly responsible for changing reflex strength are not open to observation or direct control. Hunger spasms and other physiological effects of deprivation are likewise difficult to observe, and Skinner's preference is for formulating laws in which such constants as number of hours without food or number of food units consumed enter into the observation.

The practical difference between his system and the systematic stand taken in this book is not always discernible. Electric shock can be dealt with as an experimenter's operation and its strength and frequency related to the strength of operants or respondents. My own preference is for recognizing that the effects of shock are mediated through proprioceptive stimuli in the contracting muscles or their central equivalents. I prefer to recognize that the effect of administering food is mediated through receptors in the stomach, that hunger may have as one of its components the hunger spasms of an empty stomach which may serve as direct stimuli responsible for an increase of tonus in many skeletal muscles, and that such increases are the ground for increased vigor of response, for the restlessness and increased activity characteristic of hunger. Skinner's attack on the problem reduces it to laboratory terms and to a far more manageable system for the type of laboratory experiment to which he is given. He objects to interpreting hunger in terms of stomach spasms because in his own experiments on the effect of food deprivation (1938, page 375) hunger can be demonstrated in the absence of hunger pangs.

One further major concept is offered by Skinner. This is the concept of *reflex reserve,* or amount of available activity in a reflex. The reflex reserve is diminished or exhausted by the elicitation of the reflex. The strength of a reflex at any moment is proportional to the reserve. A reflex starting at a sound may occur once or twice and then require a long period of recovery. This is a case of very low reserve. In conditioned reflexes of both Type S and Type R reflex reserve is built up by reinforcement and exhausted by unreinforced occurrence.

Skinner's system, which is probably the most consistent yet formulated, considers another important problem and offers an answer consistent with the general direction of the system which is, above all, oriented toward the discovery of quantitative laws of behavior. This problem is: What is the unit of behavior which shall constitute the response of record in an experiment, and what part of the environment or what change in a part of the environment shall be the item of record? His answer to these questions is practical and simple: "A specification is successful if the entity which it describes gives smooth curves for the dynamic laws."

Skinner finds, for instance, that "pressing a lever" by a rat, though it can be accomplished by an indefinite and very large variety of movements, is a specification or class of response that can be made the item of record and result in lawful changes. The smoothness of the curves would decrease if the rat's behavior were more specifically described. "The curves would have been destroyed through the elimination of many responses that contributed to them" (1938, page 38).

To this I am tempted to say that in my opinion a different and possibly more important lawfulness would have appeared. The record of highly specific movement patterns in the rat would have betrayed a lawfulness governing their appearance. This opinion is based in part on a view of a film produced by Neal Miller in which successive bar pressings by a rat exhibit predictable idiosyncrasies in style and manner that lie completely outside the concepts or laws of Skinner's system. The observations Horton and I made on the behavior of cats in a puzzle box used methods very different from Skinner's. We arranged everything so we could get a maximum amount of detail of the movements made by the cats. Skinner enclosed the rat in an opaque box and recorded only the behavior of the box mechanism, assuming, rightly enough, that the animal must have done something to actuate the lever.

Skinner does not deny that the determiners of response include such components as proprioceptive stimuli from the animal's own movements. He is interested "only in the degree of consistency that can be obtained while [the forces affecting the organism] are still by no means completely determined. This consistency is so remarkable that it promises very little improvement from further restriction" (1938, page 39).

The satisfaction with his results is well justified. Skinner's method has produced very interesting demonstrations of lawfulness in behavior. The basic method of observing conditioning of Type R is described by Skinner himself in an illustrative case (1938, page 67).

The rat was first placed in the box and pellets of food were discharged from a magazine into a food tray. After 50 to 100 pellets are thus discharged, the rat responds to the sound of the magazine by going to the tray.

For the first record shown here, after the training just described the rat was placed in the box with the lever in an operating position. The first response of pressing the lever took place after 5 minutes; the second occurred 51.5 minutes later, the third 47.5 minutes after the second, and the fourth 25 minutes after that. There was then a rapid increase in the rate, which became roughly constant (15-second intervals) for a time and then diminished as hunger was alleviated by the pellets eaten.

With this apparatus and method Skinner has been able to attack a great variety of problems. If a rat, previously conditioned to respond to the box by pressing the lever, is placed in the box and no responses are rewarded with food, the curve will show the rate and extent of extinction.

Each pressing of the lever moves the recording pen up a small distance where it makes a horizontal line until the lever is again moved. The record is therefore cumulative, and its slope indicates the rate of responding. (This and the next figure are from B. F. Skinner, *The Behavior of Organisms*, Appleton-Century-Crofts, 1938.)

Extinction is an exhaustion of "reflex reserve." Skinner does not attempt to formulate the curve of extinction, but irregularities in the process of extinction tend to be corrected for in a fashion that makes the curves return to an "envelope" such as is indicated by the dotted lines in the second figure.

The processes of forgetting and of spontaneous recovery from extinction, the effects of periodic reinforcement and of punishment, the formation of discriminations between situations, and particularly the behavior of drives can all be investigated by this method. It is perhaps worth noting that in discussing discrimination of the stimulus in Type R conditioning, which is operant behavior and therefore not regarded as *elicited*, Skinner finds it necessary to say that in operant behavior stimuli may act as occasions for response but do not elicit response. It will be recalled that the stand taken in this book is that stimuli are in no case to be regarded as causes of response but only as occasions for response, and the distinction between operant and respondent behavior is therefore not made. There should be no distinction in

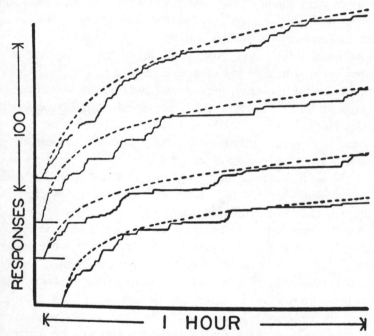

Four typical extinction curves. No responses were reinforced. The curves appear to conform to an "envelope."

meaning between "elicit" and "occasion." Neither can mean "cause" in the sense of being the sole determiner of an event.

More recently Skinner has undertaken a very original and promising variation of his box apparatus. Pigeons were substituted for rats and the box was opened to observation. In an article entitled "Superstition in the Pigeon" (1948) he described the behavior of pigeons when food is mechanically dropped into a food hopper at regular intervals "with no reference whatever to the bird's behavior."

Under such circumstances the hungry pigeons in most cases developed well-defined responses which were highly individual. One bird turned counterclockwise around the cage, another thrust its head into an upper corner, a third developed a peculiar tossing of the head. Two developed a quick swing of the head with a slower return. Another made incomplete pecking movements toward the floor. Nearly all these responses were repeated in the same part of the cage. Each bird was responding to some aspect of the environment and not merely executing a movement. The odd movements were repeated rapidly between reinforcements.

Longer intervals between the automatic "reinforcements" were less effective than intervals of a few seconds, probably because the bird's behavior shows less variation just after the food is taken from the tray than after a long interval. Systematic changes in the response developed with practice.

Skinner interprets this behavior as "a sort of superstition," and believes it analogous to such human rituals as are used to change one's luck at cards. Actually there is no essential difference between such behavior and the acquisition of behavior that is really effective in bringing reinforcement. Thorndike described the result of releasing cats from a puzzle box whenever they scratched—on being placed in the box the cat soon learned to sit down promptly and scratch. The modern householder who "flunked" physics in high school and never resumed its study but who can push a button on his automobile's instrument board and have this regularly followed by the opening of his garage door is very little different from the scratching cat or the nodding pigeon.

It has been the contention of this book that reinforcement and reward are not irreducible categories of explanation. Like Hull, Spence, Neal Miller, and others, Skinner so regards reinforcement. His scientific model is so constructed that when a stimulus is followed by a response and this in turn by reward, the stimulus becomes effective as an "occasioner" of the response if not as a cause. The original definition of operant behavior as "emitted" rather than responsive has been in effect discarded by Skinner with the admission of stimuli as occasions for operant response. Stimuli are only occasions for any responses.

There are close analogies between the behavior of Skinner's pigeons and the cats which Horton and I watched escape from a puzzle box. All the cats' escape movements were operant behavior in Skinner's terms, in the sense that the experimenters had not specified and elicited (occasioned) the mode of escape. A fundamental difference between the two studies is that Skinner's interest was in the effects of hundreds or thousands of repetitions of the behavior and the lawful changes that can be demonstrated in such long series. Our interest was in a play-by-play account of changes from one exposure to the next; we also noted gradual changes as the cats were repeatedly placed in the box. But to us the important feature was the appearance of complex new behavior patterns in the situation which *on the next occasion* were repeated in great detail, or which, having been completely absent from intervening trials, showed up nine trials later in an astonishing duplication. This we believe to be the important issue in understanding learning: Under what circumstances may complex behavior patterns be expected to recur?

The concept of reflex reserve, which is the basic concept of Skinner's system, may prove to have extremely interesting and important applications to human behavior, to problems of addiction particularly; but we can raise the question whether in that concept and the attending notion of drive as independent of stimuli Skinner has not discarded a useful analysis which distinguishes motivation from learning and does not lump them in one package. My own preference is for an analysis of drive into stimuli and certain physiological states, even though we have difficulty in quantifying this conception and must accept Skinner's device of using hours without food as a measure of drive.

Human and animal learning is not normally exposed to the artificial reduplication of situation used by Skinner and Hull. If repetition were the essential of learning, this chapter should have the musical notation *da capo* to encourage that it be read over and over. The reader would not actually profit from that. There are a number of ambiguities in Skinner's system. His distinction between conditioning of Type S and conditioning of Type R makes their distinction depend on "whether the reinforcing stimulus is correlated with a stimulus or with a response" (1938, page 62). Does "correlated" as used here mean correlation between events or correlation in the observations of the experimenter? If the latter, the distinction is required to carry a heavy burden of consequences for what is acknowledged to be an accident of observation and not independent of the observer's attitude. Reinforcement means radically different processes in respondent and operant conditioning. In respondent conditioning reinforcement means the application of the eliciting stimulus for the response in question. In operant conditioning reinforcement means that after the response in question has taken place (and it may be many minutes after, or perhaps hours), a stimulus which has no part in eliciting the response but has reward value is effective in causing the response to occur, not as a result of any eliciting stimulus but dependent on occasioning stimuli.

For this my own thinking, which tends toward finding some mechanical analogy, some scientific model, requires two radically different conceptual schemes. Skinner's diagrams of the two modes of learning are very different and give no hint that the real difference is only inherent in the method used by an experimenter.

He diagrams conditioning of Type S as follows:

$$S^0 \diagdown \quad \cdot \quad (R^0)$$
$$S^1 \quad \cdot \diagdown R^1$$

This symbolizes the contiguous occurrence of two stimuli, S^0 the S^1, and the irrelevant response, R^0. The line means that after the pairing of the two stimuli, a reflex that had until then existed in zero strength is increased. We have no way of knowing how much.

Operant conditioning is symbolized as follows:

$$s \quad \cdot \quad R^0 \longrightarrow S^1 \quad \cdot \quad R^1$$

Here s $\cdot$ R^0 is "some part of the unconditioned operant behavior" and S^1 is a "reinforcing stimulus." The arrow indicates "is followed by."

One of the ambiguities I find in this description is the fact that operant behavior is obviously always elicited in the presence of a complex of stimuli (whose presence Skinner acknowledges by the small "s" in the diagram of operant conditioning). *Does Type S conditioning fail to occur* when the experimenter chooses to disregard the stimulus situation and to wait for an emitted response? If Type S conditioning does occur *according to Skinner's law*, his account of learning becomes essentially the same as the one in this book. If Type S conditioning does not occur, we are confronted with an organism that has two mutually exclusive mechanisms for learning and we have no criterion for knowing which will operate in a given situation.

We are faced with this problem in Skinner's account of chaining (on which Horton and I depended so much for our interpretation of the behavior of the cat in a puzzle box), which recognizes that long series of movements like those involved in seizing food with teeth, chewing, moistening with saliva, swallowing, are respondents. Once started, such series carry themselves on because one movement furnishes the stimuli which elicit the next. Only the first response to the lever is an operant response. Chains can be broken and reëstablished. Skinner breaks a chain by removing the lever and disconnecting the magazine, or leaving it empty. Breaking a chain is roughly what in this book has been referred to as "sidetracking" a habit. What is there about the first movement in a chain of behavior which makes it radically different from the others? What makes the initial movement independent of stimuli and not subject to association by contiguity, but a radically different process requiring reward reinforcement? The same initial movement could obviously be involved in a chain under other circumstances.

It is possible that Skinner's distinction between operant and respondent behavior can be maintained only as a description of the experimenter's method and not as a description of behavior. His acceptance of both reward learning and contiguity learning does not really settle this controversy. The experimental reconciliation of reward and contiguity theories may be ultimately hit upon by closer observation of the details of response and situation. Skinner's work with pigeons, which demonstrates a remarkable control over behavior, may lead to a reconciliation of the two views. Or such an experimental line as that taken by Estes in his studies (1943, 1948) may demonstrate a possible reduction of the reward category to contiguity.

We should note that Skinner has effected a notable thinning out of what Woodrow (1942) has listed as "mental sets and cortical sets, traces, residues, synaptic resistances, inhibitory and excitatory substances, inhibitory and excitatory tendencies, mental attitudes, sentiments, wishes, tensions, field forces, valences, urges, attributes, instincts, and so on and on."

In a recent article in the *Psychological Review* (1950) Skinner raises the question whether or not learning theories are necessary. In a somewhat abbreviated paraphrase, his answer is "no." He chooses to reject any notion of scientific model and does not believe that even the generalized curve is useful at the present stage of development of our knowledge about learning. We have not, he believes, determined by experiment the relative importance of the very large number of relevant variables.

In reply to this it may be pointed out that his experimental method assumes a theoretical position of which, if we accept his refusal to theorize at its face value, Skinner is unaware. He defines learning as change in behavior; but his basic experiments, by disregarding actual movements and recording only the movement of a lever which could have followed an indefinite variety of movements by the rat, evidently accept adjustment to goal achievement as a fundamental explanatory principle of learning and not as the very thing that is to be explained. He assumes, in addition, that the learning process is describable as a continuous function of a number of variables. The assumption of the theory presented in this book is that stimulus patterns acquire a functional unity with one occurrence and that similarly, with one expression, a complex of movements is organized into a functional unit (by cross-conditioning of its parts or serial conditioning of its successive phases) so that the complex movement pattern has an all-or-none character. The result is that a complex of stimuli which happens to be present at the time of the initiation of response becomes a signal for that response or, in other words, will elicit the response. This basic event does not have degrees. The response occurs or does not occur. The features used by most experimenters to measure the degree of learning, such as reduction of response latency, increase of response vigor, increase of response certainty, are complex products of the special circumstances of the experiment. This is true also of Skinner's basic datum, *rate of responding.*

If, as I believe, the basic datum of learning is the appearance of a response (movement complex) following a stimulus complex which was formerly not followed by the response but was thus followed on one intervening occasion, Skinner's method would guarantee that this basic datum is not observed. Only certain regular changes in the rate of the response itself would be observed. The basic fact of the sudden appearance of associative responses after one occurrence of a response in a given setting is clear in Skinner's descriptions of his pigeons. The pigeons' development of "superstitious" acts which always take place in a certain part of the cage is an instance. These are not gradually built up; they appear full-blown and are maintained if, by reward, the pigeon's attention is withdrawn from the situation to which the superstitious response was being made and therefore no unlearning could occur.

Mowrer (1947) has taken a position very like the dualism of Skinner. Mowrer suggests that there are two radically different mechanisms of conditioning. The conditioning of movements involving the skeletal muscles he believes is dependent on reward; and the reactions mediated by the autonomic nervous system, the general states that go to make up emotion, he believes are subject to association by contiguity. This theoretical position has implications very different from Skinner's distinction between respondents and operants, because, by making the distinction derive from the physiological mechanisms involved Mowrer is, like the writer, committed to the belief that the basic association is between stimuli and movements or glandular secretion, not between stimuli and goal achievement or goal striving as such. Hence Mowrer, like the writer, must seek to explain the obvious goal character of behavior in terms of organic structure and response repertoire and association, rather than make goal striving a fundamental law of behavior. Skinner's theory is noncommittal on this point. He selects as his response in a basic experiment not movements of skeletal muscles but the accomplishment of a change in the environment.

CHAPTER XX

Cats in a Puzzle Box

———————

IN THE years following the first publication of *The Psychology of Learning* George P. Horton and I entered on a long series of observations of the behavior of cats in a puzzle box to see whether the general theory of learning described in that book seemed to be a practical description of behavior. We were particularly concerned with finding out whether all the observed behavior was consistent with the principle of conditioning or whether behavior appeared which that principle would contraindicate. Is it a general principle, or is it only one of a number of behavior mechanisms which adapt behavior to the conditions of life?

There is a great weight of opinion to the effect that association is just an occasional feature of behavior and that alternate principles are involved. This was the opinion of John Locke, who believed man a creature who was governed mainly by reason but who occasionally fell into associative thinking and so into error. In our own day Allport has expressed the belief that insight and association are mutually exclusive processes. The stand taken in this book is that insight is achieved through association. Tolman holds that there are at least six types of connections that are learned; the theory presented here can be entertained only as explaining one of these types, the acquisition of motor patterns. Wheeler, Koffka, Köhler, Lewin, Razran, Culler, Hilgard, Skinner, Mowrer, Maier, and numerous others either reject association of cue and movement as a principle or hold that the effect of association in making a stimulus a signal for a movement is an alternative mechanism of learning and that association has two alternative forms. Allport, Wheeler, Koffka, and Köhler all refer to association as a low or primitive mode of behavior change which is occasionally in evidence, usually with no result of value to the animal. Culler believes that conditioning could associate some appropriate action with a signal, whether or not that action was the practiced one. In 1930 Miller and Konorski suggested a distinction between classical or Pavlovian conditioning (association between two stimuli, a new and an old) and instrumental conditioning in which a response is rewarded when it appears. Skinner (1938) based his argument for two different mechanisms of association on the highly practical ground that two radically different experimental methods are in use for studying association which of necessity result in different laws. One of these, the classical Pavlovian method, observes the application of a new stimulus signal such as the sound of a bell along with a stimulus which can be depended on to elicit a response, as food elicits the flow of saliva. The result is the association of the signal with the response. The bell acquires the power to elicit salivary flow.

In contrast with this are the experiments in which no attempt is made to observe or control the situation that occasions the response, but which provide that if and when a particular response occurs it will be rewarded.

Probably the best-known and most quoted experiments in learning, after Pavlov's experiments on the conditioned response, are Thorndike's studies of the behavior of cats in a puzzle box, which were described in his *Animal Intelligence* published in 1898. These studies were widely quoted in elementary texts and exerted a strong influence in directing the development of American theories of learning toward the use of reward or reinforcement as the basic concept in learning. A whole generation of American teachers were trained in Thorndike's views, and his ideas were the foundation for the theories of Hull and Spence, of Skinner and of Mowrer, and in general for the theories which reject straight association for a concept of reinforcement.

The box which Thorndike used was a wooden one with slats across the front and top. The escape door was held shut by a catch which could be released by pulling on a loop hanging in the box, or, in some models, by turning a button from a vertical to a horizontal position.

The cat was placed in the box and the door was latched. The cat's movements were watched through the openings between the slats, and the time between entrance and final escape was recorded.

Thorndike reported that on being placed in the box the cats were excited and active, biting at the slats, clawing at various points, trying to push their heads between the slats. He referred to these as random movements or as trial and error. The word "random" has been misinterpreted by numerous writers as "chance" or lawless. This is of course not what Thorndike meant. He meant that from the point of view of an observer the movements can not be described as aimed at operating the mechanism because the cat has had no previous experience with the mechanism. Thorndike conceived the whole process as consisting essentially of the acquisition of an association between the sight of the loop and the movement by which it was pulled. "The time curve," he said, "is obviously a fair representation of the progress of the formation of the association, for the two essential factors in the latter are the disappearance of all activity save the particular sort which brings success with it, and perfection of that particular sort of act so that it is done precisely and at will. . . . The combination of these two factors is inversely proportional to the time taken, provided the animal surely wants to get out at once. This was rendered almost certain by the degree of hunger."

Some cats learned the successful movement of escape in two

or in three or four trials. For the majority there was an irregular but generally progressive decrease in the time required for escape. Thorndike interpreted this as proof that the cats were establishing an association and not using ideas or thought. This assumption, that associations are not made all at once but are built up by repetition, is in my own opinion an error founded on the habits of thought established in the early studies of learning, in the acquisition of nonsense-syllable series as in Ebbinghaus' experiments. These activities are better described as complex skills than as simple associations, but such studies firmly established in American psychology the general concept that the strength of an association is a function of the number of repetitions and not an adjustment achievable on a single occasion.

Thorndike held that the cat's learning consisted of establishing an association between a sense impression and an act "with the impulse leading thereunto." This was eventually described by him in terms of bonds strengthened according to the law of effect.

In 1929 Donald Adams published an account of a repetition of Thorndike's puzzle-box experiments and of experiments of his own design which avoided certain objections to Thorndike's method.

Adams worked on the assumption that animals use "ideas" in ways not consistent with "mere" association, and this theoretical assumption directed his factual observations. The canon guiding his theory was adapted from Lloyd-Morgan. Adams' amended version was as follows: "Any experience or mental process in another organism can be inferred from structure, situation, history, and behavior only when a similar experience or mental process is or has been invariably associated with similar structure, situation, history, and behavior in oneself; and the probability of the inference will be proportional to the degree of the similarity." In other words, Adams' scientific model is himself. To the choice of such a model there is one very important objection: We do not know enough about Adams' behavior (or our own behavior) to use him or ourselves as predictive models. It is really Adams (and also ourselves) that we set out to try to understand in the first place.

Horton and I began with a very different theoretical orientation. We were seeking to describe the cat's behavior in terms of public facts rather than in terms of our own consciousness. A useful theory of learning must start with such public facts and derive or construct a set of principles or a model with known behavior on which can be based a prediction of what the animal will do. This also must be stated in terms of public facts. Laws of learning stated in terms of what the animal thinks or believes are of no value to us unless the behavioral expression of these thoughts and beliefs is open to observation and in that case the behavioral expression is a much better medium of description.

Our own theoretical position led us to observe the detail of movements and not merely record successful outcomes of movements (acts). We wished to know whether or not the detail of movement is predictable as well as the end result. The "goal" psychologies (Köhler, Koffka, Lewin, Maier) have no basis and no provision for predicting such detail. Because common sense is interested not in how things get done but only in whether or not they get done, many psychologists have failed to show any interest in means; they are interested only in the attainment of ends.

There was another theoretical bias which directed our experiments. We were not concerned with improvement for its own sake (which many psychologists have identified with learning) but we were concerned with the nature of the changes in behavior whether they were improvements in behavior or not. We were therefore interested primarily not in the curve of learning which Thorndike considered the important result of his observations, but in the changes in the pattern of the animal's movements from one trial to the next. Thorndike believed that the curve of learning showed a gradual reduction in the time required for escape and that this represented a gradual increase in the strength of an association between situation and successful response. Our theoretical position was worlds apart from this. Thorndike himself had noted that the successful response often occurred on the first or second trial and that no learning was required. This is no evidence for the strengthening of an association. The association appears to spring full-blown like Minerva from the head of Jove. By Thorndike's own acknowledgment, the lessening of the time required for escape is due to the omission of movements that do not contribute to the escape, although these movements appear and are repeated just as the final movements are.

The unsuccessful movements do not fade out or show any gradual weakening. The successful movements are often as strong at the beginning as at the end, and often appear in an early trial and continue indefinitely.

It was our conviction that there is evidenced in both animal and human behavior a strong tendency for action to exhibit a certain all-or-none character, a strong tendency toward dichotomy of choice. Just as people either sit or stand, either rise or remain seated (with occasional but atypical amusing compromises), either go to the right of the obstacle or go to the left, either speak or remain silent, either say the word or do not say it, either go to the party or stay home, so do animals, once a movement pattern has been executed, tend to exhibit the whole pattern or none of it. Compromise responses exist—Stevenson Smith and I described them in 1921—but behavior tends strongly to be organized into definite patterns and these patterns occur or fail to occur.

Horton and I therefore began our observations with the intention of observing not the total time required for escape, or the curve of diminishing errors, but whether or not recognizable patterns of behavior appeared according to any rule, and whether such patterns could be best described in all-or-none terms or showed evidence of waxing and waning consistent with the general concept of habit strength or of response as a continuous function of such variables as elapsed time, trial number, number of previous practices.

Our choice of a puzzle box rather than a maze was based on an interest in specific behavior in one situation. Studies of maze learning have by the nature of the experimental device strongly prejudiced theory in favor of the learning curve as a basic concept because the maze discourages observation at specific points and lends itself to records of total errors, total time required to traverse. We believed that the phenomenon of learning was lost sight of in such observations. The recording of total errors conceals such essential phenomena as the shift to a correct turn at choice point E and the subsequent adoption of the correct turn for the balance of the experiment. Miss Voeks' experiment (1948), in which this feature, so far as I know, was for the first time made a matter of record, showed that the response at a maze choice point could be predicted with significantly greater certainty from the response last made at that choice point than from the amounts of previous practice of right and wrong responses at that point. For instance, if a subject turns left at point E (wrong) on trials 1 to 10 and on trials 11 to 20 turns right, the prediction of trial 12 on the basis of previous practice will be strongly in favor of "left" as it will on trials 13 and 14; and even on trial 20 the conventional betting will be 10 to 9 on the false premise that habit strength is a function of previous practice.

But it is characteristic of maze behavior that, except for such special patterns as a tendency to alternation or to exploration, responses at a choice point change suddenly and the new response is maintained. By recording only total errors, a completely artificial continuity is introduced into the record and association is given a false appearance of depending on the number of previous trials.

We were equally discontented with the classical conditioned response experiment which we believed was likewise highly misleading in its results. The fact that response certainty (the percentage of trials in which the signal is followed by the response in question) shows a gradual curve of increase with repetition we thought did small justice to the learning capacity of dog or man or even lower animals. We know very well that in everyday life animals as well as man characteristically acquire new behavior in one trial. The rat probably never repeats on the same trap if it escapes the first time. It does not require 100 springings of the trap to learn caution. Once handed a hot bone by his master, the dog refuses to take the next bone. This refusal is not a response whose strength gradually builds up with repeated burnings. Hudson's rats (1939), once shocked while eating from a metal dish, one month later when again exposed to the situation started (13 out of 14 of them) toward the dish and then withdrew before touching it. Köhler (1925) so takes for granted that a solution once hit upon will be repeated that he makes a special note when one of the chimpanzees fails to act accordingly.

The puzzle box which Horton and I chose for our experiments had certain advantages. Its front was a large pane of glass which allowed us to observe all the animal's movements, to photograph the final successful movement, and (so far as our funds would allow) to take motion pictures of all the behavior.

The release mechanism by which the cat could cause a glass door in the glass front to open and thus permit escape, was either a post on the floor or a tube suspended from the top of the puzzle box. By an electric contact or by the interruption of a beam of light, a slight movement of the post operated the release of the door.

At the rear of the puzzle box was a starting box in which the cat was placed. In this way we avoided putting the cat in by hand, which would have introduced a great variety of initial behavior.

The movement of the post which opened the door also operated the shutter of a Contax camera and took the cat's picture in the act of effecting its release.

The animal was placed in the starting box and kept there from ten seconds to a minute. A pull on a lanyard opened the doors into the puzzle box. For the first three trials the glass escape door was left open. A saucer containing a small bit of canned salmon was outside, in view of the cat.

The routine of the experiment consisted of setting a visible electric timer at zero, closing the escape door, setting the still camera, placing the salmon in the dish. The doors of the starting box were then opened by a lanyard and notes taken on the actions of the cat.

In most experiments in maze or puzzle-box learning the experimenter's interest has been on the decrease in the total time required by the animal or the gradual reduction of "errors." We considered these to be results of learning, not learning itself. We were interested in the process, not in the result.

Our release mechanism could be operated by an indefinite variety of movements and, unlike Thorndike's loop, permitted successive escapes by an exact repetition of movements. A loop requires very different movements, depending on whether it has one side or the other toward the operator.

When the cat moved the pole by bumping into it, by falling on it, by lying down and later rolling into it, by biting, by clawing, or by turning and touching it with its tail, the picture that was automatically taken was supposed to represent a cross section of the escape movement. In spite of our hopes, this was not always taken at the same point of the escape movements even when these represented startlingly exact repetitions. The escape

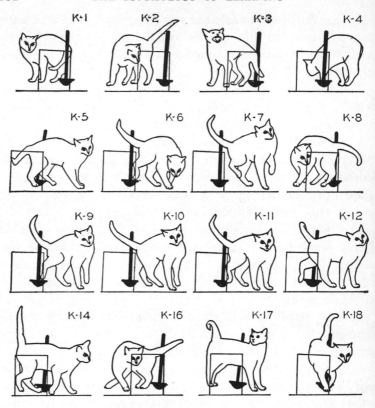

Record of Cat K

In trial 4 the routine used in the first three escapes was repeated, but without success, and the cat escaped by striking the pole with the left shoulder. On trial 5 the original routine again failed to

movement might be practically identical with the preceding one but initiated from a position an inch farther from the post so that the picture was taken farther on in the series; in some cases the exact repetition of the movement series was begun from a point too far away and failed to operate the release.

There were therefore many more close repetitions of escape movements than our camera record shows.

operate the release and the cat continued to turn. Striking exceptions to the prevailing routine can be seen in trials 8, 16, 26, and 45. In each of these the cat had backed out of the starting box and followed a routine different from the usual one, but remarkably the same in

We observed and photographed about 800 escapes. One of the noteworthy features of the escape behavior was its conformity to the descriptions by other men. All the features noted by Thorndike and by Adams were noticeable in our own cats. Lewin's general description of behavior at a barrier also applied. The cats spent most of their time at the front of the box through which they could see the salmon or the "outer world." It would

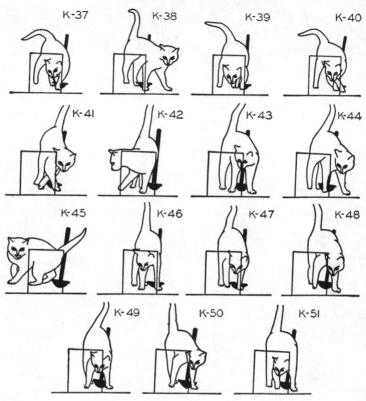

the four isolated cases in which the start had been through backing into the box. Motion pictures of this cat are included in the film, *Cats in a Puzzle Box*, by Horton and Guthrie.

have been very difficult to describe the cat's goal, which was not an object, but escape itself. Only when the cat had spent considerable time at the glass front did it turn to other parts of the box; and the post, as Lewin would probably have predicted, was not noticed until the whole periphery (barrier) had been thoroughly explored over and over. The cats were also promising subjects for description, in Tolman's terminology, of cathexes (the attachment of interest in escape to features of the door), of equivalence beliefs (which I have trouble distinguishing from cathexes), or field expectancies (perhaps also illustrated by the cat's evident set for escape through the door). Field-cognition modes were also in evidence—perception, at least. Perhaps the perception of the door as openable is an illustration. Our interest, of course, centered on what Tolman calls motor patterns, the cat's behavior in the box.

In general the cats, on being admitted to the box, paused at the threshold, entered cautiously, proceeded to the front door and clawed, sniffed, looked about. Any outstanding features such as the crack around the door got attention and were pushed at or bitten at. Approximately an average of fifteen minutes was spent in such exploratory behavior. This meant many excursions about the box.

Eventually most cats did something that moved the pole and opened the escape door. The noise of the door was followed by the cat's looking at the door and then (usually) by its leaving the box through the open door.

After brief freedom the cat was picked up and replaced in the starting box and the process was repeated. Evident from the very first were startling repetitions of previous behavior. If, on entering the puzzle box from the starting box, the cat had paused and sniffed at the lower right corner of the doorway there was high probability that this routine would be repeated. If, on entering, the cat turned left, this also was in order on the next trial. In some cases long series of movements—a triple tour of the periphery of the cage including numerous stops—would be repeated in detail.

The time required for escape was irregularly reduced so that by the end of the 20th trial escape usually took less than a minute and in some cases as little as five seconds.

The outstanding feature of the series of escapes was a strong tendency for escape routines (the final movements leading up to touching the post) to be repeated with high fidelity. A typical cat would have a number of these routines and its 20 escapes could be classified as consisting of 12 cases of routine B, 3 cases of routine A, 4 cases of routine C, and one unique solution. As time went on, most cats settled on one routine to the exclusion of others.

It is perhaps worth giving a play-by-play account of the first cat's behavior in a series of 34 trials with the post in one position and a series of 15 with the post in a different position. (This is quoted from *Cats in a Puzzle Box* by Guthrie and Horton, Rinehart, 1946.)

Cat A, the first animal used, represents one of the most variable records. There were certain errors in the operation of the apparatus which may account for variability. The mechanisms opening the door and activating the still camera were not so finely adjusted as in the runs of the following cats. The displacement of the pole necessary to open the door was not the same on each trial, and this proved an essential condition of some of the behavior which will be described. The speed with which the door opened was variable and the entrance door did not operate smoothly. All these factors were corrected in later experiments.

Cat A was given thirty-four runs in Box A on October 21, 1936. A motion-picture record was also made, and this has been issued by the Psychological Film Exchange with the title, "Cats in a Puzzle Box." Time records are lacking because we depended on the cinema and this had to be interrupted occasionally when film ran out.

Each cat was first placed in the enclosed starting box at the rear of the apparatus; the doors were then opened, and the cat was allowed to exit by the open door. Three such "free runs" were usually allowed in order to speed up the trials by establishing the location of the exit. All trials numbered from the trial following these "free runs."

Cat A, stopped by the closed glass door on its third trial (the camera failed on the first two trials), spent many minutes exploring the box and finally brushed the pole with its flank while moving back and forth across the front of the box. On the fourth trial the escape movement was entirely different. The cat was headed in the opposite direction and was pawing the pole. The fifth trial finds it in almost the position of the first escape except for the angle at which the tail is held. Escapes seven and eight were accomplished by what we judged to be the "same" movement, but this resembled no others in the series.

Trials 14, 18, 19, and 20 have a like substantial identity of posture at the moment of escape. The cat has approached the door with the pole on its right and gone rather promptly to the door and had struck

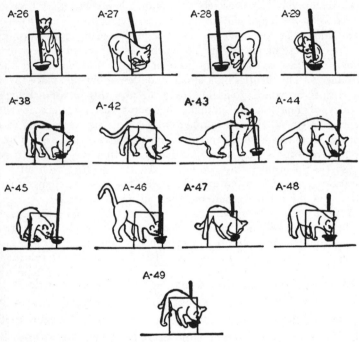

Record of Cat A

Trials 26, 27, 28, 29, 38, 42, 43, 44, 45, 46, 47, 48, and 49.

the pole with its rear while examining the door. Trials 38, 42, 44, 45, 46, 47, 48, and 49 were accomplished by almost identical movements (pawing), times being twenty, nine, fifteen, ten, and nine seconds. In trial 43, which failed to conform to this series, the time is longer, thirty-six seconds, and the action was a use of the left paw as in trial 37 but at the top of the pole rather than at the base.

It is perhaps significant that this cat had twice in the first series escaped by "advertent" use of its left forepaw. Tolman's description in terms of "means-end-expectancy" appears to fit the case very well in view of the added fact, not shown in the pictures, that the cat turns promptly from the pole to the door after pawing the pole. This action must have been prepared while the cat was pawing the pole.

But this description is highly superficial. Why should the actual movement series and the postures in which the picture catches the cat be so remarkably alike? Surely this cannot be explained in terms of the cat's knowledge of the necessary muscular contractions any more than a human being's movements can be explained in such terms. The cat does not use names for its movements and choose a movement by name. The cat has no insight into or hypotheses concerning these movements. The theories of Tolman and Lewin have no place for the movements by which goals are reached, and this occasional highly stereotyped repetition of actual movements has no place in their theories. We may take occasion here to mention that there were many more of these stereotyped repetitions than appear on the record or in the pictures because it many times happened that this repetition was not successful in operating the door. Movement series were in some instances repeated as often as forty times, but a slight change in the position of the cat now rendered the movement useless.

A movement-by-movement account of eight hundred escapes is out of the question because, among other reasons, it would not be read. This account must be limited to certain outstanding features noticed by the experimenters and in most cases based on the picture record.

How are we to interpret what the cats were seen to do in the puzzle box? The problem is not how they achieve success. No two cats in the fifty and more we watched used identical methods. The variety of names which can be given the escapes has already been mentioned—clawing, biting, bumping, pushing. The variety of actual movements is indefinitely great. Every cat has its own pattern and most cats have several patterns.

No theory of learning explains success. The actual movements which operate the release mechanism are part of the animal's repertoire, determined by the animal's structure and its neural equipment and receptor capacities and connections. Some of its movements—in an adult cat most of its movements—are the end product of much previous integration through learning. The cat has learned differential responses which will achieve pawing a seen object in a multitude of different positions. Pawing an object requires an elaborate integration of posture and limb movements. Maintaining balance while the limb is moved requires a delicate adjustment of balance in many dozens of muscles. What happens in the puzzle box is that regardless of what order these elements from the repertoire occur in on any one occasion in the box, the same order tends to be preserved on the next occasion. This is what the principle of association by contiguity would lead us to expect if we reflect that movement complexes themselves are stimuli and can serve as cues for response as well as what is seen and heard.

We can not predict what a particular cat will do on its first tour of the box except on the basis of our knowledge of cat behavior in general. A racoon will have a different repertoire to call on the first time through.

But after watching the cat through one trial we can bet rather heavy odds that the second trial will repeat most of the routines of the first. There are exceptions to this generalization. One trial is not at all what Thorndike tended to think it, namely, one association. In its wanderings around the box on the very first occasion the cat has established many associations but at the same time has replaced many of these with others. Much unlearning occurs on the first trial if that is protracted.

For instance, if the cat makes three rounds of the box and then is led to do something different, the end of a round may now have a new consequence and the cat will not keep circling.

While the cat is in the box there are continual opportunities for establishing new associations. Behavior tends to arrange itself in what we may call "episodes." These episodes are often self-terminating. When the cat sees and then bites the post, the post is in the cat's mouth and can not be seized. When a paw is raised, it can not be raised again until it has been lowered. When the cat has eaten the salmon it can not repeat the act until the salmon has been replaced. A cat that has lain down can not lie down. It can only remain lying down or rise. What we are doing is an important determiner of what we will do next, and we may be faced with the same external situation; but if we are not in the posture and action in which we faced the scene, our general situation is not being repeated. By "general situation" is meant the total stimulation that is acting.

This is a long excursion into interpretation and theory and far away from the factual description of what the cat was doing, but Horton and I believed that the behavior we watched lent itself readily to this interpretation.

There was one movement routine that changed less on successive escapes than the others. This was the final series of movements that led to the opening of the door and escape from the box. Why should this successful movement be so much more permanent than other movements which did not contribute to escape?

It is our belief that the escape routine, the essential movements of escape, are repeated because they remove the cat from the puzzle box and, being removed, *no new associations with the puzzle-box situation are possible.*

Note that this is a theoretical position radically different from the reward and reinforcement theories. The present theory holds that all response complexes are associated with their contiguous situations and will be repeated when the situations are repeated, but that the movement complexes which leave the animal in the puzzle box are subject to unlearning because, owing to changes in the external and internal situation, *the animal still confronts the box situation and may be led to different behavior which will replace the previous association.* The animal that claws at the door will eventually desist as a result of pain or fatigue. Now, looking at the door, it backs away instead of clawing. On its next approach to the door, this may completely do away with clawing. The cat has associated the sight of the closed door (and a complex of its own behavior stimuli) with retreat from the door in place of approach and clawing.

The theoretical position taken in this book is that every action performed by the cat in the puzzle box is conditioned on the contemporary cues from the cat's own movements from the box and other external stimuli. There is observable on successive trials an astonishing amount of repetitiveness, some of the routines appearing for only a few trials, some persisting through many trials. Whatever the cat is led to do, whatever new behavior is introduced by the inevitable newnesses in the situation, tends to be learned as a response to the attendant circumstances. And this wealth of detailed behavior that appears and remains for few or many trials is not rewarded behavior. It seemed to us to be any action whatever.

But this behavior is exposed to replacement by other behavior *unless it ends in the removal of the cat from the box, in which case there is no opportunity under any theory of learning for the establishment of new behavior toward the interior of the box.* Even if one adopts the reward or reinforcement hypothesis the stimuli must be present in order to establish new responses to them.

A very conspicuous feature of the cat's behavior in the puzzle box with its repetitiousness. This has been noted by Thorndike and by Adams but no significance was attached to it. Muenzinger, Koerner, and Irey noted it in 1929 in the behavior of guinea pigs in a puzzle box, though their attention was on the variability rather than the stereotyping of behavior. They did not, however, do more than note, for example, that one animal (No. 17) brushed over the release lever nine times in 550 trials; it rested its paw on the lever three times; it operated the lever with a circular movement four times, and placed the right foot over the left six times. Other animals had other idiosyncrasies. These authors concluded that the mechanization of habitual movement "is still accompanied by variability of its pattern

. . ." and that accessory movements, "while on the whole exhibiting much plasticity, show some mechanization of a brief and unstable kind."

The account given by Muenzinger, Koerner, and Irey is quite consistent with what Horton and I observed in our cats. We were interested in the routinizing, they in the exceptions and new behavior. We were convinced that whole segments of movement appear and are repeated all-or-none on succeeding trials.

It is the final movement series that is least subject to change. By the final movement we do not mean just the momentary action that operated the release. We mean a long series of movements which took the cat into a position from which the releasing movement could be made. The variety of these final movements, which were alike in no two cats and were probably as characteristic of each cat as a signature is of the human signer of a document, is sufficient evidence that no "law of least effort" was in evidence. Some modes of release consumed far more energy than others.

Our summing up of our observations and our interpretation is as follows: (1) There was a strong tendency to repeat movement series on succeeding trials and to repeat them in remarkable detail; (2) new behavior often appeared, sometimes involving a whole session in the box and a new solution; (3) the final movement series was more stable than others and was often a pattern which had appeared in early trials.

We interpret these observed facts to mean that the cat's first trip through the box is subject to accidental determiners, many of which inhere in the accidents of the entrance to the box, the features of the box, the past experience of the individual cat, and other factors. Once repeated, a series of movements in the box becomes in a sense independent of minor distractions and tends strongly to reproduce itself if it is initiated on a later occasion. This is understandable in terms of the principle of association, for each movement phase may tend to become the signal for the next phase. The possibility that temporal as well as spatial patterns of stimuli may serve as integrated signals is an issue for future research and interpretation to settle.

On the second trip through the puzzle box the cat ends to repeat its behavior on the first, errors and all, except such behavior as has been reconditioned during the trial. When the cat is in the box for a long period, much relearning tends to take place. Cats which hit upon a solution quickly on the first trial tended to maintain their pattern through an indefinite number of following trials. We could always force new behavior by holding the release mechanism so that what had been a successful escape movement now left the animal in the box with a novel situation.

Our main conclusion from the series of experiments was that the prediction of what any animal will do in a given situation is most securely based on a record of what the animal was observed to do in that situation on its last occurrence.

If it is objected that this rule applies to physical objects and is not a psychological generalization, we should add a clause which has been taken for granted, and restate the rule as follows: What an animal will do in a given situation is best predicted by the record of what it last did in that situation even though the last occurrence of the situation was long ago. Voeks (1948, 1950) has called this the principle of postremity.

Watching cats in a puzzle box raises a problem which every investigator of learning has faced. How shall he name what he sees? What elements or units shall he remark? What shall he use as the weather signs of behavior, the bases of prediction? What are the predictable behaviors? The answers to these questions will shape the observer's theory. They will determine what goes into the record and therefore into the laws developed. In his earlier experiments Skinner chose to place the rat in a closed, opaque box with a bar and a food tray. The antecedent items of record were some measure of the hunger drive, such as number of hours without food and recent starvation to 80 percent of normal body weight. The consequent item recorded was the rate and total number of movements of the bar.

We found other items of great interest but they lacked the definite character of Skinner's items. We noted that long sequences of movement around the puzzle box were occasionally repeated in great detail. This repetition by its very nature was not an item built up by practice. The first repetition was the best and most exact. If one is interested in these second appearances of complex and extended behavior patterns there is no learning curve or curve of extinction to record. The pattern appears or it does not appear. The question of degree is subordinate to the question of presence or absence.

Furthermore, in predicting what would happen next as we watched the cats, we depended on such behavior sequences. Our own basis for prediction was what we saw the animal doing; this can be thought of as a pattern of serial stimulation of exteroceptors and proprioceptors activated by the animal's movements and the consequences of those movements. We would recognize the early part of a sequence observed once before but not on recent trials. We would then predict that the cat would carry on the action as it had on the last occasion when this sequence had occurred. This rule held whether the action led to any observable reward or not. It even held when the action led to acute discomfort—for example, the cat that jumped for the wire mesh covering the cage and clung there for a time. It should be remarked parenthetically that the establishment of these sequences of movement around the box is essentially like the establishment of sequences in the maze that are the basis of Tolman's *latent learning*. The demonstration of latent learning consists in allowing an animal to stay in a maze without reward and showing later that the effect of its consequent familiarity with the maze is to reduce sharply the time required to run it when reaching the goal is rewarded by food.

Occasionally long sequences were observed in our puzzle box, but these were all eventually shortened or omitted. Most cats in time reduced their pattern to a brief series of movements. In one case at least, the series was dependent on external stimuli for its completion. This was cat K which, as shown by the motion-picture record, had been escaping by leaning toward the post. On one occasion this movement was not effective—did not result in the click of the released catch and the opening of the door. The cat made the movement again, and in succeeding trials it made a double pass at the post even when the first was successful.

Another cat used in the preliminary development of the box design had exhibited a pattern which consisted of walking across the box and stepping on the base of the post with the right hind foot and then walking out the opened door. When the post was set up in another part of the box this same routine was followed to the point of bumping into the closed glass door. In the first case (cat K), the repeated pushing of the post with the flank, evidently there were at least two serial units—the approach to the post and pushing, and, as a second integrated series, walking to the door at the signal of either the sound of the latch or the sight of the opening door.

In Tolman's terms, the double push is evidence of a negative equivalence belief (that it doesn't pay to try to exit until the door opens) and a field expectancy in that the push has acquired a "sign-gestalt" character connecting it with escape or making it the understood cause of the opening of the door, or evidence of a field-cognition mode in which the cat uses its "innately strong" tendency to infer that "if a certain sequence of events has occurred on one occasion, this same sequence of events is likely to occur on subsequent occasions." The observed event itself gives real point to Tolman's probable refusal to treat the whole series as a motor pattern. The motor pattern was broken when the door failed to click and *the push was repeated*, which had never happened before.

I contend that the eventual motor pattern, which now included a double push of no actual utility, did constitute a motor pattern and was acquired by straight association. Each movement had become the associative response to the stimuli produced by the last movement, including posture and the sight and sound of the door. The categories of behavior described by Tolman as kinds of learning all exist and are abundantly illustrated. My own inclination is to regard them as items to be explained and not as ultimate explanations.

Reflection on the behavior of our cats escaping from their puzzle box has led to some clarification in my own mind of the meaning of the word *stimulus*. There are two requirements which stimuli must satisfy in order to serve as scientific data. The first is that they must be physical changes affecting and activating sense organs. The second requirement serves a different purpose. In order to be usable as psychological data stimuli must be describable in terms acceptable to all scientific observers, whatever their theoretical position. In this particular, afferent nerve impulses do not satisfy us. At present we have no means of observing patterns of afferent impulses. Nor have we any means of directly observing any stimuli to retina or to ear or to temperature organs in the skin. What we can actually observe and agree upon are such events as "the sound of the whistle," "the sight of the pattern on the door," "the smell of peppermint," "being pushed forward," "turning the corner of the maze alley," "entering the food box," "being recumbent,"—all phrases that describe highly complex events already presumably organized by perception or organized as symbols for concepts and cognition. The only requirement for their scientific use is that we can expect any observer to accept them as described, perceptual or cognitive organization and all. When we say, "Let's get down to facts," we mean, "Let's find what events are involved on whose description we can agree." A Lewinian barrier is not a barrier in the psychological sense without being perceived or recognized as a barrier. This perception or recognition implies the perceiver's past experiences with barriers. A barrier can be accepted by the observing psychologists as a stimulus provided they can agree that it is functioning as a barrier.

Tolman's field expectancies obviously involve similar perceptions and cognitions. We recognize such perceptual and cognitive qualities of events in the common words we use for objects and events. We speak of food as a stimulus, or of the sight of the lever, or of the sound of the food pellet dropping into the tray. In actual experiment or in applied psychological work, stimuli are of necessity described in such terms. We can observe and agree upon our subject's posture and movement, which we usually also describe in terms which imply their incorporation into action and goal behavior.

As with stimuli, so with responses. The response as used in theory has two necessary characteristics. It must consist of movement or change of state in the subject brought about through the effectors, muscles, and glands. An allergic reaction is not in this sense a response, nor is a change in weight as a result of a disturbance of metabolism. The second necessary characteristic is like the similar requirement of stimuli, for, in order to qualify as scientific data or psychological facts, responses must be so selected and named and described that observers will all accept the description and agree on the use of the name. Skinner's bar pressing, which is actually bar movement with the pressing inferred rather than observed, qualifies on the second requirement but, so far as my own theory is concerned, not on the first.

The principle of association by contiguity or conditioning, as was mentioned before has possible ambiguities attached to nearly every word. *A pattern of stimuli acting at the time of a response*

will on a subsequent occasion tend to evoke that response has
many concealed assumptions. One is an absence of competing
stimuli. Another is the presence of the same general situation on
the second occasion as on the first. In fact, the principle might
possibly be stated at greater length as follows: When a general
situation which has a certain component, S_c, is followed by a
response which does not include a certain movement component,
R_u, and this general situation is repeated on a later occasion
with the presumptive addition of S_u, as well as S_c, and followed
by a response including R_u, a repetition of the general situation
without S_u but with S_c is followed by a response that includes
R_u. This is the mode of behavior change that is involved in
learning.

Even this far more ponderous statement leaves indeterminate
what is meant by a situation component or stimulus pattern. I
believe that part of Tolman's concern is that we recognize that
the stimuli act not as new elements but as perceptual or cognitive units or wholes. In escaping from the puzzle box, the post
by which the cats effected their release was merely encountered
by some cats (as by turning about and striking the post with the
tail) and not perceived. That other cats perceived the spatial
characteristics of the post is proved by the fact that without other
experience of this particular post these cats reached out with
their paws and clawed the post. The post was at sight already an
object-that-could-be-clawed.

To this contention of Tolman's I can only agree. But it is my
own contention that even if all this structuring is accepted, there
remains a strong presumption that these perceptual attitudes and
responses were acquired by associative learning where they were
not innate, and that Tolman's cathexes, which are associations
of drive and goal object, are built up out of associations and do
not represent a nonassociative category of learning at all. Studies
of perception and cognition are important, but we should undertake them with the possibility in mind that they involve associa-

tive learning. This approach will, I feel sure, prove more rewarding than the type of experiment offered by the Gestalt psychologists, who investigate perception as a phenomenon of the present moment and make no inquiry into its origins.

In the chapter on Hull's reinforcement theory mention was made of a possible tendency for behavior to be organized into all-or-nothing patterns and this was used as a serious objection to the conception of learning as a continuous function of such items as number of reinforcements or number of unreinforced pairings. In this respect Hull, Skinner in his earlier work with rats, Spence, Mowrer, and probably the great majority of learning theorists take a position different from the one here outlined. Tolman is an exception. Tolman's views admit the possibility that any one of his six varieties of learning could occur all at once, or in one trial. He has expressed no definite view on the problem of frequency.

Viewing our cats escape from their puzzle box strongly suggested that one-trial association was a characteristic of their behavior. We are reminded of Skinner's opinion that in a chain of responses only the first is open to Type R conditioning. After the first movement of the series is "emitted" the rest follow as a series of respondent movements, one movement being the signal for the next.

Consider the implications of this notion. At certain points in its first tours of the box the cat is somehow led to one of several possible movements. Suppose that one of these, A, elicits a chain, B, C, D, E, etc., in which each movement is responsible for the next because on some previous occasion it was followed by the next. All this, after A, would be *respondent* behavior in Skinner's language. Suppose that another of the possible movements, A, would have been followed by the chain B^1, C^1, D^1, E^1, etc., a chain or serial response established on some previous occasion.

There is here no question of degree or strength of the responses in either series. They occur because each of them once followed the previous response and the stimuli which that response evoked. Many such alternate series are observable in the behavior of our cats. They develop not simply alternate responses in a given situation but alternate lines of behavior. For instance, as was said earlier, in trials 8, 16, 26, and 45 cat K was caught by the camera in almost the same position, a position radically different from any others in the whole series. Examination of our notes showed that on these four trials only, the cat had turned around in the starting box before the door was opened, had backed into the puzzle box, and followed that awkward beginning by the same extended series of movements in the box.

It is here suggested that these movements did not occur because they were in any sense stronger than other responses, but because their cues had occurred. They were obviously just as *strong* on the intervening trials when they did not occur. The question of strength is irrelevant. The nonappearance of the series on the intervening trials is explained not by its weakness but by the fact that the animal entered headfirst and so there was no revival of any one of the series of movements which was begun by backing into the puzzle box.

In opposition to Skinner, it is here argued that even the initial movement has its signal, whether we discover it or not. I believe it more profitable to take a theoretical position that encourages search for the signals of emitted behavior than to assume there are no such signals, particularly in view of the fact that we can often discover them if we look.

Even in terms of Skinner's theory this conception, that elaborate response series may be set in action by the "hair-trigger" release of a single initial response which determines the rest, makes rather meaningless a description of elementary learning in terms of a continuum of response strength, a function of number of reinforcements. The fact that response probability is demonstrably a function of number of reinforcements is dependent on accidents of the stimulus situation. We can describe situations and record situations and control situations only in general terms, not in all their details. The accidental details are ground enough for occurrence or nonoccurrence of the response. The curves of learning are discovered when we attempt the repetition of situations over and over again. They are more rationally explained as dependent on the accidents of a situation that is not controlled, and as representing the development of skills, than as increasing the strength of an association.

What I am trying to say can be illustrated by the four extraordinary responses of cat K which followed backing into the puzzle box. Other responses were stronger if we measure strength by percentage of occurrence. This one odd response occurred 4 times in 60. When it did not occur, the explanation is not that it was weak. When it does occur it is obviously as strong as the responses which did not occur but which have "strengths" higher than 4 in 50. Four out of 50 really represents the observed incidence of a bad start in the trial.

If we accept this theoretical analysis and recognize that whether or not a particular response occurs depends on the occurrence or nonoccurrence of a "trigger response" which starts a chain of movements linked by the fact of one previous occurrence, we then in turn examine the nature of this trigger response. Is it basically different from the following responses in that it is the result of a different kind of conditioning? Skinner would say that it is different. It is an emitted response, whereas the others are "respondent" to stimuli.

Whether or not it is different, it is obviously of peculiar importance because its occurrence or nonoccurrence determines whole trains of action. The theory in this book represents this important determining response as an "all-or-nothing" event like the conduction of a nervous impulse or the ringing of an electric bell which depends on the making of contact in a switch. The responses made by our cats in the puzzle box were about as rigorous on the first occasion as on later ones. Their latency, in the sense of the period between stimulus and response, was not directly observed, but since a reduction in all the latencies of a chain response would result in speeding up the action, we judge that the latencies were not reduced. The action did not speed up. The total action, it is true, was enormously reduced in time and extent, but this was the effect of the progressive elimination of whole series of movements. How this elimination could occur has been discussed. The reader will remember that it was believed to follow the establishment of new associations while in the puzzle box, and the consequent elimination of the behavior involved in the old associations. This establishment of new associations and new responses to the features of the puzzle-box situation is possible so long as the animal remains in the box.

The odd behavior of cat K in trials 8, 16, 26, and 45 *did not increase or decrease its strength of association.* The association was probably just as strong six months after trial 45 as it was on that trial. The point is that the behavior simply can not occur unless the signals occur. The occurrence or nonoccurrence of responses in general need not be interpreted in terms of strength of association because their frequency is so obviously a function of situation rather than response.

The problems of perception and cognition which concern Tolman are not met in our present theory. We may note in passing that Tolman attempts no theory of how they occur but is content to call attention to the fact that they do occur. What our theory does is to recognize that somehow the learning organism can establish stimulus patterns as functional units which elicit response and that response patterns likewise are functionally integrated by one occurrence and can from then on be elicited as whole patterns. How this is achieved is not explained here. Many machine analogies are available. Research in this field has been conducted recently in the Gestalt tradition without speculation as to underlying mechanisms. The doctrine of *Prägnantz* is like the Aristotelian doctrine of entelechy which calls attention to the tendency toward a given outcome with no attention to the means by which it is achieved.

The present theory takes this ability for granted. The principle of association was stated thus: A stimulus pattern accompanying a response will on a later occasion tend to elicit that response. This assumes that the pattern of stimuli somehow becomes a functional signal *as a pattern* and that the response has similarly become a functional unit. We may note that a perception consists in the establishment of a response toward a class of stimulus patterns. We may note further that conceptions are response features or aspects attached to language symbols. We may also note that both are always instances of associative learning.

There is one further item of interest in the behavior of the cats in the puzzle box. In the original report we distinguished what we called "advertent responses" from "inadvertent responses." By this we meant that the final successful escape movement was in some instances an act like clawing or biting the post. This involved looking at the post and reaching out for it. Such an act has the characteristics that Wiener has described as involving a feedback control like the control of an automatic pilot. As the cat reaches for the post either ready to bite or ready to claw, the movement is continuously corrected by vision and therefore may be executed from a small variety of stances or of distances from the post. But when the escape was achieved by an inadvertent contact such as backing into the post or striking it with the flank in executing a turn, success was restricted to a narrower range of movements.

Advertent solutions transferred more readily to the post in a new position. The cat did not bite or claw the air in the old spot. The animal was more likely to look around and on seeing the post in a new position approach it and perform a guided act like biting or clawing. When escape had been inadvertent, this transfer to a new position did not take place and the cat repeatedly backed into the place where the post had been.

Advertent solutions obviously have many of the qualities that interest Tolman (and should interest others). They can be described as expectancies or as perceptions of means-end relationships. It is our belief that in associating the act of reaching with the sight of the post, tendencies to reach out may through previous practice be conditioned on vision and visual orientation, and serve as maintaining stimuli for a sustained reaction to the post which has the same trial-and-error components as has the automatic pilot of the plane or steamship. Reaching out and touching is a skill with much practice behind it, and it is also a behavior mode which exhibits cybernetic control. When the telephone rings we ultimately reach the instrument even if our chair is in a new spot and we must follow a course which never before has been followed. We respond to the bell by rising and by being ready to grasp the telephone, perhaps by being set to say "Hello." Seen obstacles are avoided. That avoiding seen obstacles is based on past training is evident from recent operations on children for cataract in which seen obstacles are not avoided.

In other words, association may result in acts as well as movements, and this is evident in cats as well as in men. The basic nature of the learning may be just as much an association of stimulus and response in an act that includes sustaining stimuli and cybernetic correction as it was in Pavlov's salivary responses. The automatic pilot, the thermostat, the governor of the engine—all illustrate the fact that physical analogies are available in which by setting a control we govern the later behavior of a complicated machine. In animal behavior we have only to assume that the setting, which can itself be a physical response, is itself subject to associative learning.

CHAPTER XXI

Conclusion

PIERRE JANET, in his fascinating series of lectures published under the title, *L'Évolution de la Mémoire et de la Notion du Temps,* distinguished memory from the *restitutio ad integrum* or redintegration which we have described in terms of conditioning. Animals, he said, have motor habits set up by their past experience and evoked by reminders of that past experience, but they do not have memory. The distinction lies in the fact that a memory is not a repetition of a past action but an adaptation of the reconstituted behavior to a present social situation. Its roots lie in narration. A small child may show fear at the sight of a dog that on some former occasion barked at the child. This is not, in itself, a memory. The beginnings of memory in the child lie in the beginnings of his narration of the event. It is from the time that he turns from the event and says "I'll tell mother" that true remembering dates. We remember those events to which we give a special kind of attention, those events which we observe in order to narrate. The contention of some of the psychoanalysts, that the very early experiences of infancy are forgotten because they are so tinged with lechery that later social training drives them to the refuge of an "unconscious," Janet heartily rejects.

This is very much in accord with Watson's statement that the "unconscious" of the Freudians is really the "unverbalized." Our memories are organized around verbal cues. Our access to past events is normally through their verbal associations, and if these verbal associations were not made at the time of the event they will not serve to "call up" the memory. We shall not be able to tell what happened, nor shall we be able to remember it in the strict sense of that term. We may reënact it, but the reënactment is not remembering. Remembering is a highly complex social act which involves language.

Because it is a highly complex act Janet is led to assert that it is not, like motor habit, merely an affair of association. This contention is quite right; but it is equally true that no behavior is merely an affair of association or conditioning. We have said before that the principle of association or conditioning *is not an explanation of any instance of behavior*. It is merely a tool by which explanation is furthered. A tool is not true or false; it is useful or useless. There is no moral compulsion to use any specific tool; that lies in the discretion of the workman. The contention of this book is that we may profitably search for the signs or forerunners of an act among the stimuli which were present with the act. The complete explanation of any act is an achievement which is helped on by such a principle, but it is not the principle that makes the explanation any more than it is the hammer that builds the house. In the hands of a psychologist willing to use it, the notion of conditioning is a profitable instrument, but no one can compel him to use the notion against his will.

The problem of memory is therefore not "explained" by the notion of conditioning. We shall understand memory only when we have undertaken to observe its beginnings in children, or its aberrations in adults and then its normal operation. This is also true of the nature of perception, to which the Gestalt psychologists have given most of their attention. This book can make no claim to have solved the problems of memory or of perception. It merely presents an argument that in attacking those problems we should not lose sight of the fact that past associations of response and stimuli are of use in predicting behavior. Conditioning is not the only ground for the prediction of behavior. Human nature is another source of prediction and control. Those reactions to changes in the environment which observation shows are made by persons without reference to their individual histories we can predict without reference to individual history. In many cases, however, such prediction from membership in the species can be supplemented and made specific by adding associative learning. McDougall, for instance, states that human beings are naturally imitative. Now it is true that we can observe in all cultures many instances of the repetition of seen acts. Persons have been observed to laugh when others laugh, or to cry when others cry, or to whistle a tune on hearing the tune. But it is equally true that human beings are as a rule not imitators. We do not imitate the barber; we submit to his shears. We do not whistle all the tunes we hear, but only those that we have previously learned. New popular tunes are new only in name. If we inquire the circumstances under which imitation does and does not take place we shall find the answer in terms of previous associative learning.

McDougall's principle that human beings are naturally imitative can then be refined in terms of conditioning. If we have performed an act, the stimuli associated with that act tend to become cues for its performance. We laugh when others laugh. Not always, of course. We may have fallen downstairs, or forgotten our cravat, or backed off the lecture platform and so stirred others to laughter. But without strong deterrents like these most of us can be moved to laughter merely by hearing the laughter of others and without "seeing the joke." The reason we laugh on hearing others laugh is that the sound of laughter has always accompanied laughter and thereby becomes a cue for laughing. If we have been often laughed at when discomfited, such laughter brings only annoyance.

The Gestalt psychologists have pointed out that a perception tends to be an integrated whole. A glimpse of an incomplete circle or triangle will be seen as a circle or as a triangle. We

Ink-blot figure which may be seen as a face with open mouth or as a dancing figure with arm extended. What is seen depends on the observer's previously acquired repertoire of perceptions.

tend to read meanings into what we hear and what we see. The clouds, or the figured pattern of the wallpaper displays patterns of familiar objects. In the ink blot shown we may see a human head facing the right and with mouth open, or a dancing figure with a gross body and a tiny head facing the left. In such a figure a skilled artist will discover a dozen possibilities to everyone discovered by the man who has done no drawing.

This generalization of the Gestalt psychologists is true and interesting. But its significance is multiplied many times when we discovered that what we make of the ink blot, or what we make of the incomplete figure or of the garbled letters depends on our repertoire of previous learning. The ink blot suggests more to the artist than to the layman because as the artist explores it, it has more associations with incomplete drawings of his own.

Psychologists who, like myself, speak the jargon of conditioning and association have been reproached for describing behavior in terms which leave out the main actor in the drama, the person who is giving the performance. We are charged with representing conduct as the result of stimuli alone, with no recognition of the person who responds to the stimuli. A man, for example, attends a summer lecture and in the course of it yawns. On the incoming air current rides a gnat which strikes a sensitive receptor in the throat. Nerve impulses are set up which travel to the central nervous system and out over motor pathways to diaphragm and intercostal muscles and result in a violent cough. The gnat is expelled. But it seems to have expelled itself, much as one might touch a button and turn on an electric fan. Mr. John Doe, whose throat it is, seems not to be involved at all. The incident appears only as an unfortunate escapade of the gnat's.

This is a very mistaken impression of the views presented in this book. The fact that a man is a living organism has, perhaps, been too much taken for granted; but it has been taken for granted, not denied. As a living organism, man shares the characteristics by which living organisms are defined, the tendency to maintain his pattern of structure and action for that brief interval which we call his span of life. In the higher animals, as distinguished from certain plants and from those organisms which never properly die but only divide and live on, death and the breaking up of patterns of structure and action are as essential a characteristic as is the brief maintenance of integrity which constitutes living. As a living organism man is also a member of a species, and species of plants and animals as well as individuals resist destruction and adapt themselves to adverse conditions.

The use of adverse conditions to bring about the removal of the threat of disintegration Stevenson Smith (1914) has called *regulation*. In our *General Psychology* we pointed out that responses are in general regulatory in this sense. They meet successfully the situations which contribute the stimuli that call forth responses. Sneezing is occasioned by a foreign object in the nose, and sneezing removes the object. A baby cries when he has been without food for a long period and his stomach is consequently active; his cries generally stir an adult to come to his aid. We are marvelously made and an astonishing list of vicissitudes is provided for in advance by our inherited structure.

The mere enumeration of the known regulatory mechanisms which achieve our protection from danger and maintain our integrity for our term of years would be a long task. The strategic placing of our sense organs for the reception of important classes of stimuli, the structure of the sense organs which limits and further selects the stimuli to which they respond, the wonderfully adapted system of connections between sense organs and organs of response, the physiological structures which maintain our living cells in a fluid medium of astonishing constancy in temperature and chemical balance, the structure and placing of muscles and glands through which we respond to changes in the world and in ourselves—all these regulatory mechanisms together make up a total that will never be adequately described. But the most remarkable provision of all is the intricate nervous system which not only makes possible adaptive direct response to noxious stimuli and to the disturbance of those conditions essential to life, but also enables the organism to widen the field of stimuli to which it reacts *and to make its adaptive changes in response to the mere signs of harm or the mere signs of relief.*

Through associative learning responses may be elicited by new patterns of stimulation; new combinations of response may be integrated into stereotyped acts; the organism may even cease to respond to stimuli with responses which fail to relieve it of strain but, instead, substitute new action more adequate to preserve its integrity.

All this is characteristic of living organisms which we speak of as having "minds." It is so characteristic of them that the description of *what organisms can do* appeals to some psychologists as the sole task of biological science. They will be content with a catalogue of the results which an almost hopelessly intricate structure will bring about. In the realm of behavior this amounts to a list of instincts or instinctive capacities, and the compilation of such a list is of undeniable importance. Chief among these accomplishments is self-preservation. Most of the other capacities or abilities of the organism are instrumental to this end, except those that serve another end which is ultimately incompatible with this, the end of the preservation of the species which can be achieved only by the death of the individuals. Continuance of the species might be listed as the supreme end and self-preservation its chief minor goal. Contributory to self-preservation are such tendencies, capacities, instincts, or whatever we wish to call them as food getting, defense from a wide range of dangers, the maintenance of water balance, the maintenance of the temperature necessary to life. Learning is, according to Humphrey, a process of making a systemic adjustment (1933, page 102). Self-preservation is the fundamental law of learning.

It is quite true that the whole significance of all the biological sciences is lost if we overlook the fact that living things are organized to accomplish this end. But it is equally true that we shall have very little biological science and very little control over learning if we are content merely to point this out. The same end is served by various other means. Our lives are protected by many devices other than learning. Invading bacteria provoke physiological changes in the blood which lead to their destruction. Sometimes this occurs in time. Sometimes it does not occur at all. If we have not been contented with a broad statement of the *vis naturae curatrix* but have discovered something of *how the result is accomplished* we may be able to interfere and assist the immunizing process. Dust breathed into the lungs is passed upward by the cilia of the walls of the lung passages and eventually disposed of by a cough. But not always. Haldane discovered that in certain occupations the dust was not thus eliminated and that one essential of the process was that the dust must be of a certain coarseness if the cilia were to be activated. A cure for the effects of fine dust was to breathe in coarse dust which would start the ciliary action.

We must know *how learning occurs* as well as *what it accomplishes*. Learning can not be identified with what is fortunately its common result, systemic adjustment, because learning may be responsible for maladjustment and early death. Explaining learning in terms of its hoped-for effects is to leave us helpless in its control. And to make the hoped-for effects the fundamental law of learning, or to exalt it into a universal "law of nature" is to deny awkwardness, mistakes, failure, and death by the simple device of not including them in the universal law. There have been religious cults which maintained the reality only of the good, but there have not before this been scientific cults which have attempted this solution of the problem of evil.

Teleological laws have their place in science. They are not, however, universal and general principles. They are, when used legitimately, statistical predictions. Advance in science will come from patient observation and experiment that will make clear the circumstances under which these ends will be attained and the proportion of cases in which they will follow certain antecedent conditions, the limits within which these antecedent conditions can vary and still be followed by the interesting outcome. This is the method of Humphrey and of Tolman. It is the method of what Haldane has called the New Physiology. In physiology it has had the admirable results described in Cannon's *Wisdom of the Body*. In the field of psychology it remains an ambition. The psychoanalytic movement has used such a method but without regard for the precautions that are essential to scientific investigation. Its goals are described in such vague and metaphorical terms that whether or not they have been achieved is a matter of subjective opinion. The circumstances under which these goals are to be attained are also inexactly described. And psychoanalysis is almost entirely innocent of statistical methods that are essential to any conclusions in a field in which there is so little control of circumstance. The stray and adventitious antecedent is taken for the necessary and sufficient condition.

The psychoanalysts' difficulties in adopting a scientific method derive from the fact that they are dealing with individuals as individuals. Only when the phenomena they describe can be classified without ambiguity and many cases be observed with comparable records will they be able to distinguish which among the antecedents of a neurosis will serve to predict the neurosis, and which among the antecedents of the cure will serve to predict the cure. The unique event has all that has recently happened for its antecedents. Only after it has recurred many times can observation discover those signs whose presence serves to warn that the event will follow and whose absence, that the event will default. Before we can blame neuroses on childhood traumas we must do more than show that our neurotics have had such an experience in childhood; we must show that such experiences are absent in normal individuals who fail to develop neuroses. And we must define both neurosis and trauma so clearly that we can agree on when they are present and when they are absent.

Eventually we may have a body of psychological observation from which we can draw useful information concerning what to expect from our neighbors, what the results of their learning tend to be, what they tend to learn. At present we have on our list of goals first those very general tendencies which apply alike to the whole species, if not to all the higher animals. This information is taken for granted. It is of startling little use. For the teacher to know that, whether or not she interferes, her pupils will tend to maintain themselves as intact organisms does not offer any suggestions concerning how they can be taught to read. She may even be moved to trust so little to this self-preservative tendency which is the law of all living creatures that she will take precautions so that her charges will form certain very specific habits in crossing the streets when they leave for home. In addition to these general tendencies toward self-preservation, food, temperature maintenance, etc., we can by observation of individuals note that they have their individual and specific goal tendencies. One collects stamps; another teases his schoolmates; a third is intent on pleasing the teacher. We may classify their successes in these directions as cases of insight, or we may "explain" their improvement in the pursuit of such goals as instances of maturation; but our satisfaction with such explanations breaks down when we are confronted with instances in which improvement does not take place, or when we desire to interfere and hasten improvement, or when it becomes desirable to do away with a goal tendency or establish another. In such cases *we must know the circumstances under which improvement fails and the circumstances under which it may be hastened. We must know the circumstances under which interests and desires are established or fail to be established*. We cannot rest content with statements that life is self-conservative or that improvement in the direction of least action and highest efficiency is a law of psychology as well as physics.

So far as I am aware, the only suggestions toward the description or explanation of the circumstances under which specific changes in behavior will or will not occur have been made in the form of association or conditioning.

The teleological laws which hold true of human behavior describe certain end effects which are predictable (with an error, of course), and predictable without regard to the means by which the effects are brought about and without regard to the special circumstances in which the animal is placed. We can say of all organisms that they will somehow continue alive until they die, which they will do only once. This last event will be quite unforeseen if we rely too consistently on the law of self-preservation. Teleological laws include the capacities and abilities of the species. In human psychology they make up what is known as human nature. They include all that we can expect of John Doe from the sole information that he is a man.

A system of psychology which limits itself to such teleological laws neglects the most obvious source of information about the behavior of persons, their past histories. When the past of the individual is used for predicting his behavior we find that our predictions are always in terms of associative learning. If our caller has a record with the police including a number of household robberies, we assume that there is a strong likelihood that habit, in addition to the general tendency to systemic adjustment, will be again in evidence.

The association psychology has been charged with leaving John Doe out of the picture. There is a certain truth in the charge. John Doe's quintessence, that something which constitutes his John-Doe-ness, will never be captured in any scientific account. There can be no science of the unique. We can never completely understand him but we can understand something of him and know something of what to expect of him in terms of what we know of human nature in general and in terms of what we know of his own past history and the nature of associative learning.

The problem of learning has begun to attract the attention of engineers as well as psychologists. The result may be a sudden progress in the clarity of our theories of learning, like the progress made in understanding the phenomena of sound when phonograph and radio made it important to understand the physical basis of sound. The most original and the best known of the engineering theorists who have begun to speculate concerning the nature of learning is Wiener, author of *Cybernetics* and of *The Human Use of Human Beings.* In the latter book Wiener discusses the nature of possible learning mechanisms; his discussion may throw light on the psychologists' problem. He says: "In its simplest form, the feedback principle means that behavior is scanned for its result, and that the success or failure of this result modifies future behavior" (page 69). How the modification could be achieved by a machine Wiener considers in terms of a possible gun-pointing mechanism capable of "learning" the ways of enemy airplanes: "The adjustment of the general plan of pointing and firing the gun according to the particular system of motions which the target has made is essentially an act of learning. It is a change in the taping of the computing machine of the gun, which alters not so much the numerical data as the process by which they will act and it is based on past experience" (page 73).

"Taping" here refers, of course, to the method by which data are fed into a computing machine on punched or on magnetized tape. Alteration in the patterns on the tape would be the mode by which experience is made to alter behavior; in other words, the alterations on the tape would be the physical carriers of learning, the "engrams" of an earlier psychological jargon.

Wiener assumes, as other engineers have assumed, some integrating process by which percentages of success and failure would determine the response to be evoked. This strongly suggests the reinforcement theories of the Yale school. The position taken in this book is radically different. The basic mechanism indicated is far simpler than that required for Hull's theory or for Wiener's gun-pointing mechanism. The present theory assumes that the repertoire of responses is set by the physical structure of the responding organism and the indefinitely large number of combined patterns of which the effectors are capable. It assumes also that once any pattern of response has been evoked in a stress situation (all stimuli set up stress) which includes a given signal or cue, the given signal or cue becomes an elicitor of the response pattern and remains an elicitor until the signal has been present with a new response. In any general stress situation behavior must change. Acts and movements must terminate and make their continuance impossible. One can descend the stairs but can not immediately repeat it because he is now at the bottom, not the top. The raised arm can not be raised; it can only be lowered.

In any general situation, therefore, there will be a series of responses, and each new response will alienate its predecessors from their association with any signal still present when the new response is given. In stress situation S_m (m indicates the stimuli here called "maintaining stimuli"), a series of responses, R_1, R_2, R_3, . . . R_s, R_t, is evoked. If R_s removes S_m or removes the animal from S_m, then S_m remains a signal for R_s, its last association.

This theory calls for no integration of success frequencies and allows for the characteristic tendency of human behavior to organize into patterns which either occur or do not occur. R_s is not partly evoked or evoked in partial strength. It tends strongly to be evoked or not evoked.

The analogy here is with a system of weather predicting which scans past records for a pattern of data like the one present today. The analogy is not with a weather prediction system based on a regression equation in which data are entered in terms of degrees of temperature or degrees of wind velocity. In other words, the theory of learning which has been here outlined makes learning synonymous with perception in which patterns are reacted to as present or absent, not as present in some degree.

References

Adams, Donald Keith. Studies of adaptive behavior in cats. *Comparative Psychology Monographs,* 1929, 6, no. 27.

Allport, Gordon W. Effect: A secondary principle of learning. *Psychological Review,* 1946, 53, 335–349.

Aristotle. *Parva Naturalia* (Ross' translation). Oxford Univ. Press, 1908.

Barlow, M. C. The role of articulation in memorizing. *Journal of Experimental Psychology,* 1928, 11, 306–312.

Bills, A. G. The influence of muscular tension on the efficiency of mental work. *American Journal of Psychology,* 1927, 38, 227–251.

Borovski, V. An attempt at building a theory of conditioned reflexes on spinal reflexes. *Journal of General Psychology,* 1929, 2, 3–11.

Borovski, W. M. Experimentelle Untersuchungen über den Lernprozess. *Zeitschrift für vergleichende Physiologie,* 1927, 6, 489–529.

Brogden, W. J., Lipman, E. A., and Culler, E. The role of incentive in conditioning and extinction. *American Journal of Psychology,* 1938, 51, 109–117.

Brown, R. W. A comparative study of the "whole," "part," and "combination" methods of learning piano music. *Journal of Experimental Psychology,* 1928, 11, 235–247.

Bryan, W. L., and Harter, N. Studies in the telegraphic language. *Psychological Review,* 1899, 6, 346.

Bykow, K. M., Alexandroff, I. S., Wirjikowski, S. N., and Riel, A. V. Influence du travail musculaire sur l'activité de l'écorce cérébral chez le chien. *Comptes rendus de la Société de biologie,* 1927, 97, 1398–1400.

Cannon, W. B. *The Wisdom of the Body.* New York: Norton, 1932.

Carpenter, C. R. A field study of the behavior and social relations of howling monkeys. *Comparative Psychology Monographs,* 1934, 10, no. 2.

Cason, H. The conditioned eyelid reaction. *Journal of Experimental Psychology,* 1922, 5, 153–196.

Cason, H. The concept of backward association. *American Journal of Psychology,* 1924, 35, 217–221.

Cason, H. Pleasure-pain theories of learning. *Psychological Review,* 1932, 39, 440–466.

Cathcart, E. P., and Dawson, S. Persistence: a characteristic of remembering. *British Journal of Psychology,* 1928, 18, 262–275; Persistence, II, *ibid.,* 1929, 19, 343–356.

Culler, E. Recent advances in some concepts of conditioning. *Psychological Review,* 1938, 45, 134–153.

Dahl, A. Über den Einfluss des Schlafens auf das Wiedererkennen. *Psychologische Forschungen,* 1928, 11, 290–301.

Dodge, R. Note on Professor Thorndike's experiment. *Psychological Review,* 1927, 34, 237–240.

Dodge, R. *Conditions and Consequences of Human Variability.* New Haven: Yale Univ. Press, 1931.

Dodge, R. Anticipatory reaction. *Science,* 1933, 78, 197–203.

Dollard, John, and Miller, Neal E. *Personality and Psychotherapy.* New York: McGraw-Hill, 1950.

Dunlap, K. A revision of the fundamental law of habit formation. *Science,* 1928, 67, 360–362.

Dunlap, K. *Habits, Their Making and Unmaking.* New York: Liveright, 1932.

Ebbinghaus, Hermann. *Memory.* Publication of Teachers College, Columbia, 1913.

Elliott, M. H. The effect of change of reward on the maze performance of rats. *University of California Publications in Psychology,* 1928, 4, 19–30.

Elliott, M. H. The effect of hunger on variability of performance. *American Journal of Psychology,* 1934, 46, 107–112.

Estes, W. K. Discriminative conditioning. *Journal of Experimental Psychology,* 1943, 32, 150–155; and *ibid.,* 1948, 38, 173–177.

Estes, W. K. An experimental study of punishment. *Psychological Monographs,* 1944, 57, no. 3.

Freiberg, A. D., Dallenbach, K. M., and Thorndike, E. L. The influence of repetition of a series upon the omission of its intermediate terms. *American Journal of Psychology,* 1929, 41, 637–639.

Gengerelli, J. A. The principle of maxima and minima in animal learning. *Journal of Comparative Psychology,* 1930, 11, 193–236.

Gesell, A. L., and Thompson, H. Learning and growth in identical infant twins. *Genetic Psychology Monographs,* 1929, 6, 1–23.

Goodenough, F. L., and Brian, C. R. Certain factors underlying the acquisition of motor skill by pre-school children. *Journal of Experimental Psychology,* 1929, 12, 127–155.

Guthrie, E. R. Conditioning as a principle of learning. *Psychological Review,* 1930, 37, 412–428.

Guthrie, E. R. Association as a function of time interval. *Psychological Review,* 1933, 40, 355–367.

Guthrie, E. R. Pavlov's theory of conditioning. *Psychological Review,* 1934, 41, 199–206.

Guthrie, E. R. Psychological principles and scientific truth. *Proceedings of the 25th Anniversary Celebration of the Inauguration of Graduate Studies,* Univ. of Southern California, 1936.

Guthrie, E. R. *The Psychology of Human Conflict.* New York: Harper, 1938.

Guthrie, E. R. Association and the law of effect. *Psychological Review,* 1940, 47, 127–148.

Guthrie, E. R. Conditioning: a theory of learning in terms of stimulus, response, and association. *41st Yearbook, National Society for the Study of Education,* Part II, 1942.

Guthrie, E. R., and Horton, G. P. *Cats in a Puzzle Box.* New York: Rinehart, 1946.

Haldane, J. S. *Respiration.* New Haven: Yale Univ. Press, 1922.

Hamilton, E. L. The effect of delayed incentive on the hunger drive in the white rat. *Genetic Psychology Monographs,* 1929, 5, no. 2.

Hamilton, G. M. *Objective Psychopathology.* St. Louis: Mosby, 1925.

Harlow, H. F., and Stagner, Ross. Effect of complete striate muscle paralysis upon the learning process. *Journal of Experimental Psychology,* 1933, 16, 283–294.

Holt, E. B. *Animal Drive and the Learning Process.* New York: Holt, 1931.

Hudson, B. B. One trial learning in rats. *Psychological Bulletin,* 1939, 36, 643.

Hull, C. L.   A functional interpretation of the conditioned reflex. *Psychological Review,* 1929, 36, 498–511.

Hull, C. L.   Simple trial and error learning; a study in psychological theory. *Psychological Review,* 1930, 37, 241–256.

Hull, C. L.   Knowledge and purpose as habit mechanisms. *Psychological Review,* 1930, 37, 511–525.

Hull, C. L.   Goal attraction and directing ideas conceived as habit phenomena. *Psychological Review,* 1931, 38, 487–506.

Hull, C. L.   The goal-gradient hypothesis and maze learning. *Psychological Review,* 1932, 39, 25–43.

Hull, C. L.   The concept of the habit-family hierarchy and maze learning, Part 1. *Psychological Review,* 1934, 41, 33–54.

Hull, C. L.   The conflicting psychologies of learning—a way out. *Psychological Review,* 1935, 42, 491–516.

Hull, C. L.   Mind, mechanism, and adaptive behavior. *Psychological Review,* 1937, 44, 1–32.

Hull, C. L.   Conditioning: outline of a systematic theory of learning. *41st Yearbook, National Society for the Study of Education,* Part II, 1942.

Hull, C. L.   *The Principles of Behavior.* New York: Appleton-Century-Crofts, 1943.

Hull, C. L.   Stimulus intensity dynamism (V) and stimulus generalization. *Psychological Review,* 1949, 56, 67–76.

Hull, C. L.   Behavior postulates and corollaries—1949. *Psychological Review,* 1950, 57, 173–180.

Hull, C. L., Felsinger, John M., Gladstone, Arthur I., and Yamaguchi, Harry A.   A proposed quantification of habit strength. *Psychological Review,* 1947, 54, 237–254.

Humphrey, G.   *The Nature of Learning in Relation to the Living System.* New York: Harcourt, Brace, 1933.

Humphreys, L. C.   Measures of strength of conditioned eyelid responses. *Journal of General Psychology,* 1943, 29, 101–111.

Jacobsen, E.   *Progressive Relaxation.* Chicago: Univ. of Chicago Press, 1929.

James, William.   *Principles of Psychology* (2 vols.).   New York: Holt, 1890.

Janet, Pierre.   *L'Évolution de la Mémoire et de la Notion du Temps.* Paris: A. Chachine, 1928.

Jenkins, J. C., and Dallenbach, K. M.   Oblivescence during sleep and waking. *American Journal of Psychology,* 1924, 35, 605–612.

Jenkins, William O., and Sheffield, Fred D. Rehearsal and guessing habits as sources of the spread of effect? *Journal of Experimental Psychology*, 1946, 36, 316–330.

Jensen, K. Differential reaction to taste and temperature stimuli in new born infants. *Genetic Psychology Monographs*, 1932, 12, nos. 5 and 6.

Katona, George. *Organizing and Memorizing*. New York: Columbia Univ. Press, 1940.

Koffka, K. *The Growth of the Mind*. New York: Harcourt, Brace, 1924.

Köhler, W. *The Mentality of Apes*. New York: Harcourt, Brace, 1925.

Köhler, W. *Gestalt Psychology*. New York: Liveright, 1929.

Konorski, J., and Miller, S. Méthode d'examen de l'analysateur moteur par les réactions salivomotrices. *Comptes rendus de la Société de biologie*, 1930, 194, 907–910.

Krechevsky, I. A study of the continuity of the problem solving process. *Psychological Review*, 1938, 45, 107–133.

Lashley, K. S. An examination of the "continuity theory" as applied to discrimination learning. *Journal of General Psychology*, 1942, 26, 241–265.

Lloyd, Morgan C. *Animal Behavior*. London: E. Arnold, 1900.

Lloyd, Morgan C. *Mind at the Crossways*. New York: Holt, 1930.

Loucks, R. B. The experimental delimitation of neural structures essential for learning; the attempt to condition striped muscle responses with faradization of the sigmoid gyri. *Journal of Psychology*, 1935, 1, 5–44.

Luria, A. R. *The Nature of Human Conflict*. New York, Liveright, 1933.

Macfarlane, D. A. The role of kinesthesis in maze learning. *University of California Publications in Psychology*, 1930, 4, 277–305.

McGeoch, J. A. The influence of degree of learning upon retroactive inhibition. *American Journal of Psychology*, 1929, 41, 252–262.

McGeoch, J. A. On the term "retroactive inhibition." *American Journal of Psychology*, 1930, 42, 455–457.

McGeoch, J. A. Forgetting and the law of disuse. *Psychological Review*, 1932, 39, 353–370.

McGraw, Myrtle B. Report in *Science News Letter*, December, 1933.

Maier, Norman. *Frustration*. New York, McGraw-Hill, 1949.

Melton, A. W. Chapter on learning in the *Annual Review of Psychology*, 1950, vol. 1.

Miller, N. E. Comments on multiple process conditioning. *Psychological Review*, 1951, 58, 375–381.

Miller, N. E., and Dollard, J. *Social Learning and Imitation*. New Haven: Yale Univ. Press, 1941.

Moss, F. A. (ed.). *Comparative Psychology*. New York: Prentice-Hall, rev. ed., 1942.

Mowrer, O. H. On the dual nature of learning—a reinterpretation of "conditioning" and "problem solving." *Harvard Educational Review*, 1947, 17, 102–148.

Muenzinger, K. F., Koerner, L., and Irey, E. Variability of an habitual movement in guinea pigs. *Journal of Comparative Psychology*, 1929, 9, 425–436.

Nathanson, Y. S. A conceptual basis of habit modification. *Journal of Applied Psychology*, 1929, 13, 469–485.

Pavlov, I. *Conditioned Reflexes*. London: Oxford Univ. Press, 1927.

Pavlov, I. Reply of a physiologist to psychologists. *Psychological Review*, 1932, 39, 91–127.

Peterson, J. Learning when frequency and recency factors are negative. *Journal of Experimental Psychology*, 1922, 5, 270–300.

Piaget, J. *The Language and Thought of the Child*. New York: Harcourt, Brace, 1926.

Pratt, K. C., Nelson, A. K., and Sun, K. H. The behavior of the newborn infant. *Ohio State Stud. Contrib. Psychology*, 1930, no. 10.

Razran, H. S. Conditioned responses in children. *Archives of Psychology*, 1933, no. 148.

Rexroad, C. R. Outline of the conditions under which learning occurs. *Psychological Review*, 1932, 39, 174–183.

Rexroad, C. R. Goal objects, purposes, and behavior. *Psychological Review*, 1933, 40, 271–281.

Rice, Philip Blair. The ego and the law of effect. *Psychological Review*, 1946, 53, 307–320.

Richter, C. P. Behavioristic study of the activity of the rat. *Comparative Psychology Monographs*, 1922, 1, no. 2.

Robinson, E. S. The similarity factor in retroaction. *American Journal of Psychology*, 1927, 39, 297–312.

Robinson, E. S. *Association Theory Today*. New York: Appleton-Century-Crofts, 1931.

Ruch, T. C. Factors influencing the relative economy of massed and distributed practice in learning. *Psychological Review*, 1928, 35, 19–45.

Schlosberg, H. An investigation of certain factors related to the ease of conditioning. *Journal of General Psychology*, 1932, 7, 328–342.

Sears, Robert. In *Bulletin 51*, Social Science Research Council, 1943, p. 288.

Sheffield, Fred D. Avoidance training and the contiguity principle. *Journal of Comparative and Physiological Psychology*, 1948, 41, 165–177.

Sheffield, Fred D. "Spread of effect" without reward or learning. *Journal of Experimental Psychology*, 1949, 39, 575–579.

Sheffield, Fred D. The continuity principle in learning theory. *Psychological Review*, 1951, 58, 362–367.

Sheffield, Fred D., and Roby, Thornton B. Reward value of a non-nutritive sweet taste. *Journal of Comparative and Physiological Psychology*, 1950, 43, 471–481.

Sheffield, Fred D., and Temmer, Helena W. Relative resistance to extinction of escape training and avoidance training. *Journal of Experimental Psychology*, 1950, 40, 287–298.

Sheffield, Fred D., Wulff, J. Jepson, and Backer, Robert. Reward value of copulation without sex drive reduction. *Journal of Comparative and Physiological Psychology*, 1951, 44, 3–8.

Sheffield, Virginia F. Resistance to extinction as a function of the distribution of extinction trials. *Journal of Experimental Psychology*, 1950, 40, 305–313.

Sherman, M., and Sherman, I. C. *The Process of Human Behavior*. New York: Norton, 1929.

Sherrington, C. S. *The Integrative Action of the Nervous System*. New York: Scribner, 1906.

Skinner, B. F. *The Behavior of Organisms*. New York: Appleton-Century-Crofts, 1938.

Skinner, B. F. Superstition in the pigeon. *Journal of Experimental Psychology*, 1948, 38, 168–172.

Skinner, B. F. Are theories of learning necessary? *Psychological Review*, 1950, 57, 193–216.

Smith, Stevenson, and Guthrie, E. R. *General Psychology in Terms of Behavior*. New York: Appleton-Century-Crofts, 1921.

Spence, Kenneth W. The role of secondary reinforcement in delayed reward learning. *Psychological Review*, 1947, 54, 1–8.

Spence, Kenneth W. Cognitive versus stimulus-response theories of learning. *Psychological Review*, 1950, 57, 159–172.

Spence, Kenneth W., and Lippitt, Ronald. An experimental test of the sign-gestalt theory of trial and error learning. *Journal of Experimental Psychology*, 1946, 36, 491–502.

Spight, J. B. Day and night intervals and the distribution of practice. *Journal of Experimental Psychology*, 1928, 11, 397–398.

Spooner, Alice, and Kellogg, Winthrop N. The backward conditioning curve. *American Journal of Psychology*, 1947, 60, 321–334.

Thorndike, Edward L. *Animal Intelligence*. New York: Macmillan, 1898.

Thorndike, Edward L. *The Fundamentals of Learning*. New York: Teachers College, Columbia Univ., 1932.

Thurstone, L. L. *The Nature of Intelligence*. New York: Harcourt, Brace, 1924.

Tolman, E. C. *Purposive Behavior in Animals and Men*. New York: Appleton-Century-Crofts, 1932.

Tolman, E. C. Sign-gestalt or conditioned reflex. *Psychological Review*, 1933, 40, 246–255.

Tolman, E. C. A stimulus-expectancy need-cathexis psychology. *Science*, 1945, 101, 160–166.

Tolman, E. C. Cognitive maps in rats and men. *Psychological Review*, 1948, 55, 189–208.

Tolman, E. C. There is more than one kind of learning. *Psychological Review*, 1949, 56, 144–155.

Tolman, E. C., and Honzik, C. H. Degrees of hunger, reward, and non-reward, and maze learning in rats. *University of California Publications in Psychology*, 1930, 4, 241–256.

Tolman, E. C., and Honzik, C. H. An introduction and removal of reward and maze performance in rats. *University of California Publications in Psychology*, 1930, 4, 257–275.

Tolman, E. C., and Smas, C. F. Time discrimination in white rats. *Journal of Comparative Psychology*, 1925, 5, 255–263.

Van Ormer, E. B. Retention after intervals of sleep and waking. *Archives of Psychology*, 1932, no. 137.

Voeks, Virginia W. Postremity, recency, and frequency. *Journal of Experimental Psychology*, 1948, 38, 495–510.

Voeks, Virginia W. Formalization and clarification of a theory of learning. *Journal of Psychology*, 1950, 30, 341–362.

Washburn, M. F. Gestalt psychology and motor psychology. *American Journal of Psychology*, 1926, 37, 515–520.

Wheeler, R. H. *The Science of Psychology*. New York: Crowell, 1929.

Whitford, C. B. *Training the Bird Dog*. Revised edition by Cave. New York: Macmillan, 1928.

Winsor, A. L. Inhibition and learning. *Psychological Review*, 1929, 36, 389–401.

Winsor, A. L. Experimental extinction and negative adaptation. *Psychological Review*, 1930, 37, 174–178.

Winsor, A. L. Observations on the nature and mechanism of secretory inhibition. *Psychological Review*, 1930, 37, 399–411.

Wolfle, H. M. Conditioning as a function of the interval between the conditioned and the original stimulus. *Journal of General Psychology*, 1932, 7, 80–103.

Woodrow, J. The problem of general quantitative laws in psychology. *Psychological Review*, 1942, 39, 1–27.

Yamaguchi, Harry G., Hull, Clark L., Felsinger, John, and Gladstone, Arthur. Characteristics of dispersions based on the pooled momentary reaction potentials of a group. *Psychological Review*, 1948, 55, 216–238.

Index